This

QUIET
PLACE

A Cape Cod Chronicle

Everett S. Allen

COMMONWEALTH EDITIONS
An imprint of Applewood Books
Carlisle, Massachusetts

978-1-933212-24-1

Cover image by Michael McCurdy.

Published by Commonwealth Editions
an imprint of Applewood Books
Carlisle, Massachusetts 01741
www.commonwealtheditions.com

Commonwealth Editions publishes books about the history, traditions, and
beauty of places in New England and throughout America for adults and children.

To request a free copy of our current catalog featuring our best-selling books,
write to:
Applewood Books
P.O. Box 27
Carlisle, MA 01741

Manufactured in the United States of America

To Phyllis
who discovered this place

INTRODUCTION

IN summer, if you had a nickel, you could ride the flying
horses at the local fairground. I did not choose a horse that
went up and down, for fear of getting sick or falling off, but on
the other hand neither did I resort to the seats flanked by swans
and that sort of thing, which were for ladies with small children.

Once on a stationary horse, with both feet in the stirrups and
one hand on the reins, my principal business concerned the brass
ring. After the tickets were collected and several musical revolutions had established the mood, the man who ran the flying
horses used to climb up into a wooden booth that overhung the
merry-go-round. He had a boxful of rings, all of which were
dull iron, except for one of shiny brass. He dumped the whole
box in a hopper and, one by one, the rings trickled down the
interior of a metal arm, to be snatched at by the riders as they
whirled by. Whoever got the brass ring was entitled to a free
ride.

Actually, I did not care so much about the free ride, although
there were few extra nickels in our house. But I always wanted

to see what the brass ring looked like, to have a chance to inspect it at leisure, to feel it, to see how it gleamed, to hold it in my hand for a moment. Once I saw it pop into sight in the slot of the metal arm when I was two horses away from it. The boy on the first horse fumbled and missed and I felt such excitement that my throat went dry and my pulse leaped like a trout after a grasshopper. But the boy ahead of me got it, although not before I had had quite a good look at it, shining there in wait.

That was the best chance I ever had to see it. I thought a couple of times that probably the man who ran the merry-go-round would not mind if I asked to go up into the booth with him. Had he said yes, I could have watched the brass ring lying there among its uncolorful peers, could have shared the excitement of its sliding irrevocably toward the slot and someone's hand. But I did not ask him because I did not know him. Moreover, I thought it might be quite a lot to ask because I had never seen any other boys up there with him.

Now, the days of nickels and flying horses are in the past tense, but there is this place to which I go periodically for sanctuary and although it does not look like it, being an outland of pine, caramel sand and clean tidewater, it is like the man's booth. Here, I can remove myself one step from the heady revolutions and contemplate the brass ring at leisure and in peace.

Come with me to this place.

THE FIRST DAY

I HAVE two blessed weeks of vacation and inevitably the
first day is for the house, not only because there are things
to be done if one is to eat, drink, and think in reasonable comfort,
but because it will take more than overnight to be rid of the
world left behind, and when I come to walk the bounds of this
place I do not want the remnants of what I have fled botching
the taste of it all.

The morning is overcast, satisfyingly so; it ought to be just
this way, because I do not think of the low sky as shutting me
in but rather shutting everything else out. The first need is for
coffee, and after that a full woodbox, because there is little
enough in it now but chips, splinters and a few pages from the
Scientific American on the antiballistic missile. But still, this is
enough to get something going. With both dampers open, top
and bottom, the little black stove with four paws can leap from

5

cold to roaring hot in about the length of time that it takes to prepare the coffeepot and fill the teakettle.

There is nothing spectacular about this teakettle, but it reminds me of myself because it is bent and dented. Now that it is not likely to be attractive to anyone else, I will not put it aside or condemn it to the dump; it has boiled a lot of water for me and I owe it something. Steam curls out of its spout; this is the first thing I have created here during this visit.

You may think that steam is odd stuff to be sentimental about, but in truth if you are my age — and a certain number of millions of people are — steam represents a way of life for all of us and what is more, a pace for doing things in an era when we were less clinical, more variable, and used fewer deodorants.

On a bleak fall day when I was six, in a vacant lot fenced by faded billboards ("Time to Retire," "I'd Walk a Mile for a . . ."), my father and I crossed the torn scars of new yellow earth and he boosted me into the shuddering wooden cab of a steam shovel. It was a bright merry hell with an awesome glowing firebox, and the operating devil on his iron seat, dirty sweat rag careless on his big wet neck, bit into a sausage and grinned at me. He let me touch the jumping iron throttle when his creature chewed its bright teeth into the dirt and strained. Stays, turnbuckles, drums, cogs and boom grunted and shook; black smoke belched from the lopsided stack and the boiler quivered and you knew that the earth itself was going to have to let go first.

On tiptoe, I looked through the forward dirty window and watched the shovel gulping ahead of us. I thought it was something like Sir Gawain, with whom I had recently come in contact, invincible, with lance poised. On the other hand, it was even more like the dragon he might have pursued; because, in between shovelfuls, steam within it hissed cleanly and warm, like the hot and heavy breathing of a resting monster. The devil

6

gave me a bite of his sausage and I thought how nice not to have to wear a sweater and mittens at work, not even in winter.

There was, of course, steam less brutally applied. The little pumping station, arrived at by walking down a slope of pine needles, lay handy to mayflowers and eelgrass at the head of a tree-rimmed lake where fat carp, orange and empty-eyed, came to fin quietly in season. Crossbred mallards and black ducks, which long since had forgotten whether they were wild or domesticated, conversed reedily in the dooryard.

Within the Spartan building, which seemed to have neither odor nor stain in any part of it, the steam things moved with reliable swishing and a shiny flywheel whirled quietly as a flight of swallows. Because of this gentle machine, water, clean and cold, climbed the wooded hillside to the standpipe; one understood that it would be there, dependably, for the feverish child in the night; the plowhorse, with enormous muddy feet and sweaty flanks; and the smiling gardener who made moonshine out of potato parings.

The man in the pumping station had clean fingernails; his calendars did not have naked girls on them; and he read Audette's manual on engines, marking his place with a little piece of wooden matchbox; but he said he had no wish to be promoted.

My friend MacIvers was something the same, which is to say that he was a fiercely satisfied man, being the emperor of the engine room in the belly of a Grimsby trawler that would, as the skipper said, "roll you out from under your hair," even if given no more wind than would fill a paper bag and less water than comes with the daily dew on the Humber docks.

MacIvers once invited me to take tea in his engine room, squeezed sideways against the sheathing, feet braced to avoid falling into the flying rods, and cheeks pink from the heat because the engine took all the room there was. Thus balanced, snug against the interminable pitch and trash of the Channel's crooked water and with china mug and warm bread in hand, we yelled amiably at each other over the swish ka-pow, swish ka-pow of the jewellike engine.

MacIvers was a man of Gourock (population 9,100) on the Firth of Clyde, where the livestock graze prettily with clonking bells on the August hillsides, white against purple; he was self-contained and married only to the iron and steel, sweetly warmed and oiled, that drove the ship to sea and home again. If the engine missed a beat, even when he was sleeping (if he did sleep), he stomped down the iron ladder, grimaced, cocked his shaggy head, grunted, and knew in no time where, in all those faucets, cups, cogs and bolts, the grain of dissonance was lodged.

His tea, MacIvers said, ordinarily was strong enough to hold the spoon upright in the cup, but the water they had taken on at Immingham this time out was, he said, gutless and even made steam that stank. How this could be I do not know and I spent some time thereafter thinking about gutless water, and other kinds.

Perhaps we no longer spend sufficient time with teakettles. I cannot decide, if I had to spend more time with one, whether I would prefer a copper one, spotted with solder, such as my mother used to hold me over when I woke at night strangling with the croup, or the black iron one that my grandmother had on the farm at Capigan. My grandmother's had a flanged bottom so that it sat in the stove hole over the coal fire. I remember how comfortably it bubbled and steamed on the day of my grandfather's funeral, reassuring because it said, "Well, they haven't got *you* yet."

Oh, nobody in his right mind wants to go back to the five dollar blue serge suit, the ten-dollar-a-week job, the days when they used to sell skinny little boys for chimney sweeps and a widow had to take in washing or turn to prostitution because there was no Social Security or Aid to Dependent Children, but still, there is no harm in wondering why steam takes its time and electricity is in such a hurry.

In the difference in pace lie a lot of things, including the fact that the devil in the steam shovel is no more, nor is the pumping station man who read Audette's, nor, for that matter, is Mac-Ivers. They are all gone, blown to leeward by circumstance and geriatrics, as it were, and perhaps it is good riddance, for their teeth were, after all, dirty, and they gave scant attention to man's inhumanity to man, which, as a matter of fact, they accepted as inevitable and perhaps even desirable.

Now, I shall drink my coffee.

(This is a separate sentence to demonstrate the relative importance of this act in the kind of life I have come to here. Not that coffee drinking or bowel movements or hand washing or any of these things is profound but simply that, mostly, we have a habit of doing things while we are thinking of what we are going to do next, or what we should have done before. That way, we never really know what anything is, or feels like, or smells like, or tastes like. This may be as well also; I suppose we might not like much of anything we have or do if we paid any real attention to it.)

My coffee is in a crock, like a shaving mug, that says "Father" on the side in red and gold letters. I do not know who left the cup in this place; I do not know whose "Father" it was or even whether the relationship was legitimate, but I like to drink out of it because the handle is big enough for me to hook the knuckle of my forefinger into, and most aren't.

Come walk this house with me now, cup in hand. It is a bare place, true, but therefore encourages examination of the bare bones of things, because it is not cluttered with distractions. Besides, there is so much natural decoration outside that plainness is welcome within; the Chinese knew what they were doing when they concocted sweet and sour dishes to be eaten in conjunction.

The only decoration on the walls of the kitchen (and whether it really is a decoration depends on who stands in front of it) is a square, white-framed mirror, where I shave. It is better than most mirrors, especially hotel mirrors and the mirrors in restrooms of cocktail lounges, because honest daylight from the north floods through windows on each side of it and shows you who you are and what you really look like, whether or not you want to know.

Off the west wall of the kitchen is the pantry, which smells clean and old. It contains, in addition to the usual culch, two dusty, unset mousetraps and a skinny window, through which you can see, on any clear day, the most spectacular sunsets. They are spectacular because they are seen through a natural slot in the pine forest that allows a view of the bay a half mile away, and the horizon — miles of deep-blue water — beyond that. Each night the sun burns orange, the water deepens in hue from cobalt to ultramarine, and finally the ball of fire sinks below the sea line, leaving the western sky streaked for a quarter-hour with quickly darkening patterns of warm color that change in shape and intensity a hundred times in no time and are gone, quick calm after riot.

The living room is small; the stove dominates it. The room has a half-dozen windows, nevertheless, leaving little wall space, but windows are better than walls in such a place, for they look out upon the life and times of toads, turtles, chipmunks, squirrels, nuthatches and wood ducks. The living room also has the front door in its south wall. Nobody uses the front door (although an occasional snake suns on the top step) because it opens on a treed slope that drops abruptly to the creek. I think once this house was somewhere else and its front door faced something conventional, like a street; now, the kitchen door is closest to the road and it is used almost exclusively. This is a good thing; if everybody who comes to see you has to go through the kitchen, it encourages you to keep your dishes washed.

The living room has knotty floor boards so rounded through hewing and wearing that high heels never could stand on them comfortably. A carpet of straw matting smooths out the floor somewhat, but not much.

In this room there are two folding camp chairs, a rubber-tired tea cart that came out of somebody's attic, and a Grand Rapids bookcase of indifferent maple finish with a diamond-paned top and a fold-out desk. On top of it there are two lacrosse rackets left by somebody whose views on what to do with time are at variance with mine. Inside the bookcase there are three volumes : Roger Tory Peterson's classic on birds, from which I discovered that geese do, of course, say "haronk, halunk"; something called *Humor of the Wild West,* which over the years has driven me to appreciate the humor of the wild East, and Huxley's *Brave New World.* I have read them all several times. Each time, I find *Brave New World* convincingly depressing and am relieved to have the antidote of the other two volumes.

Apart from the S-shaped stovepipe that runs up to a hole in the exposed brick chimney, the only other thing that breaks the pale yellowness of the plaster walls is a U.S. Coast and Geodetic Survey chart of the bay and its environs. On it, somebody has lettered with certain drama : "You are here," and an X next to it locates this house. It is seldom that we know where we are so precisely.

Upstairs there are two small bedrooms. Part of the ceiling in each slopes, so that you can stand erect only in the other portion of the room, but this is not a bother, because you do not go there to stand up anyway.

I am not much for sitting down, either, and so now we will

go thirty-five steps to the west, to the woodshed. As I arrive at its sagging, open door, something flies out with a flutter of wings and so fast that I cannot even see what it is. But I know what it was doing there — finding insects in the stacked logs (roof-high and, through a relatively minor error, all too long for the stove firebox). I am sorry to interrupt the bird's breakfast, but I have to cut wood if I am to eat and keep warm.

Some profess to believe that eating is not very important, yet I submit that one's attitude toward food is among the most interesting, complex and revealing things about a man. Although Samuel Johnson, according to Boswell, talked "with great contempt of people who were anxious to gratify their palates; and the 206th number of his *Rambler* is a masterly essay against gulosity," Johnson also commented that, "Some people have a foolish way of not minding, or pretending not to mind, what they eat . . . I look upon it that he who does not mind his belly will hardly mind anything else."

In any event, even if one has death in mind more than life, who wants to die piecemeal, starving a little more each day?

I start cutting wood with my shirt on, because the sky still is dubious. But I take it off soon enough. The bucksaw, rusty and with warped frame, is none too good a tool — poor enough so that nobody has stolen it in all these years — but it works better (or makes me think it works better) if I alternate chunks of hard oak and soft pine; in that way, I am able to think of chewing through every other log as sliding down hill, coasting, as it were.

My body is soon soaked with the effort, but I am pleased to discover that my arms are not quite lead and I breathe with reasonable ease even after I have accumulated a good-sized pile of sawdust and about three dozen logs. At one point, I sense movement out of the corner of the eye, and turn to see a large yellow cat come picking down the lane, hardly leaving tracks

12

in the rutty sand. He sits to watch my sawing briefly, yawns and leaves, without noise or comment. It is seldom that a creature can step into your life and out again leaving so few ripples.

When the logs are stacked next to the stove and I have made a poker out of a coat hanger (somebody always seems to have removed the one I made the year before, although, for the life of me, I cannot think what other use you could make of it after I have bent it into a poker), I look at the cloudy sky with more confidence. Rain today, if you like, I suggest. The food and fuel are in. The roof is tight. There is a board over last season's squirrel hole at the eastern peak.

Now I shall start kale soup, mainstay of the Portuguese hand-liner and a lasting nourishment that has produced generations of strong men and passionate women and has, for all I know, won wars and inspired poets.

The preparation of food and the consumption of it in this country are, as often as not, appalling and as good a reason as any for running away to a place like this. It may be that your mother memorized Fannie Farmer's perpetual best seller at the age of twelve, studied soups and sauces with Charles of the Waldorf, and was capable of constructing a lobster stew or coq au vin that would, as H. P. Ayer used to say, "set a bone." But if so, you were lucky. I have never been much impressed by nostalgic references to the delicacies that "mother used to make" and I have a feeling that most wives have a right to take umbrage (or even better, an expensive weekend alone in New York) if this subject is raised critically.

What "mother used to make" went down the hatch easily because most teen-agers are empty all the time and eat totally without discrimination, which is to say, they put catsup on everything including the floral centerpiece. Moreover, mother's food becomes heroic in stature as the years go by and is remembered astigmatically, therefore, rather than accurately. The same is true concerning the size of the fish you caught when you were seven, the distance you swam underwater at summer camp, the number of yards you ran to win the big game for old Ivy-Covered U., and all that. What I am saying is that I wouldn't be surprised if your mother made the toughest piecrust on the block.

However, I have to "take a new reading" on all this, as they say in the Pentagon, because evidence has come to light that suggests we do not, in fact, eat as well as we did, despite living in a land of plenty and an age in which we are bombed with new goodies every day including legal holidays. Dr. Moises Behar of the Institute of Nutrition of Central America has analyzed the probable nutritional condition of the Mayan Indians before Columbus and contrasted this with the known condition of Indians in Central America today. Historical and archaeological data show the pre-Columbian Mayans were probably better nourished and had a better diet than their modern-day descendants. The Indians' diet before 1492 appears to have been based largely on maize, beans and other vegetables, with some meat from wild animals. Much the same diet exists today, except that there is less meat from hunting, and some commercial food products have been introduced.

Dr. Behar's findings — namely, that the diet of the Mayans is worse now than it was in the fifteenth century — encourages some American self-examination because our own diet is sliding downhill to the level of largely fattening, totally unimaginative, mass-produced, tasteless glop. Of Dr. Behar's conclusion, Spencer Whedon, an articulate American who has eaten his last overcooked hamburger and soggy French fried potato, remarked, "So the Yanqui contagion spreads, does it? Bread bleached of color, taste and nourishment? TV dinners even worse than the televised fare they complement? Gustatorily repugnant and semantically redundant pizza pies?

"I am fully conditioned to sympathize with the Mayan Indian, but surely he can at least occasionally find a genuine vanilla bean for flavoring. I can't."

I once made an in-depth survey (seven minutes in length) of supermarket shelves and noted the following in support of Mr. Whedon's contention that we are doing our best to get away from real food: frankfurter rolls, calcium propionate added to retard spoilage; cellophane-wrapped cookies, artificial flavor; cinnamon streusel coffee-cake mix, including bleached flour; shortening with mono- and di-glycerides and freshness preserver; "real egg custard mix" with vitamins A, B and C added, and "old-fashioned" corn muffin mix enhanced by dextrose and vegetable shortening.

Oh, there are government regulations, pure food laws and all that, and I am glad there are, but there are worse things about eating, the way we do it, than being poisoned. We fill our eating places — even many of the more expensive ones — with tobacco smoke, relentless music and massive over-refrigeration (including air conditioning, as it is called) of both things and people — and insist on serving everybody far more than he needs. Much of the cooking is ill-seasoned or unseasoned, and we attempt to compensate for this by letting the eater select his own seasoning, this being a subject of which he is principally ignorant.

Most restaurants, and most customers, would be better off if salt and pepper were omitted from the table settings. Actually, most Americans would be better off if no restaurants served desserts. But I suppose, if the federal government tried to regulate this, there would be anguished cries from all over — though not, I think, from the companies that sell life insurance and are aware of the numbers who die each year of expanded waistlines.

15

What we have done to eating is to sandwich it between television programs; squeeze it into a rest room stop between Albany and Sheboygan; adopt it as a substitute for smoking, and prostitute it as a vehicle for successful business transactions. Nothing else so vital is so ignored, so downgraded.

After lunch one day, I said to my companion, "How did you like it?"

He replied, "What was it?" and I do not know whether this was because the meal was unidentifiable or because he had already forgotten what it was. Either explanation is depressing.

Now, if you want to know what I am doing with this kettle, which is a foot high and a foot wide, I will tell you. Use two pounds of linguica, which is an orange Portuguese sausage of beef and pork that smells of smoke, and cut it into one-inch chunks. Cut up a big onion and throw it in. Tear up a couple of pounds of kale; finicky people cut out the stems and all that. Throw in four or five medium-sized potatoes. (Usually, it's made with beans, soaked overnight, but I don't have any beans.) Add a tablespoon of vinegar; a tablespoon of salt; a half teaspoon of black pepper and enough water to cover, maybe about ten cups, but you will have to add water from time to time, anyway.

Cook leisurely, until everything is done. This will take several hours, during which you will fill the house with a fine smell that may be expected to improve your disposition, unless you really are beyond redemption.

Don't ask me how many this will serve. (You might suppose, for example, that five potatoes would serve five people but when John Randall worked on the farm for my grandfather, he ate five potatoes at a meal and never gained a pound.) All I know is that it keeps well and gets better each day, and I propose to eat it, in this instance, off and on, for about a week.

16

To the onion, the kale and all else that is in this soup, it is essential to add something of respect, of joy in the doing, perhaps even of some kind of love. I never cook without thinking of Nicholas, a lean little man in a white apron, who spent all of his life working in restaurants.

Nicholas was born near Kalamai, on the shores of the Gulf of Messini, a land of mulberry trees and gentle goats, a countryside of date palms, oranges and resinated wine, where the climate is always mild and he reflected all of this, and that is how he came to have his affair of the heart. It was during the war, and do not ask me which war, because all wars are the same; for the living, they are time poured extravagantly through the fingers, and for the dead, they are no time at all.

There were two things with which Nicholas was acquainted: war and food.

To him, the former was a border fight on a rock-strewn hillside that had been battled over by successive generations since the tenth-century raids of the Balkan tribes. It was a small thing, as battles go; the politicians did not know about it until it was over; there was one paragraph about it a week later in some newspaper that Nicholas never saw, and there were fewer people involved in it than live on Cuttyhunk in winter. But it was, therefore, a very personal matter and when the acrid smell of gunpowder drifted down the wind, there lay upon the bloodied stones the bodies of men whose first names he knew, and as for him, he dragged one shattered leg forever more.

As for food, Nicholas approached it with the reverence and the enthusiasm of his race, finding a particular kind of poetry that expanded his spirit in the feel, smell and sight of smooth-flowing oil from the olive; the arithmetical beauty of a fresh onion slice, and the miraculous transition of warm dough, pale and passive, to golden crust. He understood gluttony no more than total disinterest in eating, for he looked upon the preparation of food

17

as an expression of love; upon the serving of it as a form of intimate communication, and upon the consumption of it as an indication of discrimination and appreciation of life.

In these years, Nicholas was a waiter, a figure of open and ageless countenance, of spare and supple figure, who moved among the booths and tables with the warm concern for his customers that is found only in those who care about what they are doing. He not only padded about constantly in his big shiny round-toed shoes, handing out menus, brushing imaginary crumbs off the tablecloths, filling water glasses, and saying "Good evening," with an unpracticed graciousness, but no matter what you ordered, he made you feel that it was an excellent choice.

"The roast lamb?" He clapped his bony hands. "You'll be glad. It's wonderful tonight."

As wars go on, they get less exciting and more deadly. More people get killed in the front lines than at home, but those at home die a little every day because imagination is more cruel than the reality, and loneliness is erosive. Thus, as wars go on, one begins to see the women with empty eyes, whose days and nights are equally empty, and for whom life has become a plain of monotony swept bare, with neither peaks nor valleys, nor any mark ahead to break the dull horizon. It is increasingly easy, under such circumstances, to decide that nothing, neither lipstick nor a new hat, nor books nor plays, nor even eating, is worth the effort. This is the beginning of disintegration of the spirit, a process that at some point becomes irreversible.

Nicholas saw all this in the woman immediately and was wise enough to guess most of what he eventually found out. He thought, "About thirty. Husband overseas more than a year. No children. Works in an office. At five o'clock, no place to go, doesn't want to go home to a four-room apartment and cook dinner for one. Nobody to talk to."

18

Because he was, as the expression goes, old enough to be her father, but more important, because he obviously had no desire to be anything else to her, she talked to him eagerly from the beginning, and he encouraged it. He did far more. When she came to the restaurant, he was always at the door to greet her, as if he ran the place for her alone, and perhaps there was some truth in that, too. The corner booth was reserved for her.

Nicholas succeeded in making the evening meal an event; he accepted as a pleasurable challenge the task of titillating her appetite and with it, her courage for the next day. Each Saturday night, because the weekends were long for her, he placed one white carnation on her table in a vase that he had bought at the ten-cent store. The first time he did it, she put her face in her hands and wept, unmindful of others there. In dismay, he attempted to pat her shoulder, upset her glass of water, much of which poured into her pocketbook; they looked into each other's eyes and laughed, and thus was cemented something irrevocable.

The ritual of dinner lasted for more than a year, during which time he came to call her "Madame M. and B.", a small joke between them (he did not know her name and never asked her what it was), for he had discovered that mushrooms and bacon on toast would boost her flagging spirits on the dreariest winter night. When Nicholas died, his obituary was contained in precisely eight lines of type, just enough to record that he had been, was no more, and left no one behind. At the funeral parlor, the open white page of the guest book was blank except for one entry: *"Good-bye, dear Nicholas. — Madame M. and B."*

While slicing the onion for the soup, it occurred to me that I might know when or whether it was going to rain if I had brought a radio so that I could hear the weather forecast. It was not terribly important, except that if it were going to rain heavily or long, I ought to cut more wood and get it under cover, because the woodshed leaks. But I decided the risk of listening to the radio was too great; in order to get the weather prediction, I would first of all have to listen to the banalities of what we have come to call a disc jockey and, far worse, listen to a certain number of his discs.

Somebody really ought to write something about what has happened to music in this country because it is directly related to how unhappy we are, and if you do not think we are unhappy stand on any street corner and watch the poor sad faces go by.

Once, there was music inseparably related to the daily life. I remember that when we installed an oil burner we lost contact forever more with the ashman, and this was regrettable because he was a singular fellow. This ashman, who proudly refused to admit that he was a member of a dying race, was shaped like one of those round-bottomed plaster dolls that will return to an upright position if you push it over. He wore a leather apron in a swashbuckling manner, performing a dusty *pas d'action*, somewhat bearlike, every time his mate tossed down an empty ashcan from the high-sided tipcart. It was the ashman's contention that any barrel (most of them were wooden then and occasionally caught fire if the ashes were hot) could be set down, even on a cement sidewalk without smashing it beyond usefulness or waking the dead.

None of these things made him singular. What caused him to be dissonantly remarkable was his love of a song, and the phrase is used advisedly, for he may very well have had only one in his repertoire. Now that he, too, is gone beyond recall and no windy day can bring back his grinning gray countenance, it is impossible to know whether he had committed to memory any other tune than "Three O'Clock in the Morning," for this was the only one he ever whistled.

20

Admittedly, he did not achieve any note specifically. As a child, I thought of musical notes as being like plump grapes and of his notes in particular as being shaped like yellow jelly beans, an upsetting thought even at this distance.

I remember the music he produced stirred strange images in my mind, such as a whirling saber made of half a dill pickle; the scratchy confined space between the wallpaper and the plaster, and a mixture of water and egg-size stones shot through a terra-cotta pipe. Yet he whistled "Three O'Clock in the Morning" loudly enough to defeat the wind itself, and with a determination that made it plain he was less concerned with a battered tone here and there than with guiding the whole business — or perhaps "shoving it" is more accurate — with rough affection to the point (never the same point) where he could begin it again.

One cannot know, for he was becomingly reticent (and where has becoming reticence gone?), whether his whistling indicated that he was satisfied with his station in life, and found his spouse delightful in all ways, or whether he sought solace in music because he was too old to suck his thumb and could not afford to drink. But more important than what his whistling did for him is what it did to the atmosphere; hearing him was almost as good as finding a penny. It perked things up and suggested there was decent comfort in the predictable things of life (such as the fact that ash-collection Thursdays were exactly seven days apart) and that, who knows, tomorrow would very possibly be better than you expected. Using the phrase "finding a penny" dates the whole thing, doesn't it? I do not know whether today's child would pick up a penny if he found one lying there before him, or whether he would even know what it was.

So whistling has gone with the ashman, and that is not all that we miss in the way of music and the sturdiness of spirit it revealed.

It was in a small, plain-boarded church under an umbrella of horse chestnut trees and half overlooking the sea that I first came to think about the importance of men singing. What they were singing happened to be hymns. In the pew in front of me, big-boned and spare, with a nose like the forestaysail of a Parsborough three-master (which is to say, very large and triangular) was the retired skipper of a steam whaler, crows-footed from the brilliance of Arctic ice during years of chasing the bowhead. When he leaned into "Rock of Ages," his voice cracked and gravelly from a lifetime of yelling commands into the gale (and never mind the hothouse niceties of sharps and flats), it was less the strength of God than the strength of man of which one was conscious.

In truth, this was the "singing strength" of Whitman and Frost. It seemed no more than reasonable, when the last notes of the hand-pumped organ had ceased bumping about among the rafters and the captain sat down, that the pew should creak its weekly protest but would not, dared not, shatter beneath his great and bony weight.

No, we do not sing or whistle much any more and there is less human music in the byways. There was a time when Jonathan Grainey, a wraith of prodigious appetite and childlike mind, who now would be committed, but who harmed neither man nor other creature and was, moreover, self-supporting and habitually cheerful, used to make his ambling way by day and night, harmonica at the ready. Little could be said for his tunes ("I make 'em up out of my head," he said) except that they possessed the same sort of simple magic that makes a mudpie edible in the mind of its creator. Perhaps they were songs about butterflies or split smoked herring on the side of the woodshed. It was hard to tell, but certainly there were no dirges among them. This was because Jonathan found life reasonable and acceptable and assumed he would, as he said, "live until I die," and his music reflected the same combination of resignation and persistence, of comfortable accommodation to the universe that he displayed when, scythe in hand and sweat darkening his faded blue shirt, he began an impossibly long swath that stretched upslope to the horizon.

Now that most of us know more about music, we make less of it than ever. We have jammed into the vacuum created thereby a pathetic substitute, symbolic of our increased willingness to accept spectator status in virtually everything — the manufactured sound, the ubiquitous and never-ending record that assails us to the point where conversation in public places, long dwindling in health, has quietly expired.

But perhaps in the small towns, the faraway places, the quieter corners of docks and markets, there still are those who whistle, sing and play harmonicas, poorly but beautifully. I hope so.

I am writing on the oilcloth-covered kitchen table. Half of me is smelling kale soup and thinking what tremendous mileage you get out of a tablespoon of vinegar. The other half is watching a nuthatch near the porch twirling on a piece of suet that hangs from a tree branch. It is tempting to philosophize, "There is the symbol of man on his little whirling world, struggling to find nourishment and not fall off." Yet it is not an apt comparison; the nuthatch is in complete control of the situation and, what is more, could not fall anyway.

There is a sound at the window in the living room and I rise to investigate because it was a soft blow. At all hours, there are the noises of nature here, flutterings and squeakings, branches crackling, water splashing and the whistling sounds of flight, but the edges of all these are blurred. If you hear a blow, it is likely to mean something out of the ordinary.

At the south window, there is a black-capped chickadee and, as

23

I watch, he strikes the glass again, making the same feathery thump. My first thought is that he must be ill or dazed, but not so; he comes to the pane swiftly, hovers with wings in rapid flutter and snatches a bluebottle fly from a spider's web spun just beneath the center frame of the window. And this time, he is so deft that he does not touch the pane at all.

I think, "Now that's not fair; the spider worked hard to catch that fly and now, when he may be ready for dinner, his cupboard is empty." But I decide to mind my own business and withhold my judgment. Interfering in such a matter is about as unnatural as bulldozing a forty thousand-year-old marsh to get rid of mosquitoes.

It is beginning to rain, gently. The wind is light and from the southeast, a quarter very likely to bring showers in these parts, and the sky is all of one piece, something between white, gray and silver. I toss a piece of split oak into the firebox, watching the sparks fly upward; oak is worth the extra effort.

In the little bedroom upstairs, there is the gentle drumming of rain upon the roof. The birds have quieted, and beyond the woodshed I can see a hole in a tree and something moves within it. At this place, I have a habit of carrying binoculars from room to room, because you never know what will turn up that deserves to be looked at or how transient it will be. I once spotted a magnificent male wood duck for about as long as it takes to blink the eye, while he paddled past an opening in the thick creek foliage. This thing that moves in the tree hole is a gray squirrel's head, with shoe-button eyes. He is snug and waiting out the rain.

It is a good time to finish unpacking, although that is a grand word for a minor undertaking that means mostly putting things where they belong. I brought little; toilet articles (those who go unkempt when they return to nature are no kin of mine); swimming trunks, sandals, a motheaten beige sweater; my

24

paintbox and easel, with one split leg; my Underwood type-writer that is twenty years old, and about five pounds of paper.

The paper does not necessarily mean anything. I did not commit myself in advance to catharsis by writing, or pledge a stint each day. I do not care how it comes out. I feel at the moment, having recently arrived, the need to write things out of myself simply so that I can look at them.

It begins to get dark. I am glad for the dark; I am wrapped within it, the squirrel and I and whatever else paddles and lopes and snuggles hereabouts. It is time for a drink, a tall, amber Scotch in a plain amber glass, with some smell of smokiness and a recollection of malted barley.

And by and by, I shall have two bowls of soup, the aroma of which has filled this little house like silent music.

THE SECOND DAY

I AM lying in the field which is my front yard, a place about half the size of a city block that is like a room, shut in on two sides by pine and locusts, the latter never still even in light air, and on the road side by twisted scrub oak and clumps of beach plum bushes, now flaming red with the fall change. But it is warm; it is even hot. There are no clouds overhead; summer never brought a better day or a prettier one, and the dome of the sky stands still in fragile silence. Here the grasses are straw-colored and the red of pomegranate; the soil is light and sandy, shell-strewn and spotted with white and rubbery heaps of empty turtle-egg shells.

Quite early this morning, I walked a mile or so to the store for bread, a particular bread that is sour and dark and meant to be eaten without butter. Part of the route was next to a superhighway, shielded only by a fringe of stunted pine, and for some moments I braced myself against the incessant whine and roar of the traffic, each automobile tearing into new fragments the atmosphere still in disarray from assault by the car ahead of it. Where could they all be going at seventy miles an hour? I wondered and could not answer. I would have felt somewhat better had I thought *they* could.

In Detroit not long ago, Bud Guest, son of the late versifier, and another fellow dug up a rusty but recognizable Model T Ford that had been buried forty years. What a splendid idea this suggests; think of all the people it has not run over and the air it has not polluted in forty years.

One is moved to propose, indeed, that if every U.S. male over fourteen (there are 65,268,000) would bury one automobile (there are 82,699,738), highway fatalities would diminish; the air would become increasingly breathable; chickens could cross the road easier, for whatever reason, and the cries of maidens in distress would once again be audible.

On the way to the store, I thought about Papa LeTourneau, who buried his automobile and scored a smashing triumph over Field Marshal Gunther von Kluge. Oh, I am sure that Papa's victory for the allies never found its way into any World War II histories, but I could find you some likable fellows in the dark and winy sanctuaries of St. Hilaire and Cauchoise who would remember and laugh.

On June 5, 1940, while Reynaud again shuffled his cabinet, the German Fourth Army got into gear at four o'clock in the morning and struck at the Somme bridgeheads. The Tenth French Army fell back to the River Bresle, and by June 8 the rumbling tanks of the Fifth and Seventh Panzers had broken through to the outskirts of Rouen, after an advance of seventy miles in three days.

In less than a month of war the Germans were within striking distance of the Seine, and behind the thin and desperate line of the French military the civilians scrambled in terror westward, clutching handfuls of belongings and clogging every road.

In Rouen, in the quiet light of the fifteenth-century church of St. Maclou (hidden behind the cathedral that the tourist sees), beneath the magnificent carvings of Jean Goujon, huddled the hopeless, and the only sounds in that place were the frightened whispers of prayer.

Papa was a Breton, a cosmopolite, a Seine River pilot on the tricky sixty-odd miles upstream from Le Havre to Rouen, and he prayed better outdoors, while he worked. The Germans were at the gates and Papa and his friends, Messrs. DuChamps, the boss longshoreman with horn-rimmed spectacles, and Charbonne, who wore a celluloid collar and was second secretary of the Bureau de Port, were taking positive action. They were burying Papa's brand-new 1940 Peugeot sedan in his front yard because, as M. DuChamps noted, while perspiration trickled down his pipestem, "the unprintable Boches will steal every unprintable thing."

The car was expertly greased and oiled. A crate of plank and timber big enough to accommodate a pregnant elephant bound for Masqat was constructed and dropped into a hole (with dirt ramp) that took three days and two nights to dig. The top of the box was about two feet below the ground surface. Papa drove the Peugeot into the box, swaddled it in a tarpaulin, patted it on the rear fender, saying, *"A bientôt, bébé,"* spiked up the end of the crate, filled in the hole and replaced the sod on top.

"Happily," he said, "it rained for the next two days and the prefect of police himself could not have found the hole, and he knows my yard very well indeed."

The Peugeot was the war's best kept secret. Half of Cauchoise, a third of St. Hilaire and a fifth of Rouen knew about it and took pride in knowing something that the occupying Wehrmacht did not. Of course, there were winks and jokes about it over a glass of calvados, even with German soldiers sitting at the next table. "*Eh bien,* you have heard? Papa's baby, not a year old, not sick a day, but now in the grave, *hélas!*" But nobody talked, not even when to have done so would have brought a fistful of francs, for the time came when Hitler's troops were crying for transport.

In mid-August of 1944, von Kluge's Seventh Army was trapped in the Falaise-Argentan salient. The only escape routes were eastward toward Rouen, through Chambois and St. Lambert, under fire from both flanks and incessantly bombed. P-47 Thunderbolts caught the German tanks and trucks in column, three abreast and bumper to bumper, and roamed over them bombing and strafing for two days and destroying two thousand vehicles. Smoke from the massive pyre was visible for fifty miles, and soon thereafter the Germans fled from Rouen, ending four years of occupation. Von Kluge, symbol of those dark hours, killed himself.

Now, it was time for Papa's "*petite résurrection,*" attended by at least two hundred enthusiasts who sat on the fence, the front steps, the sidewalk; cheered, laughed, drank, whistled and spurred on the diggers, Papa, DuChamps and Charbonne, all of whom threw dirt into the bright blue morning with terrible abandon, each shovelful menacing somebody in the audience.

The crate is exposed. "Ahhhhh!" cried the onlookers. The end of the box is pried off. "Regard how still it is shiny!" they cried in amazement. More men than could possibly get into the hole stepped on each other's feet and rushed to push the Peugeot to the surface.

Breathlessly, they waited for installation of the new battery, the critical examination by the motor mechanic, Armand, who lived down the street; his expert touching of this and that, his

29

thoughtful "hhmmms" and his grunting "ah ha's," like a doctor probing. Finally, Armand said, "Now, Papa."

And Papa took off his blue beret, and held his glass of wine high so that the sun made it glow like the blood of life. His voice was worse than the northerly's blast in the Skagerrak, but when he began, "*Allons, enfants de la patrie . . .*" they sang for the motherland, weeping and laughing at the same time, tears running down the cheeks of young and old, until the ground fairly shook and the pigeons flew up from the cobbles in fluttering astonishment.

Then, very soberly, he got into the car, adjusted himself behind the wheel. "Only nine days ago," he said, "two German officers stood on this very grass, above this very Peugeot and asked me if I knew where there was an automobile in which they could flee. If I knew, they said, they would make it very worth my while. Ha!"

He pressed a button; the engine ground, caught, choked, back-fired — and started. How they roared, "*Vive la Peugeot!*"

And Papa said quietly, "This very day, I shall drive to Paris to see for myself that it is, in truth, liberated. This very day."

Now here we are at the store where I am going to buy the bread. It is run by a fellow named Caspar and I do not know whether it is his first name or his last. As you can see, the place is squeezed between two brick buildings and it has been there so long that if you slam the door the store probably will fall down, tin smoke-stack and all. The floor is so uneven that his cat can have only a half saucerful of milk at a time.

There is an iron bell on a rusty spring inside the door, so that if this fellow is behind the curtain in the back room it goes ta-cling, ta-cling when anybody comes in, and he comes out with a fast shuffle, to guard his cash register.

"Good day," he says in a voice that sounds like wind in the

neck of an empty bottle, and you can see that he is a shiny man; his bald head shines; his deep eyes shine like wet prunes; his ears have lobes as long as a beagle's, and they shine, too. He speaks in a quiet way that I thought went out with Whispering Jack Smith and the white dog on the phonograph record. And he stands there, with hands like dahlia bulbs across his fat apron, as if it really would top off the day for him to sell you a can of Prince Albert, a plastic bag of jacks, or a pound of lard.

In this store, there is something everywhere. Little pigeon-holes, black from age and use; drawers with white china knobs; cardboard boxes with gummed labels that you cannot read; open shelves with cans, and crooked floor displays. There are matches in two rectangular tins about as big as lunch boxes that used to contain plug tobacco; the boxes are blue and red, with gold flowers, and it says "Smokino and Chewino" on them. Caspar does not sell much plug tobacco these days, or many cigarette holders, either. It's not that kind of a town.

Only the tin ceiling, painted white with a Greek key design stamped on it, is uncluttered; it supports one neon tube, specked and sputtering.

When it rains, Caspar limps and mutters, watching the water trickle down his front window that is decorated with a sun-bleached hair tonic display that he put there about the day Neville Chamberlain had lunch in Munich. He says he limps because of wet weather, and he is the only man I know who was totally in favor of the four-year drought that we had in the middle sixties. I tell him I think he limps because of a war wound he got with Michael Angelus, in defense of Epirus against the Frankish barons, and because this happened roughly a thousand years after the birth of Christ, he waggles his shiny head and tells me I am "idiotes," which means what you think it means. But in saying it, he crooks the left corner of his mouth in a smile, because every man of his age remembers the homeland

31

with wistfulness, recalling the sun and forgetting the shadow, and likes to think he was once some kind of a dragon slayer.

I do not go to his store because it is attractive or to him because he is profound. It is simply handy — and because he does not know or care what day it is, or perhaps even what month, and because he does not rely on television or traveling salesmen to tell him what he ought to be selling, he has things that I cannot buy anywhere else. Lamp wicks, for example, peanut butter in bulk, and pink fire clay.

Over the door to the back room there is a fly-specked sign that says "Radios Repaired," but time has passed by and it is not so anymore. Caspar's son used to repair the radios; he was a quiet fellow, pale and skinny and about twenty-five. One day he was just not there anymore and Caspar never mentioned it, never said anything about him again, so I never did either. I am of the opinion that the sign remains because Caspar cannot come to the business of taking it down; it is all that is left of something.

But I remember the radio shop and especially the loudspeaker that hung out over the front door and looked like a black morning glory. Most people didn't have radios then, and one fine September night my Uncle Edward and I, with perhaps a hundred men and boys, stood in the street in front of the shop listening to what the loudspeaker had to say. We were without fear of traffic — first, because there was not much at any time of day, and also because, as Uncle Edward pointed out, "Who would run us down? Everybody's here."

From some place to which I had never been, the radio, with occasional urks of static, was broadcasting "In a Little Spanish Town" and it made the street seem quite gay.

I was being allowed to stay up beyond the usual bedtime because a Mr. Tunney (Uncle Edward called it "Tooney") and a Mr. Dempsey were fighting somewhere; I wasn't sure where. The newspaper story had begun, "History will be made tonight . . ." and I asked Uncle Edward about that while he was lighting his pipe, and he blew considerable blue smoke while he got it going in good shape and he said, "Fellows who write that stuff are paid to fill space. If they don't fill space, they don't eat." But he agreed to take me to hear it anyway. He said he thought the air would do us both good.

From time to time, Uncle Edward upset the family. He went to a dinner party once and announced on arrival that he was going to write down everything worthwhile that was said. He went about with pad and pencil, to the amusement of the many guests, and about four hours later the hostess said that it was time for him to read what he had written. Everyone drew up his chair in anticipation. Uncle Edward read: "Hello." Then he read: "Please pass the salt." And that was all he had written down.

I have to confess that I do not know much about what happened in the first six rounds of the confrontation between Mr. Tunney and Mr. Dempsey because of a competing cross fire of conversation. I was standing between Uncle Edward and another man who said his corn had been poor all summer because something "got at it" as soon as it showed its head above ground.

My uncle said he thought this could be traced to cutworms, but it took him nearly a half hour to say it, including hand motions and demonstrations with two wooden matches and his pipestem. In addition, either because of a loose wire that Caspar's son stood up on a stepladder to fix, or thick fog in the bay (Uncle Edward said, "You can't see through fog; why should you be able to hear through it?"), we had a lot of crackling interference.

Then came the seventh round, and something happened that caused several of the men to cheer loudly. In the recapitulation, the breathless announcer said: "*Fighting desperately to regain*

*the championship, Dempsey cornered Tunney in the seventh
and smashed him to the canvas with six or eight terrific blows to
the jaw.*

*"But in his eagerness for the 'kill,' he stood almost over
Tunney instead of going to a neutral corner. Five seconds ticked
away before the referee could force him there.*

*"By the time the referee finally began his count, Tunney
was coming to. At the count of nine, he was on his feet, although
he actually had been down for fourteen seconds. Then in the
remaining three rounds, he punched Dempsey dizzy and
easily won the decision.*

"There will be, believe me," said the announcer, *"a lot of
argument about this long count."*

"History was made tonight," I said eruditely, to no one.

Uncle Edward, who was in the midst of explaining to the
other fellow that most people nowadays don't know how to
handle a hoe and expect God to do all the work, turned to me and
said, "What happened?"

It was obvious that something had, because little knots of men
were arguing about whether Mr. Dempsey had been, as the
announcer said, *"robbed of a knockout victory that would have
made him the first former champion to regain the heights."*

I said, "Mr. Tunney didn't get up as fast as they wanted him
to."

"A smart man," said Uncle Edward. "If I had been in his
place, I wouldn't have got up at all."

The announcer went on, *"The second Dempsey-Tunney
fight brought boxing's biggest gate, a whopping $2,658,660, of
which the champion — and still champion — received
$990,445. It is reported he will pay promoter Tex Rickard the
difference and receive a check for a million dollars and will
frame the canceled check."*

"Think of that," said Uncle Edward. "Just while we've been

standing here, this fellow Tooney became a millionaire. In the same period of time, even if you were to count say an hour or two's bank interest and the amount that my pumpkins have grown, I don't suppose I made more than two dollars and a half."

The announcer said, *"Dempsey faced defeat with colors flying, but with his fighting machinery slowed down almost to a standstill. Unmindful of the sound of the final bell, he kept going forward; he did not realize that his last chance was gone."*

The crowd began to wander off into the dark and Caspar's son got up on the stepladder and unhooked his loudspeaker, interrupting "The Star-Spangled Banner" right at "rockets' red glare," and a few of us clapped, to thank him for letting us hear the broadcast. The street was very quiet, but there was a yellowish blob of light at the drugstore.

Uncle Edward said, "How would you like a dish of vanilla?" and as we walked along I asked, "Do you think history was made tonight?"

"I think," said Uncle Edward, "the trouble with that fellow's corn can be traced to cutworms."

And so I lie here in my hot field, with the heavy silence upon me, feeling like part of the warm earth. And Caspar's son is gone, and Uncle Edward; surprisingly, since it seems so long ago, Mr. Dempsey and Mr. Tunney remain, but still, they are not at all the same people, are they? Nor am I.

Even without lifting my head, I can see the large dead elm near the house; it is taller than anything nearby. It occurs to me that if death is an outrage in winter, it is monstrous in the warm months, when every part of nature spills life, full-blown and sensuous, upon the landscape, as if there were no end to it.

Yet this tree that I have known for years, an old, gaunt figure that has been friend to me and to generations before I was dreamed of, is dead; it now stands without sense or meaning, a discordant skeleton, damp, gray and rattling, in a bright world of chlorophyll. By day it leans lonely as a Puritan image, an unfriendly reminder to the drowsing mouse and the wayward grasshopper that one may not leap lightly in the noon sun forever. And by night, especially in moonlight, the fragile tracery of its branches against the sky is a thing of wonder, yet it is the bloodless beauty of Poe, and not that of Frost.

I suppose an examination of its annuli at the butt would reveal that it was planted before Robert Fulton's paddle-wheeler *Clermont* steamed upriver to Albany, or Napoleon was exiled to Elba, but this does not interest me. I have loved the living poetry of this tree, and I will leave its autopsy to sawyers, historians and those who manufacture paper.

It is far more rewarding to wonder about the man who stood, spade in hand, on some morning when the nation was younger, the air sweeter and the world less mad, pondering where to plant this tree. For tree planters are people of quiet and magnificent conviction; they not only believe in tomorrow, but are determined that there will be a place in it for trees. And a man who will set out a leisurely growing tree is thinking far beyond himself.

This tree was planted by a man who lacked no confidence in himself or it. For the old house was here then, too, and when he stuck the sapling in the ground he had to think, "Not too close to the house. This one's going to be here for a while; it'll need room." And more than a century later, although it is far taller than the slightly buckled kitchen chimney, the tree still does not overhang the roof, its drippings do not rot shingle or gutter, nor have its long roots penetrated the huge fieldstones of the cellar wall.

During hurricanes, the elm rocked like a beleaguered square-

36

rigger. Its tortured roots lifted and fell, and the wet sod for yards about the trunk hove as if the earth were struggling for breath. Once, when the bottom was dropping out of the barometer and the tightly drawn disquiet that precedes a hurricane warned of the storm's coming, a gray squirrel scrambled to the elm's first crotch. He sat up, twitching uneasily, decided he had chosen the wrong place, flowed down the gnarled trunk and ran for other sanctuary. "He knows that tree is going to come down this time," said the farmer next door. "Elms have shallow roots."

All during the daylight hours of the storm, the children peered through the rain-beaten windows while the elm fought for life. "Will it fall?" they asked every half hour, and when the darkness came there was no way of knowing whether it had, for the roar of weather was louder than the shattering of a trunk.

But in the ragged gray morning, there the tree was, drunkenly canted to the northeast forevermore, minus a half ton of sodden leaves and minor branches, the ground raw and torn from its battle; but still it stood, gallant in dishevelment.

In summer its grace was exceptional for anything so large. It was a tree that looked satisfactorily like a tree, neither possessing nor lacking symmetry, yet combining dignity and a pleasing flow of line. A half hour of lying on one's back in the grass, studying the never-still greenness of its thousands of leaves, now revealing, now obscuring the clean blue of the sky (with which it seemed to achieve, artlessly, a perpetually satisfactory composition) contributed greatly to peace and perspective.

In the warmer weather always there were birds in the elm, nesting, trilling, scolding and tapping its branches for insects. It was a sanctuary, being far too high for cats and too close to the house for hawks and owls. At such times it was a busy, green and pleasantly noisy world, sheltering its population, yet not in such manner as to leave the rest of us shut out.

But this year, the season grew later and still there were no birds nesting in the elm. There is nothing about death to attract life, and the tree stood naked and silent. It was ugly and dangerous; chunks of it plunged to the ground every day. It had to come down; there was no excuse for delay.

Still, this was a friend, and in the shattering whine of the chain saw is the voice of Armageddon. Moreover, the manner of the tree's death was infuriating. What the droughts and gales of more than a hundred years had been unable to do was brought about by a sexless fungus, a mold's cousin, without mind or muscle.

Still, there was no reason to postpone the elm's transition to sawdust and junk. That is, there wasn't until the other weekend, when I drove down here to make sure the house was still habitable. Staring at the tree for the hundredth time, attempting to wish life back into it, I saw, high up, the head of a bird popping out from a dark hole beneath a branch. "She has a nest there," I said aloud, hardly believing. Yet it was so.

Of all the birds, one, perhaps a late arrival who found the better places taken — or a relaxed mother, casual about such things — had decided a dead tree was all right. And so, for just one more time, the elm will shelter young until they are big enough to leave it.

There is one more thing to be said. Each day, especially at sunrise and sundown, the male bird perches on a bare branch and sings his three or four evenly spaced liquid notes as if he were determined, single-handedly, to make up for the tree's lack of sound, leaves, life and beauty. In so doing, he provides a better requiem for my friend, the ancient elm, than I could create on an iron typewriter. I am much moved by his solitary faithful-

38

ness. He might easily be sitting on a greener branch, surrounded by his fellows.

I am sitting very still, swirling sunlight in a glass of white Rhine wine that has been cooled in a bucket of creek water. I cannot remember when I last sat still for so long, and I am rewarded. Like fluffy baseballs, a dozen quail rocket out of the pine shadows, cross the sandy road about four feet off the ground and plop into this field, no more than fifteen feet away. When my arm or leg goes to sleep and I make so much as a single movement, they will roar out of the short grass and away, but for the moment I can watch them, bobbing and pecking like plump little matrons doing their housekeeping, and they do not know that I am here.

This field has been plowed, although not for some time, and now it is hubbly and overgrown. I remember the last time it was plowed, because Faris and I did it together, he well and I poorly enough to make him smile and shake his head; yet we were still together and heard the same crows scolding in the distant beeches.

Faris is some English, some French (and perhaps some Indian, for all I know, since something gives him complete communication with the land and he knows what a hawk is thinking about when it soars against the sun). I went with him one time to the side of a rock-faced mountain, half a mile straight up from the house where he was born. You could not see China or Mexico, but if Emerson was right in concluding that travel is an illusion, you probably could see enough of things and people from that slab of granite to make a fair guess at all the rest of the world.

On this day, both wood and mountain were snowbound and so was all the countryside. Blue smoke plumes rose straight and slim from the occasional farmhouse; the river twisting across the valley was black in the few places where swift-running water had not frozen, and the red barns, brow-deep in drifts, appeared likely to remain that way until spring.

But it was not cold, nor was there bitterness in the winter noon. It was warm enough so that, from time to time, great plops of snow dropped from the sagging firs, releasing their branches that sprang up and startled the birds — juncos, grackles, grosbeaks and a half-dozen varieties of sparrows — into an excited fluttering that ended abruptly as they swooped back into the deep trees.

Faris walked, sat and stood as if he were part of nature. He knew this place far better than I, for it was his, and he has been coming here ("to think about things," he said) from the time he was a boy and the farm was owned by his father. He stands here now in his calf-high, laced boots; inevitable overalls patched at the knee; belted red and black mackinaw jacket; his white hair curled over the coat collar because he has been too busy cutting wood to get to the barber; and he seems cradled against the steep mountainside without actually touching it.

We had not spoken for some time, but this is not unusual with us. ("I doubt if anybody has something to say all the time," he said once, "but most people don't let that stop them.") I was looking at his hollow-cheeked profile, thinking about the strength and dignity of its composure.

Faris has no mannerism, no extravagance of facial expression; I think I have never known him to move purposelessly. His face could have been cut from the rock on which he stood except for one thing: in the eyes, there is a warmth sufficient for anything or anybody likely to come along.

Finally, he said, "I ever tell you about me and the war?"

"No, Faris."

"Well, by the fall of '17, father wasn't dead, but he was a sick man and so used up that he couldn't do much around the

40

place. I suppose I could have told the government I was needed at home; it would have been true enough."

He halted, raised his arm slowly in the direction of the wooded slope. "Look there," he said quietly, "just there; you see that fat rabbit watching us? Right there, where the pine branch comes down thick to the snow, right underneath."

Faris went on. "I remember getting the letter from the government. I knew what it was when I took it out of the mailbox and the first thing I thought of was not about the war, but that I didn't want to leave this place. I don't mean like homesickness, but it just didn't seem to me I could think as well somewhere else. I wondered whether I would know as much in another country."

He patted a lump of soft snow in his leather mittens. "Well, mother and I sat in the kitchen that night and talked about it. She was afraid something would happen to me, but she managed to make a small joke and said, 'If you go, you'll probably meet one of those girls in Paris and marry her, and I shan't even be able to talk to her so that I can tell her how to keep house.' But finally she said, 'It's your life. I know what I wish, but you have to live with the decision, so you must make it.' "

Somewhere across miles of snow, there was the muffled roaring of a plow clearing the back roads and he listened to it absently for a moment. "What bothered me," he said, "was what I owed myself and what I owed my country. The thing was, I'd been hunting all my life, and we ate what I got, and relied on it in winter. But I didn't see how I could kill a man, not even in anger, and what's more, how could I hate somebody couple of hundred yards away that I'd never laid eyes on until I got him down the barrel of a rifle?"

He sighed. "Believe you me, I struggled with it. I never had any trouble sleeping before, but I did then. And finally, I told

41

mother and father that I had decided to go, because I supposed that nobody wanted to go any more than I did, but still, somebody had to go. They were both pretty good about it, especially since all of us knew father wasn't likely to be there when I got back . . . which he wasn't."

Faris squinted at the lowering sun, now milky as the day began to cool. "It was right here that I decided how I was going to do it. And I have never told anyone to this day what I did. I'm going to tell you."

He turned to me. "You've seen me shoot a little. You know I hit what I aim at?"

"Yes, Faris."

"Well, I jiggered my rifle sight so that I went through the whole war aiming at what I was supposed to, but knowing I wouldn't never hit it so long as I aimed at it. So I didn't kill nobody, but I served my country, and don't tell me what you think about it, because I don't want another opinion at this late date."

Not long ago, while he was snaking cedar logs out of a swamp, I tried to talk to him about Vietnam and draft resisters, but he wouldn't have any of it. If I said fifty words to encourage his comment, he just grunted, and when I had about given up trying he put down his axe and said, "Look, I'm a simple man. I have led a simple life, some good, some bad, but I guess no worse than most anybody else.

"The world ain't simple anymore. I used to think I had common sense enough to keep a roof overhead and out of trouble. It seemed to me that most times, if anybody got in trouble, you could see clear enough why they had. That's not so anymore. It's a whole new kind of people. It's a whole new world, maybe worse, maybe better. I don't know. But I sure as hell know that there's little enough place in it for me.

"Most of the time, I don't even know what it's talking about, and I'm glad I'm as old as I am. Now that's the way I feel about it."

So the wine is gone; the bottle is empty, and the quail are gone, because I finally had to move or get stiff in the joints. The sun is sloping off westward and soon it will be below the tops of the pines and it gets cool quickly after that. I will go in soon, and light the fire. The blue heron already are flopping up the creek to roost.

I did not bring any books to this place this time. I was talking to an acquaintance who runs a bookshop the other day and he described his customers as "fluttering among the shelves." He said, "They take armloads of books. I have no complaint to make about the sales volume, but I just have an uneasy feeling that they aren't reading them, that they can't, even though they would like to, because they can't achieve the peace of mind that is essential if you're really going to get something out of a book. If you're going to get anything out of somebody else's thoughts, you have to keep your own from getting in the way."

So perhaps I did not bring any books because I knew that, this time especially, the world being as Faris described it, my own thoughts would keep getting in the way.

What I mean to do this evening is think about tomorrow, because there are several courses open to me. I can walk, paint a picture, sail in my little boat if the weather is fair, or catch a fish for baking. These are all good things to think about.

THE THIRD DAY

O N the way to the beach, I met this fellow on the bridge
that spans the creek. The bridge is so narrow that it forces
one to speak, and had this not been so I believe neither of us
would have, being in that place at that hour for peace, not
conversation.

It was not the bridge that van Gogh painted at Arles, being no
more than a sway-backed pole and slab affair with one end of
the deck adrift and afloat at each high water. Yet van Gogh came
to mind. This was because, approaching the weathered span
across the wet flat, the marsh was golden in the fall sun, its rich
grasses shimmering in bright and restless windrows.

Having spoken, we paused at the railing, reluctant to make
talk for the sake of doing so, but, in civilized fashion, unwilling
to rebuff a man intelligent enough to be found in that place.

I was not particularly pleased to see him. I was thinking about something and I did not wish the process interrupted. What I was thinking about was that it was just starting to get light when I began my walk, and the high western sky reflected the sun's pinkness even before it could be seen over the heavy black pines in the east. Every time I come to this place I try to see a fox, and you have to get up early to do that; I had, as a matter of fact, never seen one, but today was the day.

I came to the marsh edge and, so quickly as to take the breath, I suddenly saw him, the shiny red fox whose den is on Try Island. Very quietly, he sat up on his hind legs, peering over the clump of bayonet-edge eelgrass. In a moment, he leaped, as beautiful as wind, light and water, and seized something. I suspect it was a fiddler crab; purple-black, with bowlike starboard claws, they scuttle on the marsh by the thousands, popping in and out of holes in the mud.

I thought I would tell this fellow about seeing the fox, but then I thought I would wait a little to see whether he deserved it.

"I heard a rail this morning," he said. "Have you seen him?"

"I'm not a bird watcher," I said.

He made no comment and we watched the water. Under the bridge, Silver Spring Brook surged seaward on the ebb. At tide's crest, this beach is a frontier, drowned and swirling, sandpipers and herring gulls by the hundreds roosting on its narrow bars. When the water goes back to the sea, it pours in runnels that each twelve hours ruthlessly recast the architecture of the soft tideland.

Finally, this fellow said, "I found a gull the other day, in the road to the cottage. I got out of the car to move it, realizing that it was too weak to fly. It had half swallowed a fishhook and the line was hanging from its mouth. I got the hook out. I'm feeding it. I think it's going to come along all right."

A pair of mallards, handsome with violet-white wing patches,

45

rocketed from the pond nearby and wheeled toward the bay. He went on, "When I cannot help in the world of man, sometimes I find the problems in this other world of creatures here simpler by contrast, and I am encouraged to try to do something about them. As with the gull . . ."

Abruptly, the man turned and left the bridge, not saying good-bye, not asking my name. Nor was it rudeness, for there seemed no need of either. Nor was there anything more to be said. There was not, because as he walked to his car, parked just beyond the bridge, I saw that its Massachusetts license plate bore the letters "M.D."

All kinds of people are attracted, or at least think they are attracted, by the things that are here, as my friend the beach poet could tell you. Where he lives, the sea stretches beyond the fish traps, where the bony-shouldered cormorant hunches on a lime-spattered spile, and even beyond that, where the dark-green Portuguese dragger named for a saint leans to her deep, wet work.

"Before Eugene O'Neill had coffee money," they will say to you, "that is where he used to write." And they will point to one window in paintless frame and black-paned in the afternoon light, high in an arkish waterfront house in Provincetown's East End. These days it is a place where tourists come, and probably they do not write much more than, "Having a fine time. Wish you . . ."

Next door lives the poet, with a somber tomcat, a sliver of driftwood that looks like a grilled bonito over the fieldstone fireplace, a tall blue bottle that catches the sun, and books enough, broken-spined from constant assault, to overflow three wheelbarrows.

Blue water comes under the porch decks of these houses when the tide is high. When it isn't, you go beneath the decks on

46

plank steps, dark and mossy; through a peeled forest of piling, silvered at top and lisping weeds at bottom; walk halfway to the horizon on hard sand, and halfway again through warm, ankle-deep water, to come to swimming depth.

"I would have understood," said the poet, dipping a garlic-bread crust in his lentil soup, "if they had been underprivileged. But obviously, they were the 'American Family' right out of one of those slick national magazines that, for reasons obvious at least to me, finds its own survival the month's most difficult assignment."

This is what happened:

Their car, with stereophonic sound, was named either for a wild animal or some dismal form of weather. The father had Italian sandals, matched golf clubs, a *Playboy* subscription at Christmas, twenty-three extra pounds inside the waistband of his Arnold Constable shorts and, about the eyes, still a touch of the wet-dog friendliness that had characterized him as a sophomore.

Mother and the children were the helpless by-products of success. She was still handsome, although slightly dried out from oversunning and martinis starting at 11 A.M. The three boys obviously understood they could do whatever they liked, and that anyone who said no to them was ignorant of modern psychology and the delicacy of the formative mind — and anyone, parental or otherwise, who laid a hand on them was operating counter to a present or future Supreme Court decision.

In a phrase, then, the family was attractive, unquestionably bright, well bred and, as the poet said, "the inevitable social wreckage of complete permissiveness."

So the poet munched his bread and he said, "They arrived next door at noon, after a long, hot trip from the city. They skinned out of their clothes and into bathing suits. Then they transported to the beach swim fins, inflatable raft, six-foot plywood boat with sail, red-and-white-striped umbrella, folding beach chairs, transistor radio — oh well, you know, all the bare necessities.''

He scraped the bottom of the soup bowl. "They dumped this pile of expensive junk on the beach and ran for the water. Then there was this uproarious shrieking and laughter. I went to look and they were kicking, splashing, raising a welter of foam, forming a semicircle and heading for the shore — driving something in the shallow water before them. I went down to the beach like a shot, furious.''

On the kitchen wall, the wooden clock with a gold schooner on the lower glass banged brassily four times, and he looked at it reflectively.

"In their first five minutes here, they had kicked ashore a blowfish, a comical little creature that can inflate its white belly when it's scared and make it harder for bigger things to swallow it.

"These people didn't have anything better to do than try to kill, needlessly, the spirit of the very thing for which they had driven five hundred miles. Five above-average products of our affluent society, without purpose, had reduced this frightened, somewhat ugly little being to a helpless lump of life struggling for breath.''

He shook his head, remembering. "I gave them hell, I quoted Thoreau and also a friend of mine in the Marine Corps.

"When I had finished, the children looked at their parents to see which way they should react. The father was uncomfortable, but he said tartly, 'This fish belong to you?'

" 'In a way,' " I said. " 'Creatures on earth with less intellect are in the trust of those who theoretically have more. It belongs to you as well.'

"The woman started to walk away. She said, 'I told you we

48

should have gone to Maine.' They all followed her, and one boy looked back and stuck out his tongue."

The poet rose, went to the window on the sea. "With a start, I realized I had forgotten the most important thing. I ran to the blowfish and put it back into the water. I hate to lose my temper; my head ached, and my heart was pounding.

"The little fish lay belly up and I thought, 'Oh, damn, all this for nothing!'

"But then, Allah be praised, his small eye, brown, gold and green all at once in the sun, popped open; he flicked his tail, blew three large bubbles of relief and slithered off into the sparkling sea."

And the poet looked at me then, saying, "I will write something about that sometime if you think there still are those in America who will read it with empathy."

All right, we shall proceed toward the shore, and barefoot is the only way; high water has not been that long gone and much of the way is puddly and squishy, depending on whether it is sand, clay or marsh mud. Now here, cradled behind a dune, I direct your attention to a matronly catboat called *The Three Sisters*, and especially to the boatman's brown hands. They move strongly over the hull in the sunlight and there is pleasant rhythm in his scraping, which is neither so loud nor so unnatural as to inhibit the sandpiper in his damp rounds. Blond sawdust powders the backs of his fingers and the curled hair of his wrists below the khaki shirt sleeves rolled to his corded forearms.

He is talking about a four-foot-wide strip of purple-black bunker oil or bilge pumpings that coats a long stretch of the waterfront. It is a snakelike band between the high and low water marks, darkly violating the sand and coating the rocks with ugliness. Impervious to salt water that covers it twice daily, it stains the harbor deadly brown and the little fish of last summer, darting and shining in the shallow water, are not to be seen any more. At the nearby moorings, a film of bubbles, washed off the shoreline and thickly stirred by the ebb and flow, coats and recoats the white boats' boot tops, banding them with a dirty stripe the color of tobacco juice.

The boatman filled his pipe as if he had time, tamped it with subconscious reverence and struck one of those big wooden kitchen matches that few carry anymore — only those who have to light up in the wind. He ignited the match by scritching his horny thumbnail across the blue and white tip; when he puffed, the pale flame wavered like a silent dancer in the bright light of the morning.

"That's no five gallons," he said, waving the match northward where the sludge line stretched to the far point. "Whoever dumped it let go a lot. Ought to jail him. Better still, make him damned well clean it up. Won't burn off; won't scrape off. Five years from now, you turn over a rock and there it is on the underside, messy as ever."

Hook-nosed and hungry, a gull seesawed over the float stage and plopped onto the blackened gravel. He found a chunk of gurry and it swung like a bony pendulum as he flapped off to the deck of a shiny cruiser, swinging at her buoy, to eat it in peace.

"He'll leave the best set of tar footprints on her you ever saw," said the boatman and he shook his head, and turned back to his scraping.

So I remembered Ida, and you will pardon the fact that her name is a poor pun, and frightfully obvious, because these were simpler days, long before anybody had sniffed amphetamine, and people really used to laugh at things like, "I'm a little stiff from Bowling . . ."

Nor was it so long ago — but before there were laws against pumping ship bilges into the clean sea — that my friend and I, trudging an empty beach in the clear wind, found a female eider (Ida, of course), sick and soiled from the gummy oil plastering her feathers.

The eiders, hundreds strong, rafted at sea for the night, and the oil scum floated down about them while they slept. When they tried to wash it off, they contracted a bird's version of dysentery and died miserably by the scores.

If you do not know the eider, except for its quilt-stuffing reputation, it is a large marine duck, and the female is dark reddish brown, barred with black. It nests from the coasts of Newfoundland northward, and do not be misled because it looks clumsy, for it flies fast and dives admirably.

Ida squatted on the beach, barely beyond the sea's reach, too weak to flee the enemy, too near death to care whether man hastened it. We looked at her; bill under wing, she refused to look at us.

In short, we put her, unprotesting, in a burlap sack on the back seat of the car; drove twenty miles home; squirted gin in a medicine dropper down her throat ("She can't be any worse off," said my friend) ; scrubbed her with kerosene, hot water and yellow laundry soap, and made a bed for her in a little house formerly inhabited by a wayward Belgian hare gone spring mating.

I did not sleep that night. Several times I went to the bedroom window, squinting futilely into the deep shadows of the back-yard, where Ida waged the battle that each of us must fight essentially alone. There was no sound; no movement; nothing but terrible and interminable silence. I thought of her dead; one big, funny foot outstretched awkwardly and her soft head unmoving on the wooden floor of the house, and I could neither stand the image nor put it out of mind.

51

At daybreak I ran out, bracing myself.

Behold, she stood, the wild sea rover. Her eyes were like jewels in the fresh morning; feet apart, chest out, and bill high, she made one demand of me — and I knew what it was. I shucked and hand-fed Ida a pint of quahaugs, joyous at the arrogance of her reborn appetite, unmindful of the fact that she nipped me unmercifully and unintentionally.

That was the beginning of days of quahaugs and quickening convalescence. I cannot say we became close. She was one with the lonely offshore swell, and kept her distance. Still, when we freed her, strong and eager, she rocketed aloft — and yet, and yet, took time to make one swift circle of farewell over our heads before beating seaward forever, a black dot in the sun path.

Interpret that single circling of a free, wild thing as you will (the ornithologist will suggest it was navigational orientation); yet I have my thoughts about it, too, and that is why I have not forgotten Ida.

In this marsh house with the terra-cotta chimney wired to withstand the gales of February lives Charles, and as he said once, "I've lived here quite a long time. I can't say I've lived here so long that I own the house, but it sure owns me."

Charles is an admirer of James Fenimore Cooper and stereophonic sound, and this simply demonstrates the adjustability of the human creature, as does the fact that officially recorded temperatures at a given intersection of Boylston Street in Boston ranged from one hundred degrees to five below zero, in one twelve-month period.

I could do with less of both Cooper and stereophonic sound, but I like Charles because he is comfortably irrational. Furthermore, although past retirement age he has the agility of a grasshopper, and at this particular moment was attempting, with a bent coat hanger and other objects, to snake a wire up through a plastered wall so that he could pipe such melodic offerings as "Tracy's Theme" into his bedroom.

Grunting with the effort, he asked irrelevantly, "You remember the day we found that damned tree stump on the beach?"

It was, in fact, a day to remember. After a week of late-season humidity and fog that did not burn off until midmorning, the wind had hauled into the northwest, producing an incomparable blueness of sky and an atmosphere of incredible clarity. The sea, flicked into little touches of motion, sparkled something like ten million times between the wet sand flat and the horizon.

There was a nice choice for walking barefoot; above the high-water mark, clean, fine-grained beach that poured between the toes with each step and was warm from the sun; below the mark, a damp, hard road that encouraged firm strides and recorded very satisfactory footprints.

Something natural there is, namely, a determined current, that guides floating objects from the Maine coast to a beach on Cape Cod. The process may not be wholly predictable and it undoubtedly takes months, but in this instance it had floated an extraordinary tree stump the many miles between, and the receding tide had stranded it on the flat. Charles first saw it, far off, and decided it was a petrified octopus, so we waded out through the shallows to examine it.

It had been a large tree. Where the saw had felled it, the butt was more than two feet in diameter. Presumably it had stood at the top of a bank of sand and gravel near the water's edge, and once the stump was dead, and its roots had lost their holding power, it succumbed to years of erosion and eventually slid gently downslope and overboard, until it was afloat.

53

The circle of roots, worn by waves and groundings, still was formidable and even beautiful. Each root was more than two feet in length, although broken off short, and the total effect was flowerlike, as if the stump possessed wriggly petals forever frozen in their pattern. Stump and roots were smooth as glass and silvered with the patina that comes only from long weathering.

Apart from his pension, Charles's income is derived from "the summer people," and he concluded immediately that the stump, inverted and fitted with a circular glass top that spanned the root structure, would make a coffee table that ought to sell for five hundred dollars. "I don't know how many years this thing has been in the process of creation," he said, "but you don't find more than one in a lifetime, if that."

So nothing would do but that we must round up two additional stalwarts, a truck, block and tackle and other ponderous gear, and spend the remainder of the day — to use Charles's expression — "jack-assing" the stump a half mile along the beach and two more miles across creek and marsh until it lay, newly damp with our combined perspiration, in his front yard.

"I remember the day, and the calluses, very well," I replied.

He chuckled and said, "Good for you. Well, just the other day, I got rid of the stump. Fellow wanted it for a coffee table."

"Fine," I said. "Now you can make the down payment on that pickup truck you want."

"Um," he said. "Not exactly."

"You didn't get five hundred dollars for it?"

He hemmed two or three times, rebent the coat hanger and went fishing for the wire again. "Well, you see there were these two fellows. When the first one came, he had his checkbook in hand and pen at the ready before he even got through the front gate.

"Said his wife had just the spot in their living room for it and

54

he knew somebody who would cut the glass for him, and all that. Didn't even ask if I wanted to sell it.

" 'What'll you take for it, fella?' he said to me.

"Now if there's one thing I can't stand, it's being called 'fella.' One time I was thinking about Nelson Rockefeller for President and he came around and put his hand on somebody's shoulder — I forget who, but it doesn't matter — and he said, 'Hi there, fella!' and I said to myself, I said, 'Governor, as far as I am concerned, you have had it.'

"Anyway, here was this overbearing pilgrim from inland somewhere who was bound to buy the stump, and all of a sudden I decided I wouldn't sell it to him if he covered the damned thing with cut diamonds.

"As I think back on it," said Charles, "I must have been out of my mind, because I need that pickup truck in the worst way and this stump didn't cost me anything, unless I count your calluses."

"So what happened?"

"Oh, he kept upping the figure until it was ridiculous. And I kept getting madder, although I was glad none of the neighbors could hear what kind of money I was turning down. Finally, he got all red, mad and ugly, and said he thought the stump probably was rotten on the inside anyway. Which it isn't, of course."

"But you did get rid of it?"

"Ye-e-s," said Charles, somewhat reluctantly. "The other day, a young man stopped by to give me his mother's regards. She's my age and went to high school with me. He's a schoolteacher, little town in Indiana. Probably makes about half what I do, even if I don't work much. Wanted the stump for his wife's birthday. Said he could pay as much as ten dollars for it.

"I said I couldn't take money for it because it hadn't cost me anything. I gave it to him and helped him load it in his car. He protested that I shouldn't be so generous, but I told him stumps like that came ashore every day and we had to burn 'em to clear the beaches."

Charles cleared his throat and he said, "Now, if you don't mind, I'd just as soon change the subject before you're tempted to offer some high-flown moral comments on this piece of idiocy." He bent to his coat hanger business, grunting some more, and added, "You might go see if the stew is hot; I'm getting empty. And rustle up a bowl for yourself."

Come sit here in the lee of this dune; it is a bowl of warmth, golden in the sun. I am always surprised at the number of people who do not know which is the lee side of something; most creatures of nature, except sheep, know. If it snows, you have to go after sheep and get them in; otherwise they will drift to leeward with the storm until they come to a stone wall, and there they will pile up and die. Why nobody taught them to buck the storm until they came to a wall, in which case they would be on its lee side, I do not know. I suppose a moralist could draw a moral, but I am not a moralist; I just like to crawl out of the wind and wet when I can.

What I have to think about is composing a letter which, in a very general way, has something to do with Agrippina the younger, who was the mother of Nero. For all I know, you may entertain a certain provincial prejudice against her because she married her uncle and had a penchant for felony with her honeyed figs.

Yet I submit she is a classic example of a mother who success-fully taught her son that he could not lallygag indefinitely at the end of her apron strings, but must cultivate independent thought and activity. How seriously he took this advice may be judged from the fact that he invited his mother to spend a weekend at his summer place in Baiae, which is a cannon shot and a half west of Naples, and arranged for her to go sailing in a vessel ingeniously contrived to founder.

The suggestion is that Nero expected her to drown, especially since, when she did not, he had her assassinated. But it seems to me that, in so doing, he was demonstrating little more than over-reaction to the lessons he learned at her knee. Clearly, there can be such a thing as too much independence of thought and action, but this is, after all, only a question of degree, isn't it?

However, in this instance, it is not the family portrait that interests me; it is Baiae, once a pleasant watering place on the Gulf of Pozzuoli named after Baios, the helmsman of Ulysses, to which affluent Romans retreated to bathe in the curative sulphur springs. It may be helpful to think of it as a first-century New-port, the principal difference being that in Baiae, the rate of induced mortality obviously was much higher and the wine came in terra-cotta jugs instead of glass magnums.

I am indebted to the erudite *Christian Science Monitor* for observing that, "in the days of the Caesars, Baiae was the swingingest spot of the Roman world . . . The life led there and the money spent make today's 'jet-set' activities look like a strawberry lawn fete."

But *hélas*, as Papa LeTourneau, the Seine River pilot, used to say, Baiae fell upon evil days, or vice versa. It was first devas-tated by eighth-century Saracens, and in 1500 was deserted because of malaria. But the worst and final calamity arose because Baiae was on uncertain land, and, as a result, much of its ancient site, still containing the impressive ruins of domed bath-ing temples, now is under twelve feet of water.

Frankly, these things confuse me, and I do not know whether Baiae, like Venice, is sinking into the sea, or whether the sea has risen twelve feet because some frightful force in the earth's bowels is shoving up the sea bed. But the important business is that Professor Giovanni Ovannosky, Naples' superintendent of antiquities, has asked Rome for enough money to raise Baiae from the sea bottom.

In a century dominated by the unimaginative (witness congressional debate and the American version of French dressing), I find this a brave and bold notion. I regret that we have no modern counterpart of Lucretius, who made great poetry out of scientific matters, to write something of heroic proportion about it.

Now I propose to write a letter to Professor Ovannosky, because I would like to know how he proposes to make Baiae dry again. Is he intending to have divers go below and bring it to the surface piecemeal, so that it can be numbered, lettered and put together again on higher ground? Will he build a dike or cofferdam about it and pump out the water?

I have a particular reason for wanting to know, because there is a piece of watery ground I should like to retrieve for my own personal and particular purposes.

In a quiet byway of the Atlantic, near enough to this place to be comforting, and south and by east of a shoal old enough to have an Indian name, there is a strip of stubborn sand with nothing on it but the green and graceful eelgrass that helps to hold it there from one tide to the next.

I have spent hours watching this sun-baked flat from a boat, marveling at the rhythmic peace of its existence. By day, the wet sand is the color of maple sugar, and the water rolls upon it, rumpled lace of foam, and then is sucked back, surely and regularly, into the lime greenness of the shallows. Its population is never large and, if it is not always compatible, it is at least complementary; in other words, I know that some things present sometimes eat other things present, but this is an equation older than even I, and besides, I have observed that this sort of thing is done with such consummate grace that even the quarry is only momentarily affronted.

58

I could get along with the creatures there. I have seen rows of black-capped terns nestling, at a distance looking like a twenty-foot piano keyboard. Sometimes there is a damp, drowsy seal hauled out close to the water's edge, and he raises his cannonball head, stares at me with the bright eyes of the innocent, to see whether I am coming too close, which I am not.

By night, this tongue of sand lies in the black water like a silver staff of truth on an impenetrable sea of the dark unknown. It gives off its own calm light, about which there is a comforting aura of great age, a mute suggestion that some things are beyond the rigors of the daily hurly-burly and will outlast them.

Where I now sit, in the lee of this dune, is sanctum. The little grass-covered spit could be sanctum sanctorum. However, at each high tide, it is, unfortunately, submerged, and this is what I have to talk to Professor Ovannosky about; if he can dry out Baiae, I ought to be able to do as much for the strip of sand, or at least enough of it to sit on and eat a sandwich.

The stone building that you can see at the head of the wharf over there used to be Jonathan Bourne's countinghouse, in the whaling days. I never see it without thinking about a man I saw only once, with whom I had little conversation, but whom I shall remember always for his uncommon dignity, from which he obviously was inseparable and to which he, therefore, had to give no thought.

He came, a shambling figure half-blown by the shrill easterly, along the shadowy side of the countinghouse. The too-long khaki overcoat, once intended for some American soldier in some war since 1940, drooped to the tops of his battered work shoes. He was hatless and the thin strands of black hair squirmed in disorder across his half-bare scalp.

His arms were outstretched and he carried, somewhat

gingerly, a long and floppy package in brown wrapping paper, the pieces of which were untied and in rebellion. He came closer, brown eyes evaluating, his aged, toothless mouth half-cocked in a grin. He was a man of the Cape Verdes, perhaps seventy-five, lanky and weathered, easy-moving and soft-footed, such as have, at least since the days of Jonathan Bourne, walked the decks of every type of vessel this port has had to offer, in search of everything from eels to ambergris.

He came over and said, "Hi boss," and you will not assume anything by the use of this word. There may be people somewhere who say "boss," and in so doing, are tugging at the forelock to acknowledge the presence of their betters, but not so here. It represented no more than good spirits and a desire to let me know that he wished me well.

He wanted a piece of string, to subdue his package, yet he did not even wait for an answer, but added, "Good day, today." Obviously, since the red small craft warnings whipped straight out across the river, and silver needles of rain lanced the street puddles, he wasn't talking about the weather.

"How's that?" I asked him.

"Look," he said, and held down a wet flap of the paper. His grin widened.

He held a haddock across his arms, plump and fresh, about four pounds, and with the head and tail still on.

"Good soup," he said. "Tell by the eyes."

Of course, any old handliner such as he would know that the eyes of a fish are a good indication of how fresh it is. Too old, too frail to pull a skiff off to the ledges for sea bass or tautog, too poor to own a boat with power, he was one of the fraternity that waits each day for the draggers to take out their catches. With luck, on the "good days," somebody tosses him a fish.

It was tempting to ask him whether he was aware of the Great Society, or Social Security, or government surplus foods, or aid

60

for the aged, or the United Fund, or virtually dozens of sources which would have made available to him food, clothing, shelter, heat and, undoubtedly, money, for which he qualified by virtue of his years. Such a question would have been sensible and humanitarian, for he might have been unaware of all these things — people still are — and he might have been glad to know about them.

Yet call me craven if you will, there was something in his face and bearing, something that began not yesterday, or even at birth, but somewhere long ago, in another era and another country, that restrained me. His race and his genealogy were older than mine, older even than the nation that could provide him with security if he chose to ask for it.

The moment when I considered talking to him about assistance evaporated when I looked into his eyes, in which, if there was something of Job, there was a bright spark of colossus as well. The spontaneous surge of compassion for this man, who looked so frail in the wind-blown rain, was replaced by the uneasy suspicion that he might never in his life have felt he needed help of such nature; that he probably did not think he needed it now, and that he would be surprised to learn that it was available or that anyone ever accepted it.

It seemed supercilious in the extreme to ask him whether he could care for himself when he obviously had been doing it for decades longer than I. Besides, he had not stopped for the purpose of complaining or wheedling, but only to ask, sensibly, whether I had a piece of string.

Once, in times that he could remember well, men carried useful things like string and jackknives in their pockets. Today they don't, because they don't want to bulge, and they carry only useless things like combs and little flat tins of antihysteria pills. I didn't even have either of these.

Along the shadowy side of Jonathan Bourne's building, the

wind flicked something at the foot of the rusty fire escape. It was a length of fuzzy yellow wrapping twine. The eyes that had spotted for years the dark flurry of schooling mackerel in the bay caught the movement. "Ha," he said, knelt on the wet gravel, tied the brown bundle securely with such deftness as is second nature to a sailor, and crunched off. He turned once and waved, calling, "Thank you, boss."

I do not know what he thanked me for, because I did not do anything for him; as a matter of fact, I failed him in the smaller sense and perhaps in the larger, too. Surely I gained more from the encounter than he: I gave him neither string, help nor inspiration, yet he thanked me, and I suspect that is the way he goes through life.

It is something to think about.

THE FOURTH DAY

I DO not know yet what wind and weather will do this morning, so we shall sit here at the mooring for a while and bask in the snugness of being afloat without having to be alert. This sloop is the *Guinea Hen*, so named by somebody long before me, because she is slow and fat, but easy to get along with. The cabin always smells salt and damp. It shouldn't, but it does because I have never been able to make it as tight or dry as I would like to, pounds of paint and seam compound notwithstanding.

I cannot count the times I have banged my head, moving about in the cabin, even though I know from years of habit precisely where everything is — but she is small. You peel potatoes sitting on the foot of the port bunk, over a counter that I built next to the sink. You wash dishes sitting on deck with your feet in the cabin, and thus do not have to bend double because of the cabin's low overhead.

Even though there is a door that will close, there really is no privacy in the head at all, unless, as a guest once suggested, "The party of the second part jumps overboard and swims alongside at a respectable distance." And when *Guinea Hen* is stowed for a weekend, with bedding, icebox, food, kitchen utensils, foul-weather gear, shore clothes and books, crawling into a bunk is a chore for a contortionist.

I remember the first time, bringing her home. Small craft warnings were up; the three-foot sea was lumpy and had a couple of days of brisk wind behind it; tatters of fog obscured both buoys and shoreline, and it rained heavily.

From the start, she leaked; the first warning I had of it was when I picked up a floorboard and found a half barrel of water sloshing in the bilge and spraying off the revolving propeller shaft. She also leaked from the top; solid spray and rain poured over her and trickled down below through the seams; everything was soaked within the first hour. She leaped through the gray seas, every third or fourth one of which threatened to overwhelm her. Mindful of the fact that she had no self-bailing cockpit and carried a half ton of iron ballast — that she would, in fact, go down like a stone if she filled — I stared constantly at the electric pump and entreated anyone who might be watching over me to continue to do so, because I do not know anything about electric pumps, except how to turn them on and shut them off.

I finally had to take in sail as it blew harder. I doused the jib, getting soaked in cold spray a half dozen times, clinging to the foredeck with broken fingernails, and after another struggle clawed the mainsail into submission and tucked in a double reef. Then I started the little engine again and thus she drove, slammed and inched her way to windward for a painful six hours.

At day's end, lame in every muscle, I brought her to an anchorage, close to home. Once anchored, the pump choked twice and died; the instrument panel disintegrated into saltwater rust; the engine stopped, and the throat halliards parted, letting a certain amount of canvas, blocks and running rigging dump in disarray into the cockpit. Yet she had behaved gallantly in the face of adversity; I know of no boat of comparable size that crossed the bay that day, and she held on just as long as she could, and it was just long enough. She has always been like that, sufficiently gallant for the demands upon her. At such times as this, at anchor or at the mooring, she gives a deceptive impression of lightness and agility, of swinging with a certain spirit, almost ebullient in her gentle noddings.

There is much merit in sitting aboard a boat at a mooring. It allows you to look back at the land you have left, and if you would find a new country within an old one, you need only look at it from the opposite direction. Now it is very early morning and what is so breathtaking, apart from the crystal quality of hour and season, is that, being land-based creatures, our view of environment usually is from shore to sea — but on this day, we swing at anchor and look to the land as if it were another world.

Two differences afforded by the change in perspective are astounding. Even at this short distance, helped by the dawn's stillness, what yesterday was familiar and even dull now well might be a foreign country. Although only a half water-mile away, its edges are smoothed and there are beauty and mystery hidden within them. It is easy to imagine that the inhabitants ashore bear no resemblance to those of yesterday, and for all I know they may speak a foreign tongue, wear doublets, and traffic in Eastern spices.

It is pleasantly incredible that, tucked into the shoreline's blur, there actually are such unimaginative things as gasoline pumps and laundromats.

Creatures, one is obliged to observe, sometimes are no more polite than humans. Two terns, black-capped and sharp-tailed (do they cry "reed, reed," or is it "greep, greep," and why should two birds of the same kind say precisely the same thing, for men do not?) squabble over the slime-green, weeded end of a mooring buoy on which both want to stand. In the southwest there still are gray masses of night, but the wind is northeast, with a certain sharpness, and gradually the clouds whiten, become puffy, and finally are blown like enormous leaky pillows hull down over the sharp horizon, and the whole sky is bright blue and magnificently uncluttered.

It is good to live close to the weather; in watching the poetic machinery of the bowl overhead there is both peace and adventure. I once knew a man who deliberately had no windows in his office, and I felt that he had sacrificed a great deal in choosing not to be distracted by sun or rain, or the wet and silver splendor of late fall fog.

Now over all is morning quietness, except for the sad and raucous two-toned laughter of a gull; or perhaps he is not laughing, I do not know. How bright is the coming sunlight on white boats; on smooth wood it sparkles, and on the sea's face it is dappled and interspersed with the darkening wind ripples.

Here comes a gravel-voiced duck, breasting a little V of wake and leading his talkative flotilla, six in line, with purple and white chevrons, to the attack. The proffered doughnuts are a day old and slightly passive from the mists of dawn, but the ducks do not mind and snatch for them greedily, their quick bills snapping. I think, "Nature did not intend ducks to eat doughnuts," and have some misgivings, but then I think, "Nature did not intend college boys to eat goldfish," and although there is nothing reasonable about this approach, it is comforting because at least for this moment I do not have to be reasonable. It is sufficient to let all the things this morning is flow over me, without worrying about why it is, or whether it ought to be.

The quality of atmosphere is changing from day to day at this time of year and the new kind of world is particularly noticeable in the early hours. There is a clarity, as if everything were freshly washed; it is a powerful beauty and it etches, as with a diamond-bladed cutter, the sharp ridgepoles, the spires, and even the tree clumps against the sky's line.

Like the mute, moving targets of a shooting gallery, lines of clumsy, impatient vehicles push along the distant highways and it is happily strange to see them so far away as to be noiseless and fumeless, their insistent horns too weak to reach me.

Coffee, rich in a white china mug and light dancing on its dark surface, titillates every sense and is an experience of the spirit as well. Steam from the cup rises to embrace the nostril; married to the wind of daybreak across the cheek, to the warming sun that prompts an emotional uncoiling, it infuses an attitude of well-being — not ambition, just well-being.

The quiet houses ashore are tucked in and out of stately elms so ancient that they must remember all the long-lost idioms, the leisurely provincialism of some earlier life. That is the key to the spell; this morning, time is pushed back at arm's length for a moment and the values — lapping of water, the equation of sun, sea and sky — are much the same as they have been for hundreds of years. That is why, when someone ashore slams a screen door, I wonder how he could bear to do it, but I remind myself that he has not made this journey I have made; has not lost time as I have lost it, and his sleeve of care is still raveled.

The mind — my mind anyway — is occasionally too insistent to be denied. Over the years, I have never sat here at the mooring, looking ashore at this beach, without recalling in exhaustive detail much that I would rather not remember. This is because, in a war largely forgotten because there have been other wars since, I spent weeks memorizing the configurations of the Normandy beach called Omaha which this one unfortunately resembles more than any other I have ever seen. It is an irony, for this is a place of peace; it has never known war; yet it pulls the trigger of recollection for me and I shall tell you what I remember, because I must.

The raw taste and smell of fear began with the time of dawn or earlier, when the crumpling explosions, dull blast of mine in mud, singing shell, and roar of flame commenced to transform the summer land into wounds, and man into shapeless, black-wet mounds, lapped by the tide.

It was chilling in the fresh northwesterly. Four-foot breakers curled along the beach, and the steel gunwales of bobbing landing craft scraped off the sides of the transports those shivering soldiers who forgot how to come down a scramble net properly. Smoke and dust from naval fire and a slight mist made the land purple and the enemy therein more terrible by virtue of invisibility. Landmarks we sought were obscured, undoing our assignments catastrophically. The fuzziness of shoreline contributed to the unreality of the blistering shattered air, the headless infantryman bobbing by, the boat disintegrating in a fountain of white water.

Offshore were the great gray hulls of the fighting ships, *Texas*, *Arkansas*, *Ancon* and *Augusta*. Inshore, a dozen rolling destroyers slammed five-inch shells into the strongpoints, for we could not land artillery and all but two of the thirty-two "swimming tanks" foundered short of the beach. A French cruiser, muzzles blazing orange, broke out an ensign of incredible size, a tricolored assurance to those natives ashore who had refused to evacuate, that they were being shot at by friends.

Most of the landing craft grounded on sandbars. Under fire as they came within a quarter mile of the shore, the infantry suffered its heaviest casualties just after touchdown. Rapid gun-fire beat on the landing crafts' bows, and when the ramps were lowered you could see the spatter of bullets whipping the surf just beyond them. Some soldiers dove underwater or went over the sides of the ramps to try to duck the machine gun's pattern.

Chilled from cold spray, stiff from cramped positions, green-faced from seasickness, and often loaded so heavily that they sank when they waded into a deep hole, the debarking troops could not move fast in water knee-deep or higher, and they stumbled on the runnels, crossing the tidal flat. Many were exhausted before they reached the shore, where they faced two hundred yards of open sand before gaining the seawall or shingle beach. Those who made it did so by walking into or crawling under heavy fire; most of those who stopped to organ-ize, rest or take shelter, joined the dead.

Behind the survivors of the beach crossing, the rising tide was drowning the wounded who had been cut down on the sand. At Sector Dog White, LCIs 85 and 91, which had sailed with us, were mined and shelled; clothes burning, the living jumped or fell into the sea and tried to swim in under the artillery fire. The ships burned for hours under palls of black smoke. As the tide rose, underwater obstacles — posts, angle-iron "hedge-hogs," gatelike "Element Cs" and log ramps — all carrying teller mines, blew up more boats.

Up ahead were wire and minefields to get through, the ex-posed beach flat and, beyond, bare and steep bluffs with enemy strongpoints. In addition to mines, there were fougasses, TNT charges set off by trip wire that ran along much of the beach. Enemy pillboxes, casemates, rocket pits and antitank guns poured plunging and grazing fire along the tidal flat and beach shelf.

At 0830, approximately two hours after the landing, de-stroyers were no longer able to bring fire to bear on the German strongpoints for fear of hitting our infantry clinging to the foot of the smoke-obscured cliff. The tidal current and poor visibility had caused innumerable units to land in the wrong places; heavy casualties among commissioned and noncommissioned officers produced further confusion.

Sometime during those hours of fear and interminable explosion, of outrageous introduction to an outrageous world — and do not ask me what time, for time was gone — something offshore in that gray, milling armada caught my eye. What a remarkable thing it is that a split-second glance at some familiar line or shape prods the subconscious. What was it I had seen that called to me to look again?

Then I saw her, bright bone in her teeth, threading her way through the fleet and bound inshore, the two-hundred-and-fifty-foot steamer *Naushon*, once queen of the New Bedford, Martha's Vineyard and Nantucket Steamship Line, and requisitioned in 1942 by the War Shipping Administration for use as a hospital ship. She had come to Omaha Beach to take back the first wounded to England.

Oh, she too had changed; gray paint for white; no insignia on her black stack, and reinforced steel plating where none was before. But her lines were unmistakable as she stood in, and it just happened she was starboard side to and turning, exactly as I used to see her, day after day, as she rounded the breakwater at Vineyard Haven, with a long and two shorts of the whoomping whistle to let everybody know she was coming.

Squatting among the broken poppies and the junk of war, I wept until I vomited. It was sacrilege for this symbol of tanned women in summer hats, of children playing in sand to be in such a place and on such a bitter errand. It was unbearable to be reminded of a time when my principal concern was whether the mackerel were biting at the steamboat dock — and to try to relate that time, or myself, to the new corpse upon the sand six feet away, a thing of open mouth and vacant eyes.

All aspects of war are, of course, not of such intensity; otherwise, I suppose, no one would survive it. Within their vast and terrible framework, all wars embrace a multitude of human relationships, many of which, even when frustrating, serve as a kind of reassuring lubrication for the spirit that must endure the largely inhuman experience.

For example, accompanied by certain official anguish, it was established that, although there was a shortage of medical supplies in Vietnam, the Army-Air Force post exchange service had utilized scarce cargo space to import there 500,000 to 600,000 cans of hair spray and 15,000 women's plastic raincoats. Since there were an estimated 750 women in Vietnam entitled to post exchange privileges, this worked out to about 675 cans of hair spray and twenty raincoats apiece. That should have taken care of the monsoon season nicely.

However, I suggest that wars, foibles in themselves, are characterized by such foibles, and I direct you to Rouen, the ancient capital of Normandy, eighty-seven miles northwest of Paris, to prove that today is more like yesterday than may be desired.

The time is the gray and bitter fall of 1944.

This old French city, where Joan of Arc was burned, lies in an amphitheater of hills bordering the Seine valley. It is surrounded by the suburbs of St. Hilaire, Beauvoisine and Cauchoise. Here, black steeple-finger sharply pointed to the noon sun, is the ancient cathedral with its Tour de Beurre (Butter Tower), square stone pierced by high mullions, and so named because funds for its building were given in return for permission to eat butter in Lent.

The recently departed Germans had left Rouen's port a mess

of sunken hulks full of explosives. But a real port, to ease the load on the invasion beaches and supply the fast-moving Allied frontline, was needed until Antwerp could be opened. British and American salvagers went to work with sixty-ton cranes to clear the river wreckage.

It was a critical time.

On the shoulder of the wooded Ardennes plateau, Patton's Third Army tankers, a quarter million strong, had reclaimed Lorraine for the French, placed heavy pressure against the enemy in the Saar, and were pushing to break through the Siegfried Line. At this point, Allied interrogators of prisoners of war secured evidence of an Ardennes counteroffensive plan, designed to regain German initiative in the west. The primary objective was Antwerp. If its potential supply source could be cut off, the Germans would have isolated four Allied armies. For this push, von Rundstedt, Hitler's brilliant field marshal, was mobilizing thirty-six divisions, including six hundred tanks and four crack panzer outfits of Sepp Dietrich's Sixth Army.

It was vitally important to get Rouen, unused as a shipping port for the four years of occupation, back into business. The major role thrust upon it — supplier to fighting men who hoped to forestall the counterattack and, if the German thrust were successful, substitute for Antwerp — inspired British, French and Americans, who worked side by side around the clock to clear the channel and berths.

In record time, the job was accomplished. It was a proud moment when the port command sent the dispatch to Britain: "Ready for the first cargo vessel." Rouen, restive under the iron hand of her conqueror since 1940, was about to join the fighting.

The U.S. Naval Port Party went virtually sleepless with anticipation, visualizing this vital first ship — symbol of France liberated by Americans; of Rouen restored to her dignity and destiny; of the opening of a new lifeline to the battlefront —

boiling across the Channel at flank speed bearing shells, grenades, petrol, mines and guns for freedom's cause. Every longshoreman in Rouen swore, on the name of the beloved Maid of Orleans, that the ship would be unloaded in lightning time, to buttress Patton, to blunt the enemy attack.

Rouen was ready when the rusty little coaster turned the river bend and headed for the quay. *"Voila!"* cried the crowd, tossing its hats and kerchiefs aloft and giving three ragged rousers for God and country.

A thumper of a brass band struck up "Hymne de Marseilleis" and everybody wept, even those from Boston, Mass. The deputy mayor, in a weskit of pool-table green, bared his bald head in respect; following suit, every docker yanked off his beret and slammed it against his chest in salute. Up went the American and French flags.

Joe College, the French docker chief from Cherbourg, whose cropped hair, roaring motorcycle and striped blazer obscured his real name, put on his horn-rimmed spectacles, raised his hand (as large as a bunch of bananas) and quieted the crowd. The first man to go aboard, he readjusted his fountain pen and started up the gangplank. He personally, with ("sirty-six years, *mon vieux*") experience — *"mon vieux"* being a warm term such as "old shoe" — would supervise handling of the first slingload of the war cargo. A battery of rumbling trucks already was lined up for loading; drivers were poised for the long haul to Ardennes.

Monsieur College placed his handkerchief on the ship's deck to protect his trousers; kneeled, and peered over the coaming of the open hatchway into the vessel's dark interior. He rose, a puzzled look on his face, and announced, *"Eh bien,* it ees not gons."

"Not guns?" the crowd cried, amazement in every Allied face.

"Non."

73

The cargo pallet rose out of the hold, swung skyward on the boom for all to see. It contained two wooden office desks, a chair and a wastebasket.

"Monsieur," the crowd yelled, "is it the same with all the rest?"

"*Oui*," replied Monsieur College glumly.

Silently, they left the dock, walked quietly to the café in the Rue du Gros Horloge, and spent the rest of the day drinking in Allied perplexity.

One of the things the war did to or for me was to make me hopelessly prejudiced in favor of the French people. So I was sorry that there came a time when General Charles de Gaulle did not like us very much. I submit that, although differently shaped, his nose was no larger in area than that of George Washington, which ought to demonstrate to you my determination to be fair.

In late years, after Ben Franklin, that is, I think we have not shown much imagination in our diplomatic relations with France, and this is a vital quality to Frenchmen. Who but the imaginative French would make it possible for you to take a girl to the Place de la Concorde in the dead of night, snap your fingers, and cause the lights to come on, the fountains to glow, and the girl to fall gasping in your arms in sheer amazement?

You can do this for $12.20 an hour, by contacting (two days in advance, *s'il vous plait*) M. Calvet, Direction Technique de la Voirie Parisienne, 9, Place de l'Hotel de Ville. Other monuments cost more; the Eiffel Tower, for example, $55 an hour. Some can be lighted for as little as eighty-eight cents, if it's just your in-laws from Duluth.

But if you really want to knock the eyes of your beloved out by lighting up the whole city of Paris, it will set you back four hundred clams. I would have to see whomever you are trying to impress before deciding on this one; four hundred dollars will buy an awful lot of truffles.

But I am sorry that M. de Gaulle somewhat fell out with us because I have eaten buttered mackerel with a cousin of the mayor of a little French town and discussed with him his glass-cased brass clock that never needs winding, for whatever reason I do not understand, either in his language or mine. Which is to say that I regard the French with fondness, especially this cousin of the mayor, who acquainted me with the only horse ever decorated by the World War II French underground, the maquis.

"This horse," said M. Dalbec, spearing a piece of mackerel and staring at the transparent wafer of afternoon moon, "was a creature of Alsace-Lorraine and, *naturellement*, of great perception, as are all those who come from there, including my beloved mother-in-law, who selected me as her son-in-law.

"Have another pickled egg," he said, darting his fork, adder-like, at the plate painted with overblown pink roses. "I have to begin at the back, in telling you about Marcel."

"Fancy name for a horse," I remarked.

"Fancy horse," he mumbled through his egg and mackerel. "In late '44, Marcel removed himself from Alsace-Lorraine and came to Honfleur, where he went into service for a friend of mine. Who makes a formidable omelet," he added, apropos of nothing.

"Briefly, then, Marcel was pulling a wagonload of turnips and turned left into the very path of an American jeep filled with two colonels. Two wagon wheels (unhappily, on the same side) were fractured, so that my friend tumbled into the road, shattering the crystal of the gold watch given to him by his father, a devout Christian farmer of Calvados, on his deathbed. His father's deathbed, that is."

M. Dalbec waved his fork at an insistent bumblebee. "My

friend engaged me as his solicitor, because I am privileged to be bilingual, although I explained that to speak English does not necessarily mean to be able to converse with Americans. No offense," he added quickly.

"Of course not," I said, deciding thereupon that I would, in fact, take the last piece of mackerel. "I've said far worse on the subject."

He went on, "Because my friend did not know why the accident occurred (he said he had told the horse to turn right, not left), I interrogated the horse."

I arched an eyebrow. "You are trilingual. You speak horse, too?"

"It's not difficult if you know more than the horse," he said curtly. "Most Frenchmen are imaginative enough to converse with animals. Also, this was an important matter, because the colonels were not inclined to reimburse my friend.

"But happily, the horse saved the day. The horse said, 'For almost four years of the enemy's occupation of France, I have gone to the left when told to go to the right, and right when told to go left, to the constant exasperation of the Wehrmacht which, happily, now has gone home. It was the least I could do for my homeland, the resistance movement and the Allies, *n'est-ce pas?* Everything the Germans wished me to do took twice as long.' "

Dalbec sighed with pleasure. "It was superlative. The horse had been so little time in Honfleur that he resorted to his underground tactic automatically, without thinking — hence the accident. Of course it was a natural outgrowth of his aid to the Allies and so it was forgivable. The colonels agreed, and gave my friend a new watch crystal and a handsome settlement."

"But why did they decorate the horse?" I asked.

"*Eh bien,* since my friend had two unused wagon wheels behind the barn, he used the American money for the dowry of his pleasant daughter, Heloise, and six months later she married a well-to-do butcher from Villequier. Very well-to-do, indeed. They came here to live . . ."

"I still don't see —"

"The butcher discovered we no longer had a bell, or indeed a bell tower, in our little church of Saint Omer because the American guns (pardon the expression) had obliterated both in their search for a German observation post. In his great generosity, the butcher caused to be restored both bell and tower." He looked at his watch. "In exactly nineteen minutes, you will hear the bell; it is beautiful.

"Thus it was that we decorated Marcel, the horse, for 'service to countrymen beyond the call of duty.' Marcel was touched and made a splendid response, which is to say that he neighed loudly every time they mentioned his name, and in the heat of the moment even nipped my cousin, who is the mayor. But without Marcel," he shrugged, "no bell."

So what kept coming to mind while we were having our difficulties with M. de Gaulle was that we might try sending a horse to Paris to negotiate. I thought he might even begin by looking up Marcel, who must feel reasonably decent toward us.

After all, we got him decorated.

As a matter of fact, I have long since concluded that most misunderstandings — even those between nations — can be overcome by means far short of war. It is not difficult to find proof of this theory.

Last winter, I was sitting on an unforgiving bench in an out-of-town college gymnasium watching a basketball game. This is not something I do often, or knowledgeably, and I am not even sure how I happened to be there, but anyway, the atmosphere was charged with tremendous vitality and soupçons of rubbing alcohol and it was a contagious, electric sort of thing.

Actually, as it turned out, I was sorry that James Naismith

has been dead these three decades, because I think he would have been pleased to hear about this experience. You may recall that Mr. Naismith, a theology student, invented basketball, the only major sport strictly of United States origin.

Next to me, there was an amiable young man with pruning-hook sideburns, a frayed moustache and a long bang hanging over the left eye, who served as interpreter for me, and I think every generation gap should have one. He was well-spoken and very patient with me.

At some point when, I am certain, we were critically pressed by the opposition or they by us — I am certain it was one way or the other — there was an overwhelming din of horns and whistles. All the players halted in midmotion; it was like the game of "Statues" that we used to play when children, in which all participants froze in position upon signal. One player even had a huge, sneakered foot in the air, and finally lowered it, very gently.

I turned to my guide and asked, "What on earth has happened?"

"Rule Number Nothing is in force," he said. "Do you see that player over there under the basket with his hand held up?"

The young man in question, wearing a sleeveless steamy red and white ensemble with boat neck, was about eight feet tall and he was making a round O by pressing together the thumb and forefinger of his raised right hand. "O," I deduced correctly, was what had given rise to the expression "Rule Number Nothing," but what did the circle of thumb and forefinger mean?

"It means," said my friend, "that he has lost one of his contact lenses on the floor. He is standing near where he lost it. Play will not resume until it is found," he added firmly.

Here and there in the audience, some young people of both sexes raised a hand and made a similar O. My escort explained, as he put up his own hand and did likewise, "This is how you tell the referee that you know what a contact lens looks like. If you don't know, you'll never find it, and you might even step on it. In a minute, the officials will let us go out on the floor and we'll comb it, inch by inch. You know what one looks like?"

I nodded, and he said, "O.K. Here we go. Come on, you might as well help."

So I found myself on hands and knees, assigned to an area of the court floor, and crawled about, casually conversing with my acquaintance at the same time, since talk seemed more friendly than silence in such an informal atmosphere.

I was wearing overshoes, which not only were cumbersome for floor inspection, but led rather naturally to some light conversation about the recent heavy snow we had had. My young friend, who proved to be a political science major, said, "The snow had one good effect for me. It provided me with a subject for my thesis."

"Really? What possible political subject could come from a blizzard?"

"Well, four of us have one big room and a bath downtown. Two beds on one side, two on the other, and some furniture in the middle. It's an old building. The weight of the snow and sudden thawing split the whole damn building. We live on the fifth floor."

"Incredible," I said. "Is it safe to live there?"

"Well, the crack goes from the sidewalk up one side of the building, right through our room in the middle, and down the other side of the building. The city inspector came to see it and he said he thought it would be O.K. until June, and we're getting out then anyway."

"Doesn't it make you nervous? This crack through the room, I mean?"

"In the beginning it did. But it's like anything else. You know, like a girl who can't dance, or a professor with mannerisms, or a car that has no pickup; you get used to it. And finally one of the guys thought of The Game."

"Game?"

"Sure. Think of the crack in the floor as the Berlin Wall, or the parallel of latitude that separates North and South Vietnam, or North and South Korea. An artificial barrier separating two groups normally and traditionally bound by common interest."

"Ingenious," I said.

"Sure," he agreed, with splendid candor. "And when we started developing the idea, you know, making notes every day on how the crack across the floor tended to make us think we were different because we were on one side or the other of it, I asked my professor if I could do my thesis on it. Living case history sort of thing. He thought it was fine."

"Did you really stir some feelings of animosity for each other?"

"With the help of some contrived border incidents," he said. "Once in a while, we'd toss an empty beer can or a wet towel across the line of demarcation. But the most interesting thing was how conscious we became of having to step over the crack, and we really crossed from one side of the room to the other less because of it. I can't tell you exactly why we didn't want to do it, but it was not inviting to do so."

"That's too bad, considering that you started as friends, or I assume you did."

"Oh, we're friends again. After a week, we filled the crack with Elmer's Glue-All and put a skinny patch of linoleum over it. Now we pretend it doesn't exist because you can't see it anymore, and we're all back together, compatible as usual."

"Remarkable. If only your symbolic experience could be applied to international politics."

"I don't see why it can't," said the young man.

80

"Well what brought you all back together again, more than anything else?"

"Having to share the same bathroom," he said laconically.

And at that moment, somebody found Reggie's contact lens. I think they said his name was Reggie.

THE FIFTH DAY

DROPPING the mooring is one of the most final of human gestures. The vessel is no longer bound to the earth; the man in her is no more secure than his judgment is sound. Cast off from the world, they have become a world themselves, married to each other inextricably, and locked in closer embrace, because of the vast loneliness about them, than landsmen are likely to understand.

This is independence beyond the desire of many; it is founded upon self-sufficiency that requires instinct as well as experience. Very often, it allows no opportunity for a second chance. The sailor must cut the fishhook out of his own palm, or better still, not lodge it there; must splice his own parted halliard if he is to get home, or better, insure that it does not part; and he must face problems before they occur.

So there is always one eye to windward, where the future comes from at sea, whether it is gathering fog or the quick white squall that explodes with needles of rain and gusts capable of knocking the little boat down.

Leather in the gaff jaws creaks pleasantly against the varnished mast; the *Guinea Hen* chuckles her easy way through water deepening from green to blue. To the southwest, there is a flutter of quick wings over riffled water; these are the black-capped terns working over a school of bait, and surely below the little silver-sided fish are the hungry, snapping mackerel. This is Scylla and Charybdis certainly; the mackerel chases the little silversides to the surface, where he is eaten by the tern, or chased down again to the mackerel, and back and forth, across the watery miles, the meal goes on and on.

We shall drail for a mackerel for dinner, broiled and buttered, with a hint of lemon, and perhaps a baked potato. The breeze is fresh; I must take a tuck in the mainsail or we will move too rapidly for the fish to catch us. Scrape the lead jig to brightness so that it will look like a little silver fish as it is towed through the water, and over the side it goes. Now we sail alongside the schooling fish, jig towing through them, and stand alert; even a small mackerel hits hard and quickly.

There it is — the quick yank; bring in the line fast, but steadily, otherwise you will lose him. Up over the rail, flapping and torpedo-shaped, black-striped and shiny-bellied, into the bucket of cool seawater. Over with the jig again, one more of that size will be plenty, and then we shall sail with the school

83

awhile, just for the pleasure of watching it and the equation of life and water of which it is a principal component.

I am not a teacher, yet I have spent much time in and about educational institutions, and it is natural to me to progress in thought from one kind of school to another, from the school within the sea to the schools of children on the land, hidden somewhere inside the purple shoreline that I have left behind.

I suppose we all tend to think of education in terms of particular teachers whom we remember. In my case, it is not a teacher I had, but a friend of long standing, a skinny fellow named Perley, which is a Down-East name in case you never heard of it. In college, he used to be a miler and was, I gather, outstanding in mathematics. Now he smokes a pipe, raises enormous dahlias, and tries to understand why his children are so much like everybody else's. I once gave the commencement address at the high school where he is principal, and after it was all over we talked a little, and that is how we came to know each other.

He sat on the newly waxed apron of the stage, his long legs dangling between two pots of white lilies. All the auditorium doors were open, and in the twilight there were sounds, most of which can only be heard in towns, because cities are not quiet enough. A clarinet that only moments before had uttered the stately tones of Elgar's "Pomp and Circumstance" squeaked once, as if it too were now free for the whole summer; it was silenced abruptly in the slamming of a car door and a burst of young laughter that lay lightly on the warm air of the new night.

A block away, a white-spired clock struck the hour, its notes roundly muted by the acres of fluttering green leaves between bell and ear.

It had been a very warm graduation; most of them tend to be, but the temperature and the emotion had left them all, grandfathers and granddaughters and all in between, happily flushed and bright-eyed. At the end of the ceremonies, there was such a round of kissing and hugging among the families as would have distressed a bacteriologist, but on the other hand would probably have delighted a sociologist.

It seemed appropriately unrehearsed and natural that a snub-nosed tiger cat should come upstairs from the janitor's room, jump into one of the now-empty back seats in the auditorium, and sniff and crane its neck in all directions, trying to determine why everyone had not stayed home tonight as usual.

"At such moments," said the principal, "and I suppose I must have attended at least thirty high-school graduations, I feel emotionally drained and, paradoxically, spiritually brimming. There is no sight on earth comparable to that of a young face caught in the struggle between yesterday and tomorrow."

The janitor, in washed blue overalls and with beads of moisture on his forehead, came down the aisle with the cat tucked under his arm, and addressed the principal by his first name. "Didn't the kids look nice tonight, Perley?" he asked, and without waiting for an answer, walked on, saying, "This cat don't belong up here, and he knows it."

The principal smiled and said, mostly to himself, "Yes, they did look nice. They always look nice, and when I think that about them, it reminds me of what made me want to become a teacher.

"I went into the first grade at an old brick school shaped like a high-posted box. My teacher was Miss Nelson and she wore a long black dress with white, lacy cuffs and something like a little white starched apron that was always very crisp and neat.

"Because my name began with B, I was assigned to the first seat in the row next to the teacher's desk, and Miss Sherman, the principal, called me to her office upstairs. She said, 'Perley, sometimes Miss Nelson doesn't feel well. If she puts her head on her desk, because you are nearest, you must run right upstairs and tell me.'

"One day Miss Nelson did put her head on her desk, and we did not have her for a teacher anymore after that, but Miss Sherman gave to me a piece of scrap paper on which Miss Nelson had scrawled a sentence as she lay there, waiting for help. All it said was, in spidery writing : 'Perley is a good boy.' "

After we got to know each other quite well, I had occasion to visit Perley in his office, which I think is really a broom closet. As an opener I said, "I understand from a frequently reliable source — that is, the newspaper — that you seek a raise in pay." With what is intended to pass for a twinkle in my eye I added, "I don't see why you need a raise. You have all summer off . . ."

I never really did finish the sentence. I understood from certain things that my friend said as he lifted me off the floor by my lapels and barked (I think that is a fair word) at me, that teachers find little humor in this remark. "Listen, you," he gritted at me . . .

Suddenly, characteristic good nature returned to his freckled countenance. He put me down. Then he said, "You are going to play school for an hour."

It occurred to me that, at close range, he looked disturbingly like Savonarola. Or maybe Machiavelli. "You're going to sit at my desk and play principal," he said firmly. "Just to see what it's really like."

He had his hat on before I knew it and, in leaving, remarked, "I am going out and sit under a green, leafy tree in peace. Be sure not to do anything that I wouldn't do." And he left.

So there I sat, principal pro tempore of an elementary school, in a broom closet. And I couldn't close the door, which I'd have preferred to do, because there wasn't any. Abruptly, there appeared a small girl in a somewhat green dress, whose problem was obvious even before she said succinctly, "I threw up."

"Um, yes," I said, not certain whose responsibility this was.

"Help me," she said, having decided it was mine. So we made our way together through a half a box of Kleenex, discovering in the process that each of us had blue eyes and owned a dog. Then she decided she felt well enough to return to class.

She was followed by two boys with cowlicks who, recognizing that I was new, stood with hands in pockets like a couple of fast-draw artists from Dodge City, trying to figure whether they could put me on. Deciding that they could, they responded with giggles when I asked them what they wanted. Five seconds of that and I wearied of the game, deciding to belt them once or twice. Fortunately my better nature prevailed and I thought, "No, they may be related to somebody on the School Committee."

A teacher showed up and said, "What are you doing here?" to me, but without waiting for an answer added, "I sent them to your office because they were dueling in class. With rulers. Something they saw on television." She left.

I said to them, "Who won?" and the shorter one replied, "I did."

"Go stand out in the hall," I said. As an afterthought, I went to the doorway and added, "Any funny business out here and you both get promoted to a harder grade."

I went back, sat down and stared at a rubber plant in a green ceramic pot on top of a filing cabinet. There was a card scotch-taped on the pot that read: "Water every other day." I thought, "I don't even know whether I water it today or tomorrow," and that seemed to characterize my total dilemma as a principal.

Someone knocked lightly on the door casing. It was a girl

who looked, even at that tender age, at least worldly, if not seductive. She smelled of cigarette smoke, smiled disarmingly, and handed me a note that said, "Please exuse [sic] Helen from gym. She has got a bad cold."

I said, "Will you please sign your name on this, just to validate it?"

"Validate" was beyond her, as she indicated by a blank look, but she signed it, and I said, "By comparing the handwriting, I see you wrote this note yourself. Go to gym, or I'll take away your pack of butts."

She swished out in sullenness. I felt pleased with my astuteness and said to myself, "Hello, Mr. Chips, you old educator rascal, you."

This feeling did not last long. Within the next seventeen minutes:

1. The custodian, who wanted to wax the floor of the end-of-the corridor room, informed me that it had been promised to both the librarian and the remedial reading teacher for this period, and I would have to decide which of the three was to have it.

2. The truant officer arrived, seeking payment for a pair of torn trousers. Investigating what was reportedly a case of mumps, he had discovered the patient trout fishing, and had pursued him valiantly but lost the trail in a thicket of bullbriers. "The briers also ripped my leg," he said, "but I don't suppose anybody cares."

3. I had to move out into the hall because the school nurse wanted to paint some throats in my broom closet.

4. The grass snake in the Grade 4 terrarium expired (the brown paper bag in which I received him had written on it: "Edward, 1970–1970"), and a delegation gave him to me to dispose of.

5. The Grade 2 teacher said I would "simply have to do something" about a pupil who was perfect in all other respects, but who refused to sit down.

There is also much to be learned in watching the learning process itself. A classroom can be anything from a battlefield to an oasis and this particular one in which I found myself on a given day — principally because the pupils were not very old — was an intellectual byway of innocence and candor, certainly an unusual combination. The chairs were very little, and the people were very little. It was difficult to remember, perhaps impossible, when one was that small or how it felt. The teacher was very young, and this undoubtedly was a good idea, because she shared the unjaded outlook of her students and it was obvious, from the first moment of entering the room, that they liked being with each other.

The room and its population represented, in capsule, what the world might be like if the process of growing up did not have an inevitable impact on ego, equality and honesty. In their comfortable sameness, these children were like beans in a bag, still noncompetitive and unaware of any differences among them, except for a very superficial acceptance of skirts on the one hand, and trousers on the other. Their comfortable compatibility also made it possible for them to laugh and cry easily, even interchangeably; to be interested briefly in almost anything, and to answer any question in the world immediately, if they wanted to.

Someone who understands the components of learning's miraculous mosaic had transformed the four-square classroom into an atmosphere. By means varying according to the capacities of those who come to learn, good teachers at any level do this; at this primary level, things, in addition to ideas, were required to accomplish it.

89

There was a bayonet-leafed plant, flourishing and green in a glass bowl filled with white stones. On the window ledge, a pair of goldfish, suspended bright coins in their watery silence, stared large-eyed through a stream of rising silver bubbles. A plaster-of-Paris bust of Benjamin Franklin on the bookcase communicated a sense of approval of what was going on. The yellow curtains, half drawn to keep out the bright winter light of sun on snow, made the room snug and quiet. What the couple of dozen children there were doing may prove, for all I know, that a better world is inevitable.

The magazine *Grade Teacher* published two or three photographs in one of its issues. The first shows an attractive cat, out for a walk. The second portrays a mouse who, considering the propensities of mice, probably is looking for somebody's house to gnaw. The third picture is of the cat and mouse meeting, an abrupt, beak-to-beak confrontation. There are no more pictures. At this point, both the magazine and the teacher ask the pupils: "If there were a fourth picture, what would it show? How do you think this encounter between cat and mouse came out?"

In the second row, a little girl who could hardly wait to answer shot her arm into the air for recognition and cried, "They got married."

This convulsed everybody, because if there is one thing you know at this age, it is that cats marry cats and mice marry mice. The fact that you know this has nothing to do with Darwin or Mendel's law of inherited characteristics; it is simply that anything else is as preposterous as school on Saturday.

"Well," said the boy with a tooth missing in front, "they sat down and talked for a while."

It is well known, of course, that sitting down relaxes the atmosphere. That is why the principals of the Paris peace talks should have spent more time thinking about the design of the chairs and less about the shape of the table. Nobody ever fought on the school ground while sitting.

"What did they talk about?" asked the teacher.

"The mouse was looking for work."

"Why?"

"So he could buy food for his children."

Several nodded in agreement; it apparently seemed reasonable that the cat should be the employer. The teacher asked, "Do mice usually work for food, or do they just take it?"

They recognized immediately that the suggestion was that mice steal, and they would have none of it. Three or four of them said defensively, "It's all right for them to take it because they have to, and it's not very much anyway."

Another hand went up; it was a girl with braids, in a pink and white dress. "Well, the mouse begged the cat not to eat him, so the cat didn't. And then one other day the cat needed something and the mouse helped him, so the cat was glad he hadn't eaten him."

The teacher said, "That was nice," and they seemed to think it was fair, too, and were inclined to elaborate on it. One boy said, "What it was he helped the cat with was that a dog was chasing the cat, and the mouse . . ." Here he paused for thought. "The mouse bit the dog?" he finished, his voice rising in a question. Obviously, it did not suit him or some of his colleagues, who shook their heads from side to side in rejection.

"Small dog, perhaps," said the teacher.

The interesting thing was that only one of them out of the entire class offered what might be considered the adult ending. A girl with China-blue eyes said firmly, "The cat chewed the mouse's head right off."

You could hear them gasp, undoubtedly as much in excited interest as horror. They had avoided this reality by choice, but they knew it existed. Perhaps because this solution was both unimaginative and final, one sensed their disapproval of it and of their classmate for suggesting it.

In the hall, as I left, the teacher said, "Given another year or two, they will think of a possibility they now leave out. Size, of course, does not automatically determine the power of decision. Some mice are just smarter than some cats. They don't know that yet."

The bell rang and she disappeared into the classroom so swiftly that she virtually left a small smile suspended in midair.

I envy that woman her opportunity to work with the young. One reason for the somewhat lopsided accent on youth in the United States stems from the fact that too many American adults tend to become fat and unnecessarily dull, these being related forms of self-indulgence. The other is that we are producing a lot of bright, articulate and sensitive young people.

These observations were prompted by an examination of a mimeographed publication entitled "Senior Songs: A Collection of Original Poetry" by pupils in English IV at the high school here. Their instructor was Mrs. Mabel H. Knipe, of whom it may be said that most Americans who speak good English had Mabel Knipe in their public school background. Mrs. Knipe is one of the best arguments for Robert Frost's recommendation that endowed chairs of learning be established at the high school level. No one goes to college without going to high school first, and the additional security and dignity are long overdue. Achieving this is a neglected public responsibility.

The trouble is that attics all over America contain publications like "Senior Songs," each attesting to the fact that today's leaders, when young, burned with a gemlike flame that somehow has given way to the passive coals of the barbecue pit.

Listen to these youngsters talk about what moves them:

92

There is love, of course, about which one is free and willing to speak, an experience held gently and yet hungrily at that age, and without embarrassment. Of it, Jane Hiller wrote ". . . *and softly whispered words that used to fill my soul with song whenever we would meet/then quietly it left and all was still. How could I know that love had passed my way/and I, unknowing, bid it not to stay?*"

Nor is the young life saccharine, for there is no grief like the first; others may be deeper, but not sharper. And Dara Johnson wrote: "*The raindrops/how they fall upon my hand/gently . . . /as if to wash away the sorrow that life has brought to me.*"

Youth is contemporary because it has no other period to belong to. Having no past to long for, it is acutely conscious of the moment's struggle. "What color is freedom?" asked Robert Nickerson, and he warned his elders: "*Look you men of knowledge/Look you men of the world/Look here in your homeland/Look to the faces of your brothers/White means freedom; black, oppression.*"

Always the struggle for self-identity is present, and the fierce desire not to be lost, to "make something" of oneself. Ursula Ostenberg remarked: "*Forgotten!/That's the destiny/for those who won't brand/the earth's hide deep/with their names . . . Those who lifted/the heavy iron of individuality/and struggling under its weight/passed it on to/Homer,/Shakespeare, and Lincoln/ . . . They seized it, and were/remembered.*"

Like Terrence Rioux, they "*wonder at the power and majestic beauty of the angry sea,*" and Kathlyn Foley cries, "*but my cheeks are not wet . . . I sit, and try to picture with my unseeing eye a time when men will live in peace.*"

These are the thoughts and voices of potential nation builders;

here is the spark of courage and awareness. But I wonder where their earlier counterparts have gone when I survey my generation, men and women in midlife who, for the most part, no longer write or even read poetry. It is less difficult to see the results of this diminishing of spirit than it is to say why it happened.

Among men, there is a locker-room suspicion, born less of serious thought than a desire not to be thought odd, that grown males having anything to do with poetry are probably effeminate. As for the women, it is almost as if, because the dream somehow had eluded them, they no longer wished to be reminded that it might still exist somewhere, for someone.

These remarks, although sad, are in no sense cynical. For we are concerned not with dullards, not with the underprivileged and underexposed, but rather with the potential best among us. There is no reason why grown-up Americans should not find poems twice as exciting, given the experiences of adulthood, as they did in the breathless confusion of youth.

It is worthwhile wondering how this voluntary impoverishment comes about, and whether it really is related to a steady and terrible disenchantment with life or simply to habit-forming preoccupation with lesser things, until finally the sharp edge of spirit itself succumbs to a lifetime of dulling cultch.

If we have, in fact, turned our adult backs on the poets; worse, if we have turned our back on the poetry within us, what chance now have love, beauty, and compassion, at a time when they never were more essential? For poetry is the distillation of the purest truth, the fundamental whetstone. Without it, each of us surrenders to the lesser self.

This need not have happened, and I am afraid it has. Still, it need not continue to happen. What we have to ask ourselves, however, before the atmosphere of the national mentality is likely to be improved, is this question : Is the sunrise less capable of moving the human spirit after thirty? Or is it simply that we stay up so late munching potato chips and assuming the passive posture encouraged by "visual entertainment" that we never thereafter rise before dawn?

In either case, in denying the poetry we had when young, we are stumbling through life, hole in pocket, willfully dropping gold coins. That is silly. It is also tragic.

Fortunately, everything that is wrong with us is not so profound or so difficult to remedy. The last time I had to make a short talk at a school, I sat in the corridor awaiting the hour and thinking how much I like schools, even when they smell of rain-soaked children, fresh varnish, newly turned-on heat, tuna sandwiches from somebody's lunch, and chalk dust.

A short distance away, there stood two mildly penitent second-graders, male, who had been exiled for displaying anti-establishment tendencies. We did not converse, but each side eyed the other, thinking its blessedly unexpressed ideas about the generation gap.

At this point, a woman teacher strode out of one of the classrooms, closing the door behind her by leaning against it, in an attitude of what appeared to be relief. She had a pleasant, well-structured face and was old enough to remember what it was like before we had monosodium glutamate.

Because we were facing each other, and it seemed the civilized thing to do, I said, "Good morning," and she replied, "You've got to be kidding." Thus we began a conversation that included many interesting subjects, but not children or education. I carefully avoided mention of these because from time to time she said she must soon return to "the arena," and I came to realize that she meant her classroom and probably was employing the word in the gladiatorial sense. But she was a pleasant sort, nevertheless, and seemed glad to talk briefly with someone nearer her own age level. She began by asking me what I was going to speak about to the children.

I had intended to discuss this nation's breathtaking technological advances of the twentieth century, emphasizing space exploration, satellite communication, globe-girdling submarines, color television, chocolate that will melt in your mouth, but not in your hands and manmade wonders of similar magnitude.

But before I could reply she said, "The speaker we had last week discussed this nation's breathtaking technological advances of the twentieth century —"

I interrupted, "Emphasizing space exploration, satellite communication, globe-girdling submarines and color television?"

"You left out chocolate that will melt in your mouth, but not in your hands. That's what the children were most interested in." Then she asked suspiciously, "How did you know what he said?"

"Just luck," I replied.

"Anyway," she went on, "I sat there in the back of the room thinking, and I'll tell you what I had a good mind to stand up and say to him about his breathtaking technological advances and all that jazz. Look here . . ."

She took from her jacket pocket a plastic-wrapped nickel package of crackers, with peanut butter between them, I suspect. "See what it says there?" she said, accusingly.

It said on the package, "Pull tab to open."

"Pull it," she ordered. "I dare you. Live dangerously."

I pulled the small red plastic tab, and it tore off in my hand without opening the package.

"It always does that," she said. "If it doesn't do that, it's glued down so that you can't even get the tab up to pull it. Not even with fingernails like a werewolf. So then, when the tab is

gone, you either have to tear at the plastic with your hands —
and it's so tough that you smash all the crackers, because they
are so crispy, crunchy fresh that they fall apart if you snarl at
them — or else you have to go looking for a pair of pliers or
scissors or a knife to get into the thing more delicately."

"I don't eat many crackers," I said.

"Probably because you're a coward," she countered. "You
don't want to fight for what you eat. And that's not all. Yank
the string on a bag of potatoes or briquets. It breaks, and nothing
happens. Try cutting a package on the dotted line, as the in-
structions say. There are just dots there, no perforations, so you
saw away at the cardboard and what's left looks as if it had been
mauled by an unfulfilled lion."

"Well, I'm sorry," I said, "I don't know what I can do —"

"Don't interrupt," she said. "If the package says, 'Push
here,' you can push until you're blue in the face and the package collapses, but nothing pushes and nothing opens. If the can
has a key to open it, either the key breaks off or it winds up the
tin crookedly so that by the time the can is half open, the
handle is jammed up against it and you can't turn it any more.

"Breathtaking technological advances, my great aunt," she
exploded. "We have created a massive, monstrous packaging
industry so intent on preserving freshness of product that it
produces bags, boxes, tins and bottles to insure that nobody will
ever be able to open them, especially if he follows the directions,
which also are contrived to insure failure."

"I travel a great deal," I said. "I guess, mostly, other people
open things for me."

"That's what's the matter with the American man," she concluded. Then she said, much more pleasantly, "What did you
say you were going to talk about today?"

"Funny you should have said what you did," I lied. "I intended to talk about the breathtaking technological failures of the twentieth century. You know, about some of the things you have mentioned."

"Bully," she said, rising. "Must go back to the arena now. Nice to talk to you. And don't forget to mention the plastic tabs on cracker packages. Bear down on that one. All the kids eat crackers. They'll be on your side for sure."

And she departed, loping back to the arena with determination, her package of crackers still unopened.

Still, the faith remains that there is a touch of magnificence in man. I will tell you something, and you have a right to know about it, because the world we have created, or perhaps it is the other way about, is, oftener than I wish for you, a bed of nails, and what I have to say is better than that.

They began to gather at least forty-five minutes before curtain time, swarming up the steps, stomping off wet snow in the lobby, and forever chattering and laughing with the vivaciousness that is the hallmark and the prerogative of youth.

These were the booted, sideburned sweatered ones; the buckled, square-toed, suede-jacketed, wigleted ones; the artless, pink-cheeked, banged and well-washed ones, who, if you believe the magazines whose greatest stock-in-trade is solution of the nonexistent problem, distrust everybody, and for all I know everything, over thirty. (I do not believe it, but then, I successfully avoid such magazines.)

They had come, these voices and spirits of tomorrow, with the same breathless enthusiasm that they lend to a battle of the bands or a Beatle autograph party, to see the National Shakespeare Company present *Macbeth*, a program sponsored by the English department of the secondary schools.

Those far better qualified than I long since have decided what *Macbeth* is and means with reference to man, yet in this particular instance, we are dealing with something especially different.

For these are the eager, impatient and impetuous young, at an age sufficiently short of majority as to be torn each day between courage and fear, and to be dominated by the unanswerable questions born, not only of our times, but of the painful balance between childhood and growing up. You may never have seen *Macbeth,* and if you read it, perhaps it was so long ago that you do not remember about Dunsinane and all that, yet as Job is the symbol of trial, as Judas is the trademark of betrayal, so Macbeth stands for man destroyed by ambition. The play, therefore, is not something to which you go as a substitute for the Rolling Stones.

Moreover, this audience had been more lately exposed to *Macbeth* than most of us and was aware of the cold and bloody steel of its message.

(*"Nothing in his life/Became him like the leaving it; he died/As one that had been studied in his death,/To throw away the dearest thing he owed,/As 'twere a careless trifle."*)

Six hundred people in this town is a big audience and if there were six hundred there, five hundred and fifty were eighteen and under. In the tense silence, you could feel them respond to the mood and thunder, battle horn, the clashing of blades and the thundering feet of men in combat. They needed no more than the beat of distant music, the fragment of scenery that in its coarse weave and dour image signaled the ominous, the irrevocable machinery of destruction grinding through a landscape as frightening as its destination.

(*"I am thane of Cawdor/If good, why do I yield to that suggestion/Whose horrid image doth unfix my hair/And make my seated heart knock at my ribs/Against the use of nature? Present fears/Are less than horrible imaginings;"*)

Standing at the back, because every seat was filled, were the

English teachers who, in all the ways that are obvious and some that are not, were responsible for the fact that every seat was filled. If they glowed, inwardly and outwardly, one understands, for who knows in what year, at what opened page, the enthusiasm was ignited that produced an individual member of that audience?

(*"Had I but died an hour before this chance,/I had liv'd a blessed time; for, from this instant,/There's nothing serious in mortality:/All is but toys; renown and grace is dead;/The wine of life is drawn, and the mere lees/Is left this vault to brag of."*)

"This is upsetting," I said to the teacher. "Why aren't they out playing 'chicken' with speeding automobiles, or watching television, or smoking marijuana, or doing whatever it is everybody says they are supposed to be doing?"

He smiled the way my grandfather used to smile when somebody asked him how he could tell what a cow weighed by placing his hand on its flank. "I'll tell you," he said. "All the tickets were gone in no time, and the price wasn't cheap, either. No pushing, no propaganda, no enticements. They just bought them."

He walked away, an expression upon his face suggesting he had joined that fraternity which has been privileged to look upon truth and find it beautiful.

(*"Come, seeling night,/Scarf up the tender eye of pitiful day;/And with thy bloody and invisible hand/Cancel and tear to pieces that great bond/Which keeps me pale! Light thickens; and the crow/Makes wing to the rooky wood."*)

Did they, sitting there in their aura of vital youngness that pervaded the entire auditorium, think, "Well, at least today, far fewer lives hang upon the whimsy of a single mind that may not even be balanced?"

Or did they think: "This is near enough to what we have so

100

that we can feel 'with it.' You still settle your differences the same way, and as for what happens to us, either things are going for us, or they aren't."?

Probably some of both, although it was difficult to tell, because the face of youth is elastic and during the intermission, whatever had been there in the darkness of the play was gone.

("*Life's but a walking shadow, a poor player/That struts and frets his hour upon the stage/And then is heard no more: it is a tale/Told by an idiot, full of sound and fury,/signifying nothing.*")

What is more, the professional cast said afterward they had never received such applause; it went on and on, rocking all of that place as if the audience could not bear to end it, for fear of ending the spell itself, and I went home wondering, and in far better mood than *Macbeth* might sometimes produce.

And now, the wind freshens; the mackerel schools wind offshore, beyond where I want to go at this hour, and we shall come close-hauled and strike for the land.

THE SIXTH DAY

I AM not sure, but I thought I saw a cardinal this morning. If so, he is early, for I think of his magnificent extravagance of scarlet as compensatory; usually he comes in the late year's unwinding when nature, in color, pace and sound, grows increasingly subdued and his arrival in the world of dead and dormant things is a pleasant shock.

To be sure, one living splash of red in the gray of a December morning is not sufficient to make an appreciable difference in the plight of the cities, the rising crime rate, the war in Vietnam or even air pollution. Those Sisyphean burdens that sandpaper us, days without end, sandpaper still. Yet the spirit responds to the cardinal and will not let the mind do less, whether or not it is reasonable.

One thinks, seeing that bright bird sway and preen, "The day starts better because of you, even if you don't know it," and that inevitably leads to some reflection.

Once, near Hebron, up a wooded mountain so steep that the cars of that day had to be towed by tractor to the plateau of tiny pasture near the top, there was an old farmhouse. It was a never-painted, silver-shingled place with a canted chimney and a washboarded ridgepole, because nobody had lived in it for years. Where building ended and ground began, it was hard to see, for they had been married by generations of rain and snow until it was almost as if the house had grown out of the earth and thus reflected all its comings and goings.

Winter and summer, the acres of silence hung over that farm like a tight dome and during a whole week there, the only moving thing of any size that I saw was a tousled bear, who peered at me over an armful of huckleberry branches as if he had never seen a man before. I suspect he had not, because it was so lonely, and had forever been so lonely in every century, that it would have driven the maladjusted mad in the space of two sunrises.

But I talked to the leathery little countrywoman who had lived there alone past seventy and asked her, sensing what she would say, why she stayed there and how she had borne sorrow when it came in such a place. She smiled the half-smile, the hint of an upcrinkling of the mouth corners that one finds among such people because they take laughter and tears seriously, and pointed to the window above the kitchen sink.

"I look out there," she said, and her hand reached toward unbroken miles of dark green forest, tumbled mountains and piles of clouds, "or I go to my garden." The garden, by the kitchen door, was a postage stamp of fragile blues and yellows that seemed hopelessly inadequate to hold back the massive growth of brush and tree marching each year closer now that the old man, her husband, was gone and the scythe hung rusting in the woodshed.

But the point is that there was beauty, and beauty sustains, nor does it have to be of mammoth proportions. There is a film,

103

French, I think, called *The Red Balloon*. It is without words, and deals solely with the impact upon large numbers of people, young and old, of a bright red balloon carried by a little boy. It is simplistic to suggest that a balloon or a cardinal can make people better or brighter than they are, but I submit that either one can help their perspectives. Also, I think it has to be admitted that a black balloon would not have done nearly so well.

I was reminded of all this the other day because it came time to bury an alcoholic. As his one half-friend said to me laconically, "Well, it finally got to his liver, but I always say, 'When it's your time, it's your time,' and I'm not one of them that sits around waiting for it every day. Right?"

And I said, "Right," without either hearing or agreeing, but simply because this is a fellow who can talk for half a day without ever ending a sentence, with or without encouragement.

Furthermore, I wanted to go to the dead man's room alone, which I did, not for morbid reasons, but because I had known him, not well, but for a long time.

Most people live in houses or apartments, their own or somebody else's. Perhaps once, long ago, when single or going away to school, they lived in one room, but that was many years back and the experience was brief, and generally more communal than lonely. So one forgets what it is like to live in one room — not a hotel room that does, after all, relate to the world at least in the lobby through which one must pass — but one room in what used to be called a boarding house.

Admittedly, this fellow who was dead had not had a lot of money; even if he had not spent most of it on booze, he would not have had a lot. Yet lack of money was not what made the room so depressing; much can be done to improve surroundings without spending anything but time. Long before pop art, I knew a fellow who papered his bathroom with labels from cans and bottles (I remember especially the casually clad nymph from, what was it, White Rock water?) and it was much more attractive than many other bathrooms I have seen that cost far more.

But the room of my dead acquaintance was, of itself, lifeless; it did not even radiate poor taste or hostility. The naked bulb swung on a brown cord; the walls were empty; the dirty windows were better dirty, for they looked out on nothing. The room did not make him drink, of course, but I wondered whether anything might have been different, even a moment or two, had there been one touch of beauty, one cardinal or one red balloon, for him to look upon from time to time.

More often than not, you do not know why people drink, and this is probably a good thing. I am sure this was so in the case of Mr. Endicott; I do not remember his first name, because everyone called him Mr. Endicott, and his dignified bearing did not encourage more familiar address. What I do remember is the last dealing with him, and this is the way it was:

There are certain mountain towns, lonely, unpainted and scarred by rock ledge, that cling to the hard hillsides like drab tea leaves plastered against the sides of a cup. You come upon them just so, abruptly, and there they lie below in the deep bowl, looking better at a distance than closer, because poverty does not show a mile away. This was such a place Charles and I had arrived at, and soon it would be daybreak. The truck demanded a halt; it had been a hard night of hill climbing, some of it through rutted ice, and the engine was so hot that, periodically, we held the cab doors open to cool off our feet and legs.

We pulled off the narrow macadam, slowed to a shuddering halt, and climbed out, every joint in pins and needles of stiffness. We sat on the front bumper, which was rusty and peeling, an indicator of our economic level. Charles poured coffee from the thermos and remarked with more weariness than emotion, "This is a helluva way to earn fifteen dollars."

It had all started with Mr. Endicott, who looked something like the late Dr. Schweitzer, described himself as a rhetorician, and earned a living, if it could be called that, by reciting excerpts from popular literature in the town halls of shut-away New England villages. I suppose Mr. Endicott is now dead, because he looked so old even then. But I would not count on it. He once suggested to me that he had not decided whether he would die at all and he was, among many other things, dramatically convincing.

You should have heard him, this bony, white-maned Dirksen of a fellow, with a cut-glass stickpin in his purple tie. Standing alone on a dirty little stage, his long arms sweeping the air in gestures that I suppose went out with Chautauqua, he would have those farm people ram-rodded and squirming excitedly on the edges of their seats in about a minute and a half.

Poe he loved especially, and I can remember him thundering, *"While I gazed, this fissure rapidly widened — there came a fierce breath of the whirlwind — the entire orb of the satellite burst at once upon my sight — my brain reeled as I saw the mighty walls rushing asunder — there was a long tumultuous shouting sound like the voice of a thousand waters — and the deep and dank tarn at my feet closed sullenly and silently over the fragments of the 'House of Usher.' "*

Mr. Endicott told me that when he did that one at Stony Brook, a woman in the front row screamed and fainted. If so, you must admit his ability, because the audience had not even been exposed to the full story, which builds carefully and ominously to its terrible climax. They heard only a small piece of it, but Mr. Endicott possessed, among other attributes, an almost fluid face that could shift from mirth to terror, from shock to placid-

106

ity in a twinkling, assisting him in achieving instant atmosphere.

The only equipment he carried consisted of a dozen or so small stage sets, designed as triptychs, each about eight feet high and providing him with a back and two walls of setting, within which, to use his own word, he "declaimed." This scenery was sufficiently versatile so that at least one set would apply to almost anything in the world. There were castles and moats; grazing sheep and apple orchards; square-riggers tossing in an angry sea, busy streets, rows of shops, and something that looked like the Brooklyn Bridge, and even a church interior that he used when presenting passages concerned with weddings, funerals and Daniel Webster's speech for the preservation of the Union. This latter was because he had nothing in his paraphernalia that more closely resembled the chamber of the U.S. Senate.

In any event, on this occasion, he discovered that he was without transportation to move his scenery to the next engagement, approximately seventy-five miles away. It had been nasty weather, and we did not want the job, but fifteen dollars was a lot of money then and besides, Mr. Endicott pointed out (over his fourth whisky and water) that John Greenleaf Whittier had said, ". . . *simple duty hath no place for fear,*" although I do not know why on earth it was our duty to move his gear. But he was, as always, charming and persuasive, and especially so when drinking.

The night we moved the stuff was a horror, including two flat tires, and we had no spare for the last one, so we had to patch the inner tude by a fluttering kerosene lantern, with largely chilblained fingers. About every half hour the radiator overheated and we had to stop to blow off steam. One headlight went out, but fortunately it was the left one, so we could still see where the edge of the road was.

Thus we finally came to our destination, the teacup town, and all we had to do then was to wait for the people to wake, and slide downhill to them with Mr. Endicott's scenery.

It had blown hard during the night, and we first learned how hard when the birds began to rise from the humps, hollows, drifts, roofs, trees and fields of this ugly town. Most of them were migratory; many were Canada geese, already north-bound for colder weather, and forced down by the headwind of the night. Altogether, there were thousands, crying, halunking, haronking, mewing, wailing and struggling into flight as the first burst of orange sun blazed through a hill pass and fired the sheets of ice that glassed every surface of the village.

It was so breathtaking that Charles poured the last of the precious coffee in his lap, and we both whispered, "Spring," as if speaking aloud would frighten the hundreds and hundreds of upbound birds, feathers light and dark against the new sky.

In retrospect, therefore, it does not matter that Mr. Endicott never did have the fifteen dollars to pay us. If it had not been for him, we should not have been there at that moment.

This afternoon I shall go to see Edna, who runs a personal sort of barroom, because she will be hurt if she learns I have spent a couple of weeks hereabouts and did not stop in to say hello. She presides over a rambling house that sits shabbily in mud or snow, dirty white paint peeling at the gutters, and I refer to it as "The Inn of the Lighted Horses," because Edna likes that, although when I say it, she usually hitches up her apron self-consciously and says, "You're out of your mind."

The building is pathetically gingerbreaded, and its drunken porch is wet-black with decay; this place has been staggering downhill since the last time J. P. Morgan's *Corsair* came to the harbor with the New York Yacht Club.

Inside, it is better only because there is a short bar (plastic and cheap chrome) in what used to be the front parlor, and sufficient old drugstore furniture — round tables with twisted iron legs and wicker-seated, varnished chairs — to seat a half-dozen drinkers, and there never are that many. The tables are in a kind of sun porch and the partition has been knocked out between the rooms.

Sometimes a couple of fellows in checkered woolen shirts play at the pool table in the middle of the sun porch, being careful to avoid poking their cues into the moth holes of the green felt, and there are years' worth of brown cigarette burns all around the wood frame. In the corner of the room, there is an Ivers and Pond upright with the ivory unglued from six keys. One piano leg is propped with a piece of three-quarter-inch pine, because the floor slopes that much.

Still, in the fall afternoons, even when the sky is slate, there seems to be more warmth in the porch than comes from the belching hot-air register. Perhaps it is just because the room is small. Or maybe it is because on the windowsills there are pots of geraniums, so bright red that you do not notice the cracked saucers under them, and the dark water stains snaking brownly down the bubbled wallpaper.

It is really not an inn at all, although some people live upstairs, and the lighted horses on the wall hang in a black plastic frame with a colored bulb behind them that flashes somewhat, and illuminates the name of a beer in red, black and gold letters.

Behind the bar is Edna, who is fat. She is given to short-sleeved printed ginghams and wears her stringy, salt-and-pepper hair yanked back in a way that comes easiest in the morning, and it is fastened with something from the ten-cent store that is brown plastic with sparkles in it. Her hands are red and ringless, but she squeezes out the bar rag as if she did not mind doing it.

Every afternoon at three, a man with a long pale face and no job comes in. He is about forty, but he looks fifty-five, and it does not matter that his tweed suit looks as if he had slept in it,

109

which perhaps he has. It does not matter, because he has a flat stomach and wears clothes easily, like a Harvard physicist.

"I kiss your hand, princess," he says to Edna, without even looking at her, and she wrings out the bar rag with her red hands and says, "Welcome home from safari. Your tie is crooked."

One day when he passed the pool table, the man scrooched down so that he was eyeball to eyeball with the fellow in the checkered shirt, who was squinting along the pool cue lining up a shot. The man with the crooked tie gave the fellow one sad wink the length of the cue and said, "Good afternoon, Albert." And Albert said, "Get your eyeball off the table or I'll sink it in the corner pocket." Edna laughed, only it was more like a horse snorting, wiped a glass, and held it up to the light to see if the fingermarks were really gone.

Then the pale man slid a wicker-seated chair to the piano and with his bony finger drew a small G clef in the dust of the music rack, saying, "Princess, fire the maid."

Edna said, "I keep the glasses clean. The piano's dirty, that's your problem."

He took out a long cigarette carefully, as if he did not have any more, and tapped it on his yellow thumbnail. When he had lighted it, staring thoughtfully at his shaky hand as if it belonged to someone else, he put the cigarette in a little brass ashtray shaped like a trawlerman's dory, with "Westerbeke" stamped on the bow. Westerbeke and his schooner *Vandal* once were large names on Georges Bank and I will bet you that the ashtray is thirty-five years old.

The blue thin smoke from the cigarette was flattened in the blast from the hot-air register and it trickled across the backs of his hands as he played. His music was like his face, sensitive, loose, and with the passivity of utter resignation. He went through "Cocktails for Two," and "Stardust," and "Sweet Georgia Brown." Edna rang up "No Sale" and broke open a couple of

110

wrappers of change. "He plays good," she said, "and what they wrote in them days was music, not garbage and guitars and hair hanging down over your face."

When he had finished "Sentimental Journey," the man said to Edna without looking, "It must be 3:30." And she said, "Your liver's sluggish today. It's a half a minute after." Then she poured a jigger of Scotch into a tall glass, clunked two fat ice cubes into it, and poured water from a squat blue pitcher, right to the top.

She took it over to him and put it on the piano, saying, "If I'm careful, I can set it down right on the same ring you made yesterday."

"What I like about you," he told her, "is your consistency."

She went back to the bar and stared at the calendar. "Is today the twentieth or the twenty-first?" she said, but nobody answered. The man played "Nola" and one pool ball clicked another.

I had not said a word, but she looked at me, and said, "So I don't charge him for his drinks. Let them that play pool support the place. He plays music. If I want to lose money on him, at least I enjoy it. It's my business, ain't it?"

So you can see, Edna's is a better place to drink than some. It is, for example, far, far better than the last party I went to, where this fellow with red hair was standing in front of a Picasso print and I went over to move him, because neither was doing anything for the other.

En route to the anchovies he remarked cheerfully, "I have opened my annual war of independence against encroaching bureaucracy."

"You'd do better to pay your taxes and stop struggling," I said.

"That's not what I mean. This has to do with the spirit of Christmas, and it's the town government, not Washington."

111

He balanced a slice of something on a slice of something else and popped the affair into his mouth. "For years our selectmen, or whoever it is who controls the weekly collection of unwanted objects, have decreed that all discarded Christmas trees will be picked up within a week after December twenty-fifth by trucks especially assigned for the purpose.

"No Christmas tree will be accepted for the collection thereafter. I know, because I tried it one year, and the public servants concerned threw it back over the fence into my front yard. You have no idea what disdain can be conveyed by a droopy pine tree standing upside down in a fence corner. I felt stupid, but at the same time, rebellious."

He walked across the room, stood under the Picasso, and declined any more anchovies. "You see, I have a problem. Since I was a child, my family has observed the Epiphany; we retain intact everything pertaining to Christmas until twelve days thereafter. As children, we used to like it because our Christmas lasted longer than anyone else's in the neighborhood. I still like it."

The hostess came by and asked him if he had met everyone and he said he had, thank you, and found them all, and without exception even in degree, indescribably charming. She looked at him, and his glass, with a cool gaze and replied, "You're putting me on."

He straightened the Picasso and continued. "I thought, why should I give up a lifelong tradition and take down my Christmas tree five days earlier than usual so that the town dump can be operated more efficiently?"

He jabbed a long forefinger at me. "Doesn't that seem to you a prime example of subordinating the idealistic to the materialistic — the very thing that we are warned against every day, the very reason for youth's revolt?

"Well," he said, "I went down cellar to think. I think better in

112

my cellar. And I hit upon an idea. Why do you suppose it is that I think better in the cellar?" he asked absently.

"I don't know," I said. "Maybe if you have a very tight house the atmospheric pressure is lower."

"That seems hardly likely," he said. "I believe I'll have another anchovy." We walked across to the expanse of white linen and stared down at the array of bird, beast, fish and fowl that shingled the platters in preciously precise layers.

"In any event," he resumed, "I now have adopted this practice each year. On the thirteenth day after Christmas, I take the tree down cellar and saw it into one-foot sections. Last year I had forty-six of them. I put each section in a paper bag. Each Friday — the normal trash collection day — I place one bag of Christmas tree in the trash barrel and it is, of course, collected without protest. Actually, of course," and here he winked broadly, "without knowledge."

"You're getting through to me," I said.

"Now in '65, it took me until about the middle of November to get rid of my December '64 tree, and you may say that is a long and boring program, but each week I savored the triumph and it grew more priceless.

"How well I remember the third week in July, standing there by the trash can in my shorts, waiting for the collection truck to roll down the street in all its autocratic arrogance and chuckling to myself, 'If they only knew they are still collecting my last year's Christmas tree!' Ah, sweet victory."

He eyed the docile anchovy a moment as if it were a bureaucrat, then bit it precisely in two with a quiet pleasure. "My aim now, of course," he continued, "is to cut a tree into fifty-two pieces — or is it fifty-three — in any event, I'll figure it out, so that I will have them collecting a piece of Christmas tree every single week of the year, forever and forever. Government is not a god, to be bowed down to." He hummed and tapped his fingers on the mantel. "We'll keep our merry Christmas still."

The hostess paused before him with a tray of something to be spread upon Melba toast. It looked like wet cement and tasted admirably like smoked eel and blue goat's-milk cheese from Riga. She said to the man with red hair, "I told some of the people here what you said . . . you know, that you found them all indescribably charming. They think you're putting me on, too." And she went away.

He smiled politely and returned to the Christmas tree business. "I feel fulfilled by it," he commented. "You may say it is an awful lot of work just to avoid complying with a regulation. I know I could take the poor old tree to the dump myself and avoid it all.

"But I derive a lot of pleasure from watching my neighbors scurry about to get their trees out for collection at precisely the day and hour dictated by Big Brother. Sometimes I say to them, 'I put out my tree when I like and I've had no trouble so far.' And they think I must have influence with someone in the town hall."

"It's a fire hazard," I ventured, "keeping those dry boughs in the house for months."

"Not at all," he said, munching his toast. "I store them in the freezer."

On the way to Edna's, you have to go past this piece of fallen-down stone wall, lichened and run upon by several generations of chipmunks, and I sat in a puddle of sunshine with my back against it, because I was in no hurry and I wanted to watch a good-looking horse halfway across the field who was totally preoccupied with a conscientious job of grazing. Not even any flies to bother him.

I had forgotten about the man and the horse who wore identical brown felt hats, but I walked into the Boston Public Library a little while back, and there was the man, seated at a table, and beside him was his hat, slightly squashed but still recognizable. Both hats came from Raymond's, possibly purchased at a one-cent sale, if they have such things, and they were alike except that the horse's had holes cut in it for his ears, and a red ribbon that tied under his chin. On the ribbon, which was somewhat frayed and rain-washed, it said in gold letters, "Buy American."

The man's name was Chester something, although they called him "Bombay," for what reason I cannot imagine, because I do not think he ever was anywhere east of Quincy. He addressed his horse as "Cap," but this was short for Sweet Caporal, and if you are old enough to remember the cigarette of the same name, you have some idea of the horse's age.

Each spring, horse and man sold daffodils, most recently, thirty-five cents for six, at the intersection of Washington and Winter Streets, which used to be Blott's Lane. The flowers, massed in a paintless wagon with cockeyed wheels that was falling to pieces, were a wonderful blast of color.

The first drizzly day that I came upon them, you could see the change they wrought upon the sodden, red-nosed humanity elbowing by them, rheumy and ugly from the long, dreary winter. "Here now, here now, here now," chanted Chester, and Cap would bob his head, greasy ribbons flying gaily, and all the sniffling passersby would lift their soggy shopping bags a little higher, smile at the yellow flowers, and maybe even buy some.

I stopped, and Chester said, "Going to buy some flowers or do you want to borrow money?" which was such a ridiculous alternative that I bought six daffodils. He wrapped them in green tissue with a quick twist of a bony red wrist shot out of a frayed and dirty shirt cuff.

When I paid Chester he said, "I'd have money in the bank except for him," and he jerked his chin in the direction of the horse.

"How so?"

"Horse was the only thing my father, may he rest in peace, had to leave me. Used to pull a beer wagon. Cap, that is, not Father. So when I got him, he was so used to making deliveries, you couldn't get him to go past a barroom. He smelled them, he did. And I couldn't get him to move again unless I got down off the wagon, went into the barroom, spent a few minutes and came out again. You know, as if I was making a delivery."

"Um," I said.

"If you've got to spend a few minutes in there anyways," said Chester, "well, you know . . ." He wiped his mouth with the back of a hand. "So sometimes it would take me a whole day to get across town. This horse led me to drink as it were . . ."

He laughed a short laugh, sounding like a plugged sink drain. "You've heard about leading a horse to drink, well, this horse led me . . ."

"I heard you the first time," I said.

"You don't believe the horse is why I spend my money on booze?"

"No," I said.

"Nobody ever does," said Chester. "Like another half-dozen daffodils?" I said no thank you, and he went up front, carrying a canvas feedbag of oats for Cap, who bared his teeth appreciatively before he dove into his lunch.

That was our first meeting and I saw them again a few times over the years, but Chester never remembered me because he didn't remember anything about anybody, except that everybody was a stranger.

In the library reading room, I sat down near him without speaking. The book he had open, standing upright on the table, was titled, *The Renaissance of Italy*, and it contained many pictures. On the righthand page to which it was open was a photograph of Raphael's "St. George and the Dragon." You may remember it; the saint, armored and haloed, is astride a leaping white steed and is about to dispatch the dragon with his lance.

Now you could get quite romantic about this and theorize, "Here is this fellow, who never has done or been anything; he is indulging in a Walter Mitty sort of daydream. The horse in the picture, of course, is Cap, and Chester himself is the dragon slayer, a figure of consequence and competence. You know, just by looking at the rider, at the way he sits on his horse, clean and erect, that he is capable of doing this difficult deed, and of making the world better, because of his valor and integrity."

You could say all that to yourself, but it wouldn't be real.

The truth of the matter is that, if the world is full of perpetual strangers; if you have no wife, child or relative; if you live in one room that no amount of money or imagination — if you had either — could transform into anything other than an ugly box that smells perpetually of cooked cabbage and stale beer; if there was nowhere that you had to go; nothing you had to do any morning, afternoon, or night, then you would eventually go to the library, where it is at least warm and quiet. And it does not smell of cabbage.

But does not the selection of the book, *The Renaissance of Italy*, reveal an inner hunger for, or appreciation of, richer things than the poor life ever has had?

Who knows? It is dangerous indeed to place arbitrary limits on any man's potential. But in the present instance, Chester is not reading. His eyes are closed, and if you go to a library to sleep you select a tall book (*The Renaissance of Italy* is almost eighteen inches high), stand it up, and sleep behind it, so that the attendant will not see you and wake you.

So one senses, without asking, that Cap and the daffodils are

117

gone, and that there is nothing left but a hollow-cheeked little man, with the peace of a child in his wrinkled face, dozing quietly within the pages of a large book of pictures.

Perhaps Chester could benefit from compassion but, on the other hand, I have learned the hard way to distinguish between those who want compassion and those who ought to, but don't. I discovered this at a sales convention to which, I am pleased to report, I was not invited.

I look at sales conventions the way scientists regard specimens under a microscope; they are the economic pulse beat of tomorrow, and I watch in wonderment as those who attend them trundle out their artillery of devices aimed at the American consumer, who still toys with the notion that he buys only what he wants. So, in this hotel which is a few minutes from New York, when I found myself with an idle half hour I wandered into the mezzanine convention room, well-crowded in behalf of the promotion of grease guns, insect repellent, or something equally essential.

I thought, "For all they know, I am here to buy a gross of whatever it is they are selling, so I will stand at their bar and have a free lemon squash or perhaps something smoked and succulent on a cracker. And if anyone asks me how things are in Des Moines, insect repellentwise, that is, I shall give them a report, not only in detail, but in iambic pentameter."

On the walls and booths, there were signs saying such things as "Be a Take-Charge Guy," "Success in '70," and "Join the Cash Crash." There was piped-in music that flooded the room with the aura of affluence and interminable security, founded, undoubtedly, on something astutely invested and returning at least six percent per annum.

The atmosphere of instant positivism was contagious and I stood there saying such things to myself as, "The kids are damned well going to decide within a week whether to spend summer on the Riviera or at Waikiki." I was on the point of selling U.S. Steel (I don't mean some stock; I mean the whole company) when this voice behind me said, "Well!"

I can't write it the way it sounded, because it sounded like Josephine answering the front doorbell and discovering that Napoleon stood on the doorstep. I turned around and there was Lilias, the only woman I have ever known who has really purple eyes. When we were both going to college, she sat across the aisle from me in Dr. Worthington's philosophy class and when I fell asleep, due to dietary deficiency or something, she was always kind enough to kick me before I got caught.

Seeing her brought it all back — the fly-specked yellow shades in the classroom; my scarred desk, on which someone had carved a heart with the names of Marx and Lenin within, and Dr. Worthington, a dear man in all respects, rickety with age, whose stand-up collars were sizes too large, and who made weak jokes about "cant" and "Kant."

I said, "Knowing that you are a year older than I, why do you insist on looking ten years younger?"

She said, "Keep your statistics to yourself." Then she said, "You must be freeloading here. You couldn't sell anybody anything even if he needed it to save his life."

"I am seeing how the profit-making half lives," I said. "If this is living." And I added, "Since you have caught me, I will pay for this lemon squash."

"Oh, not at all," she said. "Think of it as helping our tax situation, rather than sponging on our hospitality without an invitation." She looked at me clinically. "At least, you haven't become a nasty old man, I don't think."

"I don't think so," I said, "and what are you doing here?"

She hesitated a moment and then she said, "I entertain nasty old men. They're lonely, because here it is Friday, and they've

119

been away from home ever since Thursday, and they won't get home again until Sunday. I encourage them to order fifty thousand instead of ten thousand of whatever it is they came here for besides the bar and me. Does that jolt you?"

"I think it does," I said.

"Then," she said, "just think of it as none of your business. I never wanted a cottage small by a you-know-what, and all that. I make lots of money, and I travel every summer. My travel agent says I have been to every place in the world that isn't dirty. I'm too old to go to dirty places anymore; they depress me."

"But don't you . . .?" I began.

"Hate myself occasionally? Mostly not. I perform a service, which probably is worth more than yours, because mine tends to fulfill a human need, and probably to boost somebody's ego, at least temporarily."

She toyed with a straw, bending it about her forefinger. "Oh, the prospect of old age and loneliness bothers me some. I know time will catch up with me. I don't drink. I don't smoke. I exercise like a ballerina, but sometimes I look at myself in the mirror and think, 'A few more of those under the eyes, baby, and nobody is going to order a dozen more tractors for having spent an evening with you.' "

She looked at me. "You are just square enough to ask me what a nice girl like me is doing in a place like this. And I am just nice girl enough to tell you why I think it is.

"I grew up in New York. We lived in an apartment and I played in a cement courtyard with the other kids. At suppertime, somebody always called the other kids in. Nobody ever called me. Once, I stayed out until seven to see if anybody would. Nobody did, and I cried, and went in. My psychiatrist says parental discipline is an evidence of love, and that kids know it, and want it."

120

She crumpled the straw. "So I seek love I never had, but I seek it from lots of men, not daring to commit myself to one, who might fail me as did my father and mother."

She tapped one long, pointed nail on the bar. "Cost me five thousand dollars and three years to get all that from a psychiatrist. It's yours for nothing, old classmate."

She turned to go. "Now beat it," she said. "This is no place for a nice boy like you."

So for all the obvious reasons, I would rather drink in the atmosphere of Edna's, fat Edna's, and now I shall meander there, through the byways of moss and maple, for a quiet drink or two, and a little button-down piano, such as mother used to make.

THE SEVENTH DAY

SINCE virtually no one says anything of consequence after 10 P.M., I have acquired the habit of retiring at what my grandmother would have called a "reasonable" hour. As a result I rise early, and I suspect that the best part of every day occurs prior to noontime, in terms of one's capacity to give and receive.

There is a natural pleasure in the morning disciplines. I find nothing stimulating in preening and prinking for a couple of hours, and this is not what I mean. But there is refreshment to be had in the flow of hot water upon the skin, in walking for a quarter hour at daybreak to discover what has happened lately to the land and sky, and, finally, in the taste of coffee in the throat, even terrible coffee. (It was terrible this morning and I don't know why, either.) This, I think, is the way in which things ought to begin, with a daily retesting, if you will, of all the physical and mental senses, so that you not only know you are alive, but also that everything is working, before you begin placing burdens upon yourself.

For all of these reasons, I am disturbed by our increasing tendency to remove ourselves, by the introduction of mechanical devices, at least one step from the reality of such important personal confrontations in daily life as are likely to remind us that blood is red, fog is wet, and the cry of an owl is like wind in the neck of a bottle. I am not reassured by the degree to which we are overwhelmed by an avalanche of gadgets especially designed to deprive us of the knowledge of what things about us feel, smell, taste and sound like.

I do not suggest that defrosting an automobile window on a February morning is fun, yet I am not going to buy the "infrared heat gun" now on sale for this purpose. I will continue to perform this task with wet mittens and a plastic scraper (perhaps cursing meanwhile), simply because I am not that eager to be relieved of all winter's manifestations. A principal liability of Miami, as far as I am concerned, is that its weather is bland and boring, and its storms incredibly brief and superficial.

Similarly, I derive no great joy from shoveling snow, and would rather sit before the fire with a mug of darjeeling, black and hot. But I would be the poorer if I could never walk in snow and see, occasionally, how it festoons trees and roofs and thereby alters the whole countenance of town and city. I am not much of a friend of snowplows and snow blowers, because they noisily imply that the world will fall apart if everybody does not get to work precisely as usual, blizzard or not.

I am inclined to believe that even the President of the United States could stay home one whole day, perhaps reading back copies of *The Youth's Companion* in the White House attic, and that nobody on earth, except his wife, who would have to call him to lunch, would know the difference.

We now have forks, meat slicers, pencil sharpeners and tooth-brushes, all antiseptically powered by electricity. Just plug in the cord, stand there like a cow in the stanchion and, to the accompaniment of an impersonal and monotonous buzzing that is symptomatic of the impersonal and monotonous atmosphere we are devising for ourselves, the task is accomplished. One might almost have been absent without being missed.

I shall not buy an electric toothbrush, because I do not mind meeting my teeth every day. Furthermore, it is a personal thing and I do not want machinery intruding.

We also have a vacuum-cleaner type of apparatus that according to the advertisement, "retrieves golf balls, up to sixty at a time," so that the golfer does not have to bend over. Let us not dwell upon the fact that it would do the golfer good to bend over, or upon the bleak prospect that this invention undoubtedly is the forerunner of chairs, the seats of which will rise to meet the sitter, so that no bending of the trunk, knees, thighs or elbows will be necessary. Naturally, such a chair will be motorized to rock itself.

I remember uneasily the knot of businessmen who were discussing the efficiency of their home heating systems. One remained silent, and they asked him, "Do you have oil or gas heat?" He smiled and replied, "I don't know. I've never been down cellar."

I look upon all this as a return to the make-believe of Victorianism. I once knew a gentle lady who could not bear to eat anything, neither fish nor fowl nor spring lettuce, without eating something else with it. Thus, she never once had to endure the clear, unadulterated taste of a single food through a long, long life. We are closer to that state of mind than you wot.

124

From May through August, our lives are air-conditioned so that we may not know what heat is like. We do not read books; we read the reviews. We do not read lengthy news stories; we listen to "capsulized interpretations" of what our favorite television personality thinks has happened. Shaving lotions with such inhuman flavors as lemon and lime disguise what we smell like, and we pour catsup indiscriminately on everything except each other.

It is reasonable to try to take the booms and busts out of the national economy, but when we attempt to smooth out all the differences between one thing and another, one day and another, one place and another, and even one person and another, then I think we begin to divorce ourselves from life and living. Beware the day when a machine will chew gum for you and, I suppose, bear for you the onus of doing it in public as well.

The irony is that, for all of our ever-encroaching technology, some fundamental improvements that would really be helpful never have been made or even attempted.

A young woman phoned me one day, describing herself as having been married nearly seven years which, I gathered, she seemed to think was quite a long time. I am sure it is longer in some marriages than others. She wanted to know how to address a letter to that federal agency concerned with the American consumer, and I told her, and she thanked me. Moreover, she insisted on telling me what she was going to write in the letter, even though I insisted that I did not wish to know.

"My husband," she began, talking right over my protest, "has been with this company eighteen months and I thought it was time he had a raise. So I said to him, I said, 'Errol,' — that's my husband's name, Errol — I said, 'We're going to have a few friends in, and I'm going to invite your boss and his wife, and we'll see if we can't get him to notice you.' You know, I don't think that sort of thing does any harm, do you?"

"Yes," I said, not anxious to prolong the conversation.

"Anyway," she rattled on, "I went to a lot of pains. First, I made a list of four other couples that I thought would add something. I mean people who have something to say besides dirty jokes and baseball scores, you know? I was counting on having ten people, including my husband's boss and his wife, that is, twelve with my husband and myself . . . ."

"Funny," I interjected, "I came out with the same total."

She didn't even hear me. "So then I said to Errol that he should hint around at the office to find out what his boss likes to eat especially. Not to let him know why you're asking, you know, because I wanted it to be a surprise."

"Did you find out what he liked?"

"Oh sure. Some kooky thing his mother used to make. It's a casserole thing, like, with pork chops and peanuts and celery and about sixteen kinds of seasoning and you make it in layers like — well, like tarring a road, I guess — and I got up at four in the morning to start it, and it took me all day long. His boss said his wife couldn't make it (I'm with her, believe me) and he hadn't had it since he was a kid, and all that. Anyway, I made it and it smelled better than I thought it would."

"Sounds promising so far," I said.

That's the trouble with conversations like this. The first thing you know, in spite of yourself, you want to hang around and see how they come out.

"Oh, sure," she said. "Nothing's too good for my husband's boss, I said to myself. And I vacuumed every room in the house; I waxed the living room floor; I polished all the silver and my mother sent me a hand-done table cloth from Berlin, Germany, last summer, and I put that on the table. I even went to

126

the florists for some flowers. I forget what they were, but they were yellow and blue, and a kind of rust-brown, or something. They went just fine with the wallpaper."

"What color is your wallpaper?" I asked. It seemed to me that as long as I obviously had to hear this thing through to the last demitasse, I might as well participate.

"Pink roses," she said. "Big huge ones."

That left me somewhat shaken, because I was trying to visualize how yellow and blue and kind of rust-brown flowers would go with huge pink roses, but she was off and running again.

"That night, Errol stopped off after work for some martini mix because, I don't know, it seems to me that when he or I mixes them, they're never the same twice. You know what I mean? Who wants that?"

"Who indeed?" I agreed.

"So there we were, all ready with time to spare, and the dessert in the refrigerator. I made a nice chocolate pudding, you know, with whipped cream on top?"

I could feel the dramatic tension rising. Things were just too perfect. "What happened then?" I asked.

"I'll tell you what happened. The bathroom plumbing broke."

"No!"

"But yes. You know the handle that you push down to flush the thing? Well, it hooks onto a — you ever look inside one of those tanks?"

"Yes."

"Then you know, there's a hook thing that looks as if it had been made out of a piece of coat hanger, and it has a loop in the bottom end, and that slides up and down on a rod, and the whole thing hangs on an arm, like, and lifts a thing that looks like half a rubber ball up and down. You know what I mean? Real Rube Goldberg, all the way?"

"I do," I said, "and all of those things have names."

"I could care less. Anyway, to make a long story short, the handle fell off and all this junk inside fell into the bottom of the tank, and I even soaked my wristwatch and made it stop trying to fish this stuff up, because Errol is just no good at anything like this. It was hopeless, and company coming in a half hour."

"That's awful," I said, feeling real sympathy for her.

"Awful? Believe me, buster, it was a tragedy. I could have wept. I did weep, but I had to stop because it was smearing my mascara. And I sat there looking into that stupid porcelain tank, and you know what I said?"

"Dare I ask?"

"Oh, I said some of that, too, but what I really said to myself was, here we are, the smartest country in the world. Color TV. Send a man to the moon. Thermostatically controlled heat. No-frost refrigerators. Computers that write books. You name it. And our bathroom plumbing looks like something that a backward fourth-grader put together, and it hasn't been improved on since I was a kid, and that wasn't yesterday. That's what I'm going to write the government about."

"I don't blame you," I said. "And what happened to your dinner party?"

"It broke up early," she said laconically. "Very early. And my husband hasn't got any raise yet, either."

And with that, she hung up.

I was thinking about all this while eating a couple of eggs (poached, with butter and cream) and a strip of smoked herring and was roused from reflection by a sound that has no parallel — the thump of a log upon the tightening earth of autumn. Hearing it, I thought the day had begun most auspiciously, for this was, of course, Jacob, arrived with the annual load of September wood.

Outside, the slate sky sprinkled, not dismally, but warmly, still trying to green the spots burned brown by the drought of summer. Jacob, tough and twisted as a sassafras root, face stubbled with two days' growth of salt-and-pepper whiskers, and red bandanna handkerchief drooping out of the hip pocket of his patched overalls, stood in the back of his rusty truck and, like Jove hurling thunderbolts, hove the logs over the fence into the yard.

"Har," he said by way of greeting, showing his yellow teeth. "Up before breakfast this morning, hey?" — this being a New England remark that somewhat predates the era of Myles Standish and the discovery of Indian pudding. *Thump, thump* went two logs as he bent and swung like a disjointed machine that nevertheless knows what it is doing and will bump along until the job is ended.

"You're the luckiest man I know of," said Jacob. "Two years running now, your front yard fills up with catalpa leaves as big as elephant's ears and when they're all down, the wind backs into the northwest and blows them all under the row of lilac bushes, just where you need them for compost. And you haven't lifted a rake."

It was so. They lay in fluffy heaps, yellow and curling, rich in life-flow bound for the soil. Under the pale brick of the terrace, the fallen grapes, now black and soft, were headed in the same direction, at least those that escaped the eager beaks of the jays.

"And you've got at least one ash can that doesn't belong to you that I know of, just because it rolled down the hill on a windy Thursday and stopped in front of your house," said Jacob, leering.

"I tried to find out whom it belonged to," I said.

"Sure you did." *Thump, thump* went the logs. "You went to all the houses to loo'ard. Why didn't you go to them to wind'ard? That's where the damned thing came from."

"Jacob," I said, "you know very well that no such thing happened." But you cannot argue with Jacob, because when he has finished what he has to say and you are ready to reply, he changes the subject. "And how'd that ten-cent pine tree ever do?"

It had been odd about the pine. The garden club had had a sale, and when they came to take down the tables, almost everything was gone but one little sick pine about eight inches high. The lady said, "It won't live," but I had given her a dime and planted it in a sheltered corner of the yard, feeling as if it were some kind of friendless orphan. Most of its needles rusted, yet a clump or two held on, stubbornly, without progress, as if holding on were all that it could manage at one time. It stayed precisely the same height for one year, two years, and I despaired; still, it did not die.

But one miraculous day, it did, in fact, mate with the earth and now it was green, strong and nearly a foot and a half high, with new green needles coming. I felt somewhat proud, but Jacob would have none of that.

"Damned little you had to do with it once you spent the dime. You interfere with nature more than you help it. You're the one turns turtles around."

That had been the substance of our first meeting, years before. I had gone to Jacob's farm, to get acquainted and order wood. As we talked at the doorstep, a box turtle, up from the marsh, lumbered out of the grass. Without thinking, I picked it up, turned it around and headed it back in the direction of the water.

Jacob stopped talking about wood and said sharply, "What'd

you do that for? How the hell do you know what way he wants to go? Why don't you mind your own business? If you was on your way to Boston, how'd you like to have somebody pick you up and head you back to Truro?" And Jacob turned the turtle around again.

Thump, thump went the soft-barked pine and hard-gnarled oak. The tone of the weather, damp but not cold, reminded me of one fall in England, in an East Riding port. At a turning of cobbled street, shiny wet in the night, I had come upon a stocky woman in an apron and overcoat selling butterless baked potatoes in brown paper bags. I bought a couple, reveling in the bag's small warmth in the hands and, after she had handed the salt-shaker to me, relishing the first bite into the mealy white flesh, for it was comfort against the cold not yet felt, yet inevitably coming and thus apprehended by the spirit.

Jacob was going on, saying, "The kale in my back garden is flowering. Prettier than roses, a helluva lot. Kale has guts. I don't know why they don't sell kale flowers to girls to wear to dances. It would be pretty and afterwards they could make soup out of it, instead of just chucking it away, and all that money spent."

I had never thought of roses being gutless, but the idea of a purple kale corsage was not unreasonable. Probably very durable, too, and thus capable of standing the rigors of modern dance.

Some time back it became traditional that I should help Jacob lug the wood into the shed and stack it, even though I pay him to do it. He said the first year, while I was standing about with my hands in my pockets, "It'll do you good and besides, I'm older than you are." I recognized this as a truism, allowing neither reply nor exception, so I followed him to the woodpile, and have been doing it (without being told) ever since.

131

Stoop and grunt, feel the perspiration trickle down your stomach, smell the fresh saw cuts of the wood ends crooked in your arm, inch through the narrow door, and duck your head or bump it.

We both took pride in putting up the wood against the wall so that it would not fall, the top of the pile level, chinks filled with smaller pieces, and criss-crossed logs anchoring the end. When we had finished, Jacob rubbed the bark off his shirtfront and said, "Well, what I done looks the way it ought to; what you done looks better than I expected. Must be you're learnin', if we got years enough." That was quite a concession from him.

He swung into the truck cab, his big red hands overwhelming the wheel. "Got your wood in now," he said. "It can snow and be damned."

"There's a lot of satisfaction in a woodpile, snugly stowed against the coming of weather," I said. "See you next fall, Jacob."

"Har," said Jacob. "I'll be here, but I don't know about you. Damned if they make people the way they used to."

And his truck coughed down the rutted drive until it disappeared around a turn of huckleberry bushes.

Off and on, I have been building a piece of fence, or actually, replacing some that succumbed over the generations to the demands placed upon it by snow, rain, wind and the thumpings of sundry squirrels who galloped the length of its top rail in pursuit of happiness. I decided to spend this morning working on the project and doing a couple of other chores about the place so, with Jacob gone, I busied myself brushing stuff designed to preserve on a peeled cedar post laid on a couple of sawhorses.

I have no large dose of the optimist in me, and some days are awful, but I have to be honest and concede at the same time that there are moments when, if you will pardon the expression, it would be tragic not to be alive. This was such a moment; not for any particular reason, but because of the agreeable chemistry of several things. The air was sweet and clean; such sounds as occurred belonged there; the work was going well; the sky looked as if, by and by, it might open up enough to encourage swimming, and breakfast was digesting well.

I am glad that I do not have to fight the weather on this job, having had some experience with that sort of thing. Last October offered a classic example.

It had rained six days and nights, or something equally unlikely, and the late fall ground was like a rich green sponge. As the days passed, each with its particular kind of drenching, I had been surprised at how many different kinds of rains there are. It pelted, slashed, plopped, sprayed, seeped, splashed, drizzled and poured at various times, depending on the direction and velocity of the wind. In the beginning, the trees, still summer-dry, held their leaves crisply against the slate-gray overhead, but as the downpour wore on, they came to look more and more like thousands of little limp umbrellas turned inside out. Even when it was not actually raining, the immediate world was dripping from so many millions of water places that it was noisier than the damp birds, hunching and complaining from branch to branch in search of wrinkling, leftover berries.

But the particular morning had broken with a sense of clearing, or so I thought, scanning the patchwork sky. Actually, it was a well-mixed bag of weather signs, a day very likely to lead you into disaster if you guessed wrong. In the far east, above the sun's coming, there were strokes of hazy blue and watery yellow light that promised something better. But directly above, the clouds were roily tatters the color of soft-coal

133

smoke and shifting uneasily in a ten-knot breeze that wobbled from southeast to southwest and back. And to the north, there hung a purple-black bank of storm.

It was frustrating. There was a job to be done and once started, the whole business exposed to the weather, it had to be finished. The question was, therefore, whether one dared start it at all.

There is a shed at the end of the house and I had wanted to put a small window in the west side of it for a long time. It meant ripping off some shingle, cutting a hole, fitting the casing, re-shingling around the window, caulking and painting. Resumption of rain in the middle of the task, especially if it came from the west, would force a suspension of the project, prevent caulking and painting, and, very likely, soak all the croquet mallets, bicycles, hammocks and carefully saved back issues of magazines inside the shed.

"Well," I said, "it is a dubious day, but it is the only day I have, and besides I have waited long enough for nature to be reasonable." So I decided not to read the newspaper, turn on the radio, or dial the phone forecaster to find out what the weather was about to do — because I did not dare — but to go ahead anyway.

The shingles, half-century-old cedar soaked and crusted with oily barn paint, came off hard and split easily. Perhaps they would not have for a carpenter but then, I consoled myself as I bruised another finger, "I am not a carpenter, am I?" It took longer to get down to the boards, rough, wide and an inch and a quarter thick, than I had anticipated. Should I cut the hole now? It was not too late to halt . . . but soon would be.

Glancing overhead for some encouragement, I decided the sky looked like one of those round glass paperweights in which snow falls after you have turned it upside down. Not that snow was falling, or likely to so early in the season, but the clouds were all salt and pepper, bits and pieces and scattered uncertainly. One large, fat drop of water fell on the back of my left hand and I stared at it, wondering whether this was a message from somebody or something.

I shrugged. "This is the only day I have," and forthwith attacked the siding, tough, coarse-grained and stubborn, with the saw. After some doing that left me out of breath and soaked with my own salt, there was a hole and it seemed enormous, especially since, as the last chunk of board fell, I realized the morning had darkened, no blue was visible above any longer, and it was misting heavily enough so that when I sat on the top step of the ladder to rest, it was damp sitting.

"Um," I said pessimistically, and deep within the wisteria, a rainproofed catbird laughed.

The casing went in without large incident, and I tacked in the window temporarily, and started sealing up the outside wall again. I cut a thumb shoving the aluminum flashing under the shingles over the top of the window and lost fifteen valuable minutes while my physiology decided between coagulating and bleeding to death.

"Damn," I said breathlessly, as I remounted the ladder and began fitting shingles around the window frame, principally with my unbandaged thumb. "Damn," I said again, as gentle pitter-patters of rain hit the back of my neck.

Still, the wetness generally held off. I surveyed my shingling, being, as usual, neither satisfied nor dissatisfied with what I had done, but assuming that caulking would cover the more flagrant lapses. It seemed to me the temperature was dropping slightly; the caulking was hard to handle; it stuck to the hands like unfloured dough and was so stiff that I grunted with effort, trying to ram it and drag it into cracks between shingles and casing.

Once done with this, down off the ladder, run to the cellar,

135

open the paint, stir it, find a clean brush and trot back to the job.

The sky was blue, but it was the color of a bruise, and not the blue of June. "I suspect the world is coming to an end," I said, jabbing at the shingle-butts with the brush and covering the bright new wood with an ancient and satisfying earth-red color as old as the Pilgrims.

And finally it was finished, snug against the weather, I put the ladder and bucket inside the shed, and stood in there myself, realizing even as I did so that the drum of intensifying rain on the roof had begun; the downpour, slanting and silver, had resumed.

"I have won the race against the weather," I said to nobody, pleased with myself, and thinking how many men before me had said the same. The farmer, in sweat-soaked shirt, weary and grateful, riding the last high load of hay to the barn as the summer squall strikes, bright and purple. The lobsterman, one eye to an ugly windward, hauling the last pot in the string, and heading for home. All through the ages, man against the weather, often with only minutes to spare.

"And yet," I said, conscious of my five feet, eleven inches in contrast to the tumbling cloud-mountains of the overhead, "I suppose I have to wonder whether I really won, or whether it let me win — just for fun, perhaps, this time."

In any event, I like people who attempt things, who take pride in their self-sufficiency, who refute the notion that if you can conjugate a verb you can't drive a nail, and who know the pleasure that comes from doing for themselves many things, sometimes even unlikely things — and that, of course, reminds me of the train wreck four winters back.

As train wrecks go, it was not much. It was better attended than most and by a more interesting class of people, namely, the poor, but relatively honest.

It all started when Faris came lumbering up the snow-filled road, blowing like a grampus and wiping his big beak furiously with a red bandanna handkerchief. Faris, his tired, leathery little wife and their six children, whose principal uniform was patched overalls, lived halfway down the hill in a lopsided house to which he had been adding with each birth. Outside the house, they had piled sod blocks up to the first course of shingles to keep out the cold. Halfway up the north side, a tile-pipe smokestack squatted on a shelf and belched black plumes from the burning pine knots. Inside, the walls were decorated, if that is the word, with colored pages from magazines, and Faris said all the children learned to read just by walking about the rooms.

As a matter of fact, he said the first thing that Vernon, the oldest, learned by heart was a list of the overseas offices, including addresses and phone numbers, of the National Geographic Society. It is to the credit of Faris and his wife that there was no picture or text on the walls that was not related to some item of worthwhile information, even though you might, as he suggested, "go on for a bit" before you found a use for it.

Anyway, up the road he came, stomping the snow from his big feet and carrying a half-dozen bottles of home brew in a paper bag. Since it was not yet seven in the morning, he was obviously concerned with a matter of importance. The brew suggested that he had already planned the day's activity, since he had provided himself with the equivalent of lunch. It was a beverage he made himself; it was weakly pale as a March sun before rain, and usually had a white lump of yeast in the bottom, but it undoubtedly contained, as he often said, "as many vitamins as you can carry in both hands."

Faris said, "Fellow tells me there's been a train wreck at the junction. Carload of frozen meat smashed to hell. Railroad's giving the meat away if you get there today. My car won't start. How about yours?"

So I coaxed the old high-wheeled Reo into action with a

teakettleful of hot water and a push halfway down the hill, until finally it gurgled, coughed, barked and roared, and we swung aboard.

It was nearly eighty miles to the junction, the roads were slippery, and, as Faris suggested, "every man and his brother with an empty belly will get there soon's they can . . ."

If this doesn't make much sense from the sanctuary of a heated living room complete with television, you have to think of it in terms of Faris's background. Upcountry, which is to say the rind of northern New England, they know what winter is because they do not see the ground from November to March, and the game goes into the deep woods, and meat is difficult to come by.

People such as Faris would be the least appreciative of poetry extolling snow upon the land, not because they lack sensitivity but because it translates cruelly into a water pump frozen and burst, ears white with frostbite, winds that find every leak in a rotted window frame, and a hard life made twice as hard.

As we rode, occasionally swapping end for end in graceful parentheses as the ancient truck struggled to cling to the slick surfaces, Faris recounted the difficulties of his wife's cousin, who was spending the winter in the county jail because, in a moment of pique, he shot at a game warden. Faris acknowledged that the young man had been breaking the law by hunting out of season and said he was glad the latter had been sent to jail because it might teach him a lesson.

"You have to learn," said Faris, "not to get yourself into something that you can't win no matter how it comes out. Now if he had hit the warden, that would have been awful. But he missed him and that was awful, too, because then the warden saw him and knew who he was. Now anybody is foolish to get into that kind of situation."

And so we came to the junction, a bleak wasteland of smoke-blackened buildings, and soot upon the snow; the only color was from the strings of faded boxcars, red, blue and yellow, and the only sound upon the morning was the raspy panting of the big locomotives and the clang of a firebox door.

The wrecked car, bunted by a yard engine, had hit a frozen switch, jumped the tracks, rolled over and disintegrated. Like a felled creature, it lay with its helpless wheels in the air, great splintered holes torn in its midriff. Its cargo was sides of beef. Presumably, there was no place nearby to store it; possibly, no guarantee that some or all of it wasn't ground full of splinters, gravel or cinders; and very likely, it was covered by insurance anyway.

So some railroad employes were on top of the car, hauling out the beef and giving one side to a family, first come, first served. There must have been two hundred and fifty people there, and some of the worst automobiles you ever saw outside of a dump or a museum.

The railroad man hollered down at us, "One family or two?" and they slid down two marbly sides of beef when we said two. I told Faris he could have the bigger one, of course, because he had more mouths to feed. He looked at it, worked his mouth as if it were dry, and said hoarsely, "By God, what do you think of that?"

In due course, we had wrestled those sides into the Reo. The sun had come out and it was warm and pleasant, one of those deceptive winter days that suggests spring is close, but you know it isn't. There wasn't much room in the back of the truck, but Faris said he wanted to ride there with the meat and look at it, and think about it.

I stopped once on the way back and hopped out to make sure he wasn't congealing.

He sat between the sides of beef, and slapped one. "By God," he said, "Christmas in February and everybody can come back for seconds."

It was a good day, one of the best I can remember.

THE EIGHTH DAY

ONE of the great rewards of this interlude is that my feet may go where they will, when they will. I spent much of today in the village cemetery, although I had not intended to do so. In such places as this, either because of its smallness or its quietness — or both of these — the bond between the dead and living is a pleasant and durable thing.

I started at the shore. There is a place where the early waking gull seesaws above the empty beach, a silent shadow against the faint light of coming day, and in the white sand, the bayonet-sharp blades of grass bend in the wind and trace perfect arcs with their points, over and over.

There is such silence as purifies, heightens the hearing, clears the mind and expands the spirit; it is like being sixteen again, only better. It is better because the hope of adulthood is less breathless, less painfully personal, and more solidly based, having as part of its foundation tears and failure.

The shape of the day was imprecise — not unpromising necessarily, because that depended on what you wanted to do with it. I was not going fishing, but for the fisherman, it was not much. Rags of fog hung as low as the dripping beach-plum bushes, and the mournful horns sounded offshore; the sea was greasy-gray and lumpy — it did not break, but it was nothing to turn your back on, and rolled strong and endlessly, and was deep enough in its turbulence for the unwary boatman to trip on. There was no sun; moisture trickled and dripped on the shiny leaves. It was a good day to stay home unless you wanted to see how beautiful it was, principally because of its vast lack of dimension. There was room there to think the largest thoughts, if one were left alone.

I was, therefore, not pleased to see two sets of fresh tracks just above the low-water mark, punctuating the hard sand as far as the point, and disappearing behind it. The larger set suggested the herringbone sole of a man's sneaker, approximately size eleven; somebody who took short steps and toed out. I followed them, barefoot, and carefully stepping in each one, so that I did not mess up the beach by making more tracks, this being something I have done since the age of eight. If you are a practitioner of curbstone psychiatry, you may make of this what you like.

Rounding the point where the scrub oak and tumbled stone wall come down to the water, I came upon them, a man and a beagle. I was glad I had looked them up because they were such as had a right to be there; it was obvious that they thought as much of the place, and what it stood for, as I. Do not ask me why it was obvious, for I cannot readily tell you, but there is something in the way that a man stands and, I suppose, something in the way his dog sits.

141

The man was about sixty-five; short and stocky, with silver-rimmed glasses that you do not see much any more on people over thirty. He wore yellow oilskins and he was standing there, getting his fishing rod ready. The beagle, tan-eared and bright-eyed, was glad to have been invited; he sat and smelled the wind expertly.

"Hullo," said the man affably enough, and I thought, "He looks as if he knew something about fishing, but if he does, why did he come today, of all days?"

So we talked about the day, and the man was a fisherman all right because he said right away, "With no more sun than this, the fish'll stay down today. No day to catch anything." He stuck his rod in the sand and the dog came over close, to have his head patted. "But I didn't come to catch fish anyway," he added.

"No?"

"No." He looked at me, to see what kind I was, and scratched his chin. "No, there was something else. You see, this other fellow has lived next to me for almost twenty years. I could help him; he could help me. We used to swap tomato plants, and borrow each other's ladders and things like that. He had a table saw down cellar I could use, and I gave him a hand when he painted his house. And we got to going fishing together about, oh, I guess maybe seven-eight years ago. You know, it's good fun, and you get a meal out of it, too, if you're lucky."

"I know."

"Fact is," the man said, "we were going fishing here this morning." He stopped, looked at what you could see where the horizon ought to be, and his Adam's apple bobbed at the neck of his open shirt. "Only about midnight last night, I woke up because of the police siren, and they carried him out of his house, but he was dead when they got him to the hospital." He patted the dog's head again.

142

"My age," said the man. "He was my age, give or take a few months. Heart attack. Never sick a day in his life."

"I'm sorry," I said. "That's a blow."

"Yeah, I'm sorry, too. Sorry as can be. Well, it scared the hell out of me, and I called my doctor and told him I was scared. So the doctor said, 'What were you planning to do today?' and I told him we had been going to go fishing. The doctor said to me, 'My friend, the best thing you can do is go fishing, just as you planned. You'll feel better for it.' "

"I suspect he was right," I said.

"Yeah. Now that I'm here, I think he was right. The thing is, my doctor likes to fish. He says it's better than medicine. He's told me to go fishing for a long time. He said it probably would cut down on my doctor's bills. That's the kind of fellow he is."

"Sounds like a good doctor."

"Oh, you bet," said the man, and his voice dropped off so that I knew he was thinking about something, and not really paying attention to the conversation any more.

Then he said, "You know, I was in the war. I don't really scare easily. You must think I scare easily, because . . . well, because my friend had a heart attack and died, and I called my doctor and all that . . ."

"I don't find it strange at all," I said.

"Well, the thing is," said the man, and he stared at the horizon again and swallowed, "the thing is, I've already had two heart attacks."

And he looked at me with calm gray eyes behind the silver spectacles, and smiled a little, crooked smile. So I wished him well, and walked on, and when I had gone so far that man and dog were no more than small and dark against the sand, I turned and waved — and he had been watching me go, for he waved back.

So, thinking of the dead, I walked the East End road toward the cemetery, deciding to see how they fared. The last time I had gone there was in May, and this is how it was:

Gold letters on black, the sign at the entrance read: "Automobiles Please Run Slowly," and I passed between the square, reddish stone posts with the delicate black iron gates, and started down the easy slope toward the river. The roadside pansy bed, miniature Pekingese faces among its blossoms, was a tumble of color, dripping and trembling from the first decent rain in four weeks.

Because it was close to Memorial Day, this was the annual pilgrimage for all of those, now visible among trees and shrubs, who moved quietly, with gentle touch, brightening the graves with new flowers.

A squirrel in search of a tree to conquer led the way. The dogwood trees were soft explosions of pink and white. Every turn of the road, every green plot and half-hidden avenue possessed something of beauty, variously defined: brilliance of clumped azalea; fragility of a flowering golden lace; scarlet geraniums with accents of purple ageratum, and the crisp green knives of yucca. Over all, a roof in motion, there was the cover of trees in which the southwesterly whispered and from which petals showered silently onto the wet, black road.

Some yellowing stones were lichened; these were untended (*Captain Elijah Claghorn, Died North Pacific, March 4, 1857*) for there was no one left. But mostly, there were people at the graves, busy with clay pots and wicker baskets.

The woman across the way, dark soil on her white cotton gloves, came over. "Haven't seen you since last year. Have you been well? Isn't it beautiful here?"

I thought, here one is among friends in an extraordinary communion of what was and what is. From where I stood, I

144

could see the truck of the carpenter with whom I had gone to high school, a half-dozen potted plants in the back; at the next lot, the retired schoolteacher, fetching water for something newly planted. And beyond, the fellow who had just made sales manager at the canning plant; he would be here for his son, who was killed at Inchon.

And the stones themselves — I looked at a half-dozen, realizing that I had known all of these people, could remember what they looked like, and had eaten, drunk and argued with them.

"I like to come here to do this," said the woman, patting the earth about the plant stem. "It is a warming thing. I feel about it the same way I do when I polish grandmother's silver. She would be pleased to know that I sit in the sun on my back doorstep, rubbing, and thinking how close I am to her in that moment, and when the glow of the metal comes, it is like a response . . . a reward, almost."

She looked at the name on my family stone. "I knew him so well. When I was a little girl. Do you know what I remember about him?"

"It could have been a lot of things," I said. "He lived a long time."

"I remember early summer evenings when we lived next door. I would be eating fresh strawberries — I loved them — and through the screen door, I could see him. He would finish supper; come out into the backyard; light his pipe and set about — that is the proper phrase — mowing the lawn. I can hear the whirring of the mower — they didn't bark, roar and snarl in those days — smell the fresh-cut grass, and see him walking, not hurriedly, but carefully, for he took pains to see there were no 'holidays' between the swaths."

I dribbled water on the trowel to clean it. "I don't think it's so bad being dead. I wouldn't want to rush it, any more than he

145

did, but every time I come here, after I've been here a little while, I think it's probably not so bad." I waved the trowel at the gravestone. "You know what used to amuse him?"

"No."

"Well, I guess it was from Clarence Day's *Life with Father*. You remember the father said he wanted to be buried in a corner lot, so that if he felt like getting up and walking about, he could do it without disturbing anybody."

We laughed, yet remained conscious of where we were and why. In the damp quietness, there was the sudden sound of iron on stone and, beyond the rise, stripped to the waist, you could see the flat-muscled shoveler, bending and straightening, knee-deep in a new grave.

In the darkness of the evergreen high above us, there was a clicking and, half-floating, the fragile blue cup of an empty robin's egg dropped at our feet. In the branches overhead, there was the flutter of quick wings.

"Strange place to be born," I said.

"Better than most, for robins," she replied, and so we parted for another year, and sitting here now, these several months later, with my back comfortable against the gravestone of my forebear, I trust that she is well, polishing her silver, and that we shall meet again at this place.

In a community as small as this, you do not have to learn about a death by reading the newspaper.

If you have departed from a street five thousand or more times in the cool of the morning, and entered it an equal number of times in the late afternoon; if you have observed its cobbled gutters in February slush and July drought, and have watched children and their children spin tops on the black macadam sidewalks, then you ought to know something about what the street is.

Now this street I think of is where Faris's brother lived. It is as straight as need be, yet it gives the appearance of comfortable meandering, because it slopes leisurely to the river front. Age and the irrepressible roots of elm and catalpa insure that its sidewalks will never lie either still or flat. When a new hump or crack appears in the surface that man has smoothed so fastidiously, it is a well-deserved reminder to the pedestrian, who must adjust his gait to this latest mark of character, that little in life can be taken for granted.

Slide-rule experts might enjoy plotting the pounds-per-square-inch progress of a root that began as a pale, fragile experiment and one day expanded that last fragment required to crack wide open a two-inch layer of hot top. However, the mathematics interest me far less than the welcome triumph of nature over man. Usually, it is the other way about.

This street has lain here, dropping away comfortably to the shore, since before the days when the indefatigable ox, plodding its ruts, hauled clear pine sticks, new oak and applewood knees to the shipyards at the high-water mark. The shell and stone scatterings of Wampanoag clambakes lie no more than a spade's depth beneath the lilacs and tiger lilies, lush against the painted pickets.

No house on this street is very young and they all sit easily with each other under their broad-throated chimneys and among their hedges and fences, offering less of architectural purity than of historic record. It takes little discernment to identify the ells that were added to the original colonial rectangles in order to accommodate the third and fourth children. The outlines of the carriage shed remain beneath a latter-day second story, and in the cellars, stone "laid up" by men forgotten before Abraham Lincoln ran for a seat in the Illinois General Assembly, still supports the first-floor hearths.

Thus, it is a street that certainly has not escaped all of the twentieth century, but which, through relative simplicity of daily habit, at least holds many of the contemporary ravages at arm's length. What goes on in the street is reasonably predictable; its noises are identifiable and principally acceptable; and not only the first, but the last names of its cats and dogs are known to those who live there.

It is understandable, therefore, that on such a street, where the patterns of people and creatures have become quietly constant, the injection of an ominous note is easily achieved. One day in front of Faris's brother's house, the ominous note was struck by the alien presence of a tan sedan, door ajar; and a blue-domed police cruiser. Both were angularly parked on the wrong side of the street, haste being implicit in this. In some places, at some times, haste itself is ominous and so it was here. It forced into recollection the outlines of a face, aging and gone mild.

By night, the sudden light winking on behind a yellow shade at an hour when people who live in patterns are expected to be sleeping, can indicate a crisis. But by day, there was nothing about this well-scrubbed house's exterior, comfortably part of all about it, to indicate that the fabric of the daily routine lay torn.

Still, there were the two automobiles, unreasonably alien.

I do not know precisely how the word of death spreads through such a street — perhaps like wind through the leaves, leaving a hush behind it. If you pass someone walking, you know that he knows, and therefore begin the conversation in the middle by remarking, "Well, he went quietly, didn't he?"

In such a neighborhood, there are two reactions to death. First, the intimate recollection: "You could set your watch by him. Afternoons, he'd go for a walk down to the waterfront and you could hear that cane, tap, tap on the sidewalk. 'There he goes, I'd say to myself, right on schedule.'" Or another might say, "You know, my hound is five pounds heavier because of him. When he began not to get around so much, he liked the dog to come to see him. It was company, you know. He'd feed it, and that dog would sit there by the hour, just to get its ears rubbed."

The second reaction is primitive and stems from the need for reassurance; for no matter how many times death passes closely, it remains incredible and unacceptable.

Within the houses on the street, especially after the sun had gone, there was a wordless drawing together, a reaching out for the familiar, without our having to explain why this was. One said, "You're home earlier than usual tonight. That's good." Or, "We're going to have something for supper that you like very much." More than ever, the evidence of being was important, the flaming logs on the andirons, the taste of newly roasted meat, the stabilizing sound of a thoroughly familiar voice, and the competent and orderly strength of the brass-handled door, now locked against the dark.

It is capricious what the mind remembers and what it forgets about the dead.

There was one day when we walked to the church, snug and solid on a hillside street, through puddled ways, the air heavy-sweet with pale rose petals overhanging clean white fences. Sitting in the bare varnished pew, I watched the summer light flow through the simple patterns of the colored glass window upon the faces of those who sat there, tanned visitor and pale native. When you come together like this, I thought, each has his own approach, depending upon what he remembers and what he believes. Perhaps it is true, as John Donne wrote, that *"no man is an island, entire of itself;"* but in moments of this kind, the Donne quotation that you are more likely to remember is: *"Be thou thine own home, and in thy self dwell."*

The building, plain and strong, had known us all since boyhood; it was strange in a way to know that this very pew, shiny and sturdy as ever, had held me when I was twelve and weighed a hundred and twenty pounds. The lady organist had known us all, too, freckles and loose teeth, and watched us grow.

She was playing, "*Though like the wanderer, the sun gone down, darkness be over me, my rest a stone . . .*"

I could not remember whether Tad had pumped the organ. Most of us had; we were called "blow boys" in the record of the church accounts, and the pay was twenty-five cents a Sunday. You pumped in a little room beside the organ and behind the choir loft. On the plain board wall there was a slot with a white marker in it that rose and fell. It went up if you pumped and down if you didn't. Repenciled by the generations, there were upper and lower lines to show you where the marker ought to be, so that the organ didn't run out of breath. You could pump with one hand and read the funny papers with the other, and some did. These days, a motor does the pumping.

Well, what do you remember, I asked myself. And I knew, without turning to look, that the back pew would hold two only; in some spring far enough back so that it is blurred with other springs, we had sat there, Tad and I, after passing the collection plates. Not so much irreverently, but principally because we were young and the smell of new-cut grass came through the open windows, we were not listening to the sermon.

Without words, Tad taught me a child's game with the hands, a matter of touching left thumb to right forefinger and vice versa, faster and faster, depending on dexterity. The movement was something like a whirling wheel. It was a pleasantly ridiculous thing and reminded me of the Queen, in *Alice Through the Looking Glass*, who remarked, ". . . *here, you see, it takes all the running you can do to keep in the same place.*" And Tad could do it backward, too.

The young minister in a dark suit read, "*The things which are seen are temporal, but the things which are not seen are eternal.*"

Tad had lived in Mary Abbie Norton's house, just over the

fence from us; it was an old place, with wayward clumps of blue flag and a cherry tree bowed with fruit that drew clusters of fat, swinging birds. One year, almost too late for snow, there had been a blizzard, and afterward the sun came out; all the careless beauty of snow piles sparkled, and Lucy Cooper's yellow cat, on its way to the store, squinted at the world's brightness. For hours, Tad and I worked with the snow, wet and packable, cutting blocks for a house. We butted its squareness against Mary Abbie's woodshed, finding trash boards that were black-stained with wet to hold up the roof, and patting the wall cracks full of slush with our soaked mittens.

Somebody (I cannot remember who, my father perhaps) came upon us in the afternoon and took our picture — rubber boots, wet jackets, stocking caps and the blockish snow house. I do not know where the photograph is now, but I can remember where Tad stood, and where I stood.

"It is sown in corruption, it is raised in incorruption," read the minister.

The only other related photograph had the bones of a ship in it. There were a dozen of us, including Tad, all members of the Sunday School class, and we had gone on an overnight trip to South Beach. It was spring, and the muskrats — sleek, shiny and in search of mates — were everywhere among the clacking dried fronds and muddy paths of the marsh. Barefoot, and running the trickling sand of the dunes, we all charged up over the beach crest and suddenly came face to face with the sea's brightness and the silvered wreck.

What was left of the ship had been there for a long time; the planks, timbers and sheathing curved like the palm of a hand, with truncated oak fingers reaching upward twice the height of any of us, as if seeking release from the flat, hard sand.

Unimaginatively, we lined up in a row in front of the wreck for a picture, and two of us, characteristically, stuck out our

151

tongues. Afterward, somebody (I cannot recall who or why, but I can remember well the quick anxiety when I turned at the roaring sound and saw the leaping flame) had set fire to the ship. It was like a chimney with a dozen parallel flues; gold-orange in the clear morning, the fire shot upward through the spaces between the ribs. It sounded like a herculean blowtorch, and we wanted to run and put it behind us, but did not dare.

Some time later, how much time I do not know, firemen from the next town, drawn by the smoke column that rose straight up and a mile high, came hot and running over the hummocks and doused the flames. Panting from a futile bucket brigade, we squatted on the sand, silent and chastened, and after his work was done the chief came over and gave us hell, quietly, effectively and entirely without profanity. As I remember, the thrust of his remarks suggested a lack of common sense on our part. We accepted that, in the specific instance, and were pleased when he left.

"*We brought nothing into this world and it is certain we can carry nothing out,*" read the minister. The newspaper story about Tad had related that he had drowned while boating.

Sitting in the pew, I thought, "Is this all there is to remember?" Yet even as I asked, I knew that two photographs and a child's game were more than enough to keep intact what was.

Maybe gravestones help some people remember, but I do not know about gravestones. When I was little I thought they were to keep the people down in there, and later I thought it was a way of showing how much money you had. Now, I just do not know how I feel about them, although I had just as soon have a piece of fieldstone at my head and feet as the Indians do at Christiantown, and I suggest there are all kinds of monuments to be had, limited only by the amount of love and imagination expended upon them.

Now consider the monument to Vincent.

If it is incredible to you that a man who worked from the time he was nine could die at the age of seventy-three and leave an estate, if that is not too high-flown a word, of precisely $42.37, then so be it. The fact is, that is what happened. It probably proves that no American lives closer to social and economic limbo than the wage earner whose income is barely above those levels that would qualify him for government assistance. He is too rich to be poor, and assuredly the reverse is also true.

This fellow, Vincent, was neither skilled nor talented, yet he regarded work as manly, and the essence of life, and that was his greatest asset. He prided himself on arriving at the job fifteen minutes early; he sometimes had to be urged to go home at the day's end if he became interested in a project, and he applied himself to his minuscule tasks as if the company which employed him, all five floors of it, would collapse if he neglected the condition of so much as one paper clip, paintbrush, or wastebasket.

Next to work, his god was cleanliness. He washed his big hands after each chore was finished, and one of his few complaints against a society that had done so little for him was that his mother used to make better soap in the backyard than you can buy now. The cleanliness extended to neatness. At work, all of his tools hung, each in its particular place, on a wooden rack that he had built himself, on his own time and with his own materials. His overalls had been washed so many times that they were faded to the blue of an April sky.

At home, his were the only trash barrels on the block that were always painted and covered. He also had stenciled his initials on them, but that was not necessary; everybody could tell which barrels were Vincent's.

Vincent died as he would have preferred. He was sitting in the living room rocker; he was wearing a clean white shirt, and his round-toed shoes were newly shined. He had just placed his pipe, still warm, in the ashtray, and that was the last thing that he did. It would have bothered him if, in dying, he had spilled ashes in his lap, or if it had been the duty of some stranger to discover him in disarray.

The money he left was in a billfold that his daughter, Thelma, had given to him for Christmas: two fives, three tens, two ones, all neatly folded, and the change in a separate pocket. A lodge insurance policy just took care of burying him; there was no bank account, no other property. On the other hand, it was discovered that he did not owe anything, not one penny.

Thelma said, "It was as if he almost came out even with his money. He almost didn't have any more. He didn't need any more. He liked things to come out even. When he ate, he wanted to finish his meat and potatoes together."

Vincent would have approved of his funeral. Nothing, including the flowers and the attendance, was in such quantity as to be difficult to dispose of once the matter was ended. Those who came next, a bridal party clattering up the church's stone steps, probably did not even know what had taken place, for there was nothing left to betray it.

The club where he used to have a beer Saturday nights observed a moment of silence and then the meeting was adjourned for refreshments. His daughter had his overcoat cleaned, and gave it to the man upstairs. She said, "If it bothers you, you know, wearing a coat when somebody has died . . . but still, it's nice and warm, and he never wore it much." And the man said no, he did not mind at all.

In the cellar Vincent had a collection of nails, tacks, washers, nuts and bolts. He had sorted them, poured them into red tobacco tins, tied a paper label on each and they stood at the back of his bench like Hampshire Guardsmen at inspection. Thelma gave them to a Scout scrap drive.

Hardly ruffled, life went on. Except for the $42.37.

Thelma called it "Papa's money." She sat at the kitchen table with the green plastic cover, staring at the gold-framed motto on the wall that read, "Home Is Where the Heart Is." She said, "If it had been a hundred dollars, or a real lot of money like that, you could do two or three things with it. Like you could give some to the church, and all that. But with forty-two dollars, you know, the way things cost today, you can probably only do one thing, so it has to be the right thing, doesn't it?"

The other week she phoned, in tears. She had spent the money and somebody in the family had told her what she had done was an insult to her father's memory. She wanted an objective opinion.

The kitchen was as spotless and orderly as it had been when Vincent was alive; even its aromas were never more unleashed than those of freshly baked bread and dark new tea. Almost defensively, Thelma led the way to the white-enameled sink and pointed, "That's what I got with Papa's money."

It was a new garbage disposal unit.

She said, "All my life, every night when supper was over, the first thing Papa did was wrap up the garbage in yesterday's newspaper, and tie it, and take it down cellar and put it in the can out back. I sat here one night and figured it out — eight cellar steps and three out from the back door — in the fifty years he did it, that's 438,000 steps. It was the one job he did that he didn't like.

"He used to say, 'Out front, we have electricity come in wires, and light up a bulb so that the dark is bright as day. Out back, we still throw leftover bones into a can and wait for somebody to come pick them up. They used to do about the same thing when people lived in caves. We should be able to do better than that.' "

Thelma pushed the switch and the disposal blades whirred. She looked at me and said very quietly, "Was this a funny thing to do?"

"I don't think you could have done better," I said, " and it will last a long time."

What I am saying is that I can think of far more personal ways of remembering somebody than carving his name on a rock which, except for the accident of time and circumstance, would have been bought by someone I do not even know to memorialize someone else whom I do not wish to know.

We are concerned here with meaning; my neighbor to the southwest, a white-haired woman newly arrived from some place in New Jersey, knows much about this. In her case, it is the meaning of the end of April; obviously, what April's end means — or whether it means anything — depends on who you are and what has happened to you. If I had known what it meant to her, I would not have introduced the subject. In retrospect, however, I am glad that I did, for it produced an interlude of value.

All I had intended was a reference to the rapid changes in nature that come during this month. Things leap to life, and where yesterday there was only bare ground left over from winter, today an excitement of impatient green has broken through. Each day the wind loses some of the leanness of March, and what blows in its wake is as full of promise as the fat bud on the lilac bush.

But when I mentioned April's end, her hands, slender and competent, paused in their effort and she said, without looking at me, "My husband died a year ago tomorrow."

"I'm so sorry," I began, "I shouldn't have reminded you."

"It's all right," she said. "I don't need reminding. Doing this . . ." she gestured at the work before her, "is reminder enough, because I began it almost immediately afterwards. As therapy, or call it what you will."

She bent to examine the bright pieces of metal before her, holding them up, turning them, planning their interrelationship. "If I had had children, I might not have felt the need to take myself in hand so soon after he died, but being alone, it would have been easy to . . ." She sought the word.

"Turn in upon yourself?"

"Something like that. Shut out the world. Drown in self-pity. Rake over the ashes forever, and never see the sun again."

We were in her studio, a place of slanted ceiling, north windows and, on this particular morning, a magnificent extravagance of pale spring light. She was creating a piece of sculpture by combining parts of machinery. It is unnecessarily distracting to itemize whether they were cogs, axles, rods, rachets, or all of these, since what they were becoming is all that matters.

When completed, the figure on which she was working will stand about eighteen inches high. It is one of four pieces representing the seasons of the year. This is winter on which she is now working, and already there is, in and about it, the whirl of wind, the glitter of ice.

"A year ago," she resumed, "I had never done anything like this. Now I do everything but riveting." In her hands the little silver blowtorch hissed; like coins, the solder dropped; the wheel and shaft were joined in such manner as their manufacturer never envisioned and it seemed to me she was so engrossed in her work — no, mission more than work — as to be addressing it, rather than me.

"We were married more than thirty years," she said, "and it had, therefore, become a matter of the shared experience. More and more, words were unnecessary, because something present

157

related to something past, and we both knew it, and went from one to the other without prompting. The sharing aspect even now is so strong that I don't think of past things, good or bad, simply in terms of how I thought about them, but how he and I thought about them."

She turned a valve, and the torch's blue flame grew more intense. "I don't suggest to you that ours was an idyllic, totally harmonious, completely fulfilling and romantic union. I only say that people who live together a long time grow dependent on each other — and find comfort in this linking because life is really a lonely process. So after he died, you can understand that I looked for something comforting that would . . . take note of the fact that life unshared is simply not the same."

"You found something?"

"Yes. Have you ever read Rossetti's 'The Blessed Damozel'?"

I said I had. This is the poem in which he portrays the yearning of the loved one, who has died, for the lover, who is still living. (*"The blessed damozel leaned out/From the golden bar of Heaven;/Her eyes were deeper than the depth/Of waters stilled at even . . . 'I wish that he were come to me,/For he will come,' she said."*)

The woman picked up the piece on which she was working, cupped it in her hands and walked slowly to the window. She was not looking at anything, simply standing with the light upon her face and hands.

"You will remember," she said, "how much Rossetti made of the fact that the woman, looking forward to the reunion, dwelt upon the things they would do together, especially the things she had learned that he would not know, because she had preceded him . . ."

(". . . *and I myself will teach to him,/I myself, lying so,/The songs I sing here; which his voice/Shall pause in, hushed and slow,/ And find some knowledge at each pause./ Or some new thing to know . . . All this is when he comes.")*

The woman came back to the worktable. There was about her gestures more than just an interest in creativity. One sensed in her the beauty of self-discipline, her refusal to be profligate with the day or hour.

She said, "I thought I would show the four seasons because of their variety and wholeness; because what happens out of doors always has been of great importance to me — to us," she corrected, "and I don't say that sentimentally; I am creating not only what I feel, but what we have felt. That's why I have to be honest with it. That's why I have saved the spring piece — the April piece, if you will — until last, because it will be the most . . . the most difficult." She smiled.

I left then, and she may not even have known for a moment or two, because she was not really talking to me at all. I left, being mindful that Rossetti had concluded, *"I saw her smile . . . And then she cast her arms along/ The golden barriers/ And laid her face between her hands/ And wept."*

So ends this day, with the bright ball of sun diving past the kitchen window into the sea, but it will be back tomorrow.

THE NINTH DAY

THIS was the ninth day, not the seventh, but nevertheless it happened to be a Sunday; it goes without saying that no week is complete without one. However, I think Italian calendars are on the right track in making Sunday the last day of the week and I wonder that we do not. To my mind, the six days preceding start at a high level of energy and slide successively down the slope of effectiveness until one comes to Sunday, pleasantly unraveled and in need of restoration.

Thus, a knock at the kitchen door in midafternoon this Sunday provoked ill-tempered mutterings. This was especially true because I was inclined to suspect that whoever was there could not think of anything else to do. That is a bad start, indeed.

On the doorstep, there was a little girl in a red sweater, whose eyes were the color of Malaga grapes. At the end of a frayed

160

tether of sisal she had an amiable sharp-nosed dog, a short-haired creature the color of underdone toast who sat with his head cocked as if he were listening to the conversation. The girl brushed a blond bang out of her eye and asked, "Is he your dog?"

I said, "No I'm sorry, he isn't."

She sighed. "He's lost and he's tired and his feet hurt from walking."

As if in response, the dog oozed to the stone step, stretched at full length and lay, muzzle on paws, with his eyes watching, carefully and quickly.

"I found him last night," she said, "with a broken piece of rope around his neck. Last night, this morning and this afternoon, I have taken him to people's houses." She pointed, "This street, that street, and that street. He isn't anybody's."

She looked tired, and the dog looked tired.

We sat on the front steps with the dog between us.

"He has a license tag," I said, while he let me hold his chin in my hand. "We can find out whose he is."

"Yes, but not until tomorrow," she said. "Because the license office wasn't open yesterday and it isn't open today and my father says we can't keep him tonight because we already have a dog."

Obviously this was a crisis. In explaining its stark and inflexible outlines, the little girl had worry lines between her eyebrows. The dog also had them, by coincidence, but presumably his were genetic and not temporary.

In the living room behind me, there was an open book, an absorbing volume — Arthur Krock's *Memoirs*. There was a good, crackling fire in the stove. The thought flitted across my mind that if the little girl had lived elsewhere, had been in another town, on another road, had rung another doorbell, I

161

might still have been lying on the floor reading about Clark Clifford's memorandum to Harry Truman.

Although as a student I received some of the lowest marks in mathematics ever recorded in the history of man, I estimated quickly that probably the odds were about a hundred thousand to one against this particular little girl (and dog) coming to my particular back door. Yet they had. I felt the suddenly inhospitable breath of the fall wind from the northwest. Clearly, it was a cruel world. I do not know which is more irresistible, a little girl in trouble or a little dog in trouble.

I looked to left and right at their respective eyes, which obviously were saying, "Grownups are supposed to be smart. Now it's your problem. What are you going to do about it?"

The dog made things worse by leaning against me. I could visualize him limping through the night with that chunk of rope dragging, and how would you find him again tomorrow?

"Sit right here, both of you," I said. "I'm going to phone the police and see if they can help." The little girl looked dubious, but it was obvious neither of them had any intention of leaving.

The desk sergeant liked dogs; especially in small towns, they have a tendency to. He not only was friendly but, more to the point, after I had described the dog, he ruffled through his reports and said, "I think this is the one here, but I'm not sure. Let me phone the people who called in and I'll call you right back."

We sat on the front steps for the next twenty minutes and I could see the little girl beginning to think, "I told him nothing would happen. The only way is to ring some more doorbells before it gets dark and I have to go home."

"Wait a few minutes more," I said, "and if we don't hear I'll call again. I don't know why he hasn't called back."

The phone rang. "I keep getting a busy signal at their house," the desk sergeant said, "and I think the phone's out of order." I didn't think I could explain that to either the girl or the dog, and I had visions of driving both of them the two or three miles to the house, very possibly on a fruitless errand.

But the policeman went on, "I've sent a cruiser to tell them. You ought to hear something soon."

We waited, I not becomingly, because waiting is not of my nature, but they, both of them, with a quiet resignation that is as old as life itself and most common among creatures close to the roots of things. Even though what was about to happen was important to both of them and both were upset, each according to his capacity, there was no fretting and twitching. I once saw a farm woman sitting in a kitchen rocker, watching flood waters rising against a sandbag barrier five hundred yards away, and her hands were folded like the little girl's.

Suddenly it was over. A blue station wagon drove up with two children in the back, jumping, pointing, noses pressed against the glass. A woman opened the car door, and the dog, suddenly alive, bolted across the narrow road, rope trailing, and leaped into the front seat, lapping all the hands and faces reachable.

When they had left, grateful, reunited, and joyful, the little girl said, "I find lots of dogs. I'm going home now." Whereupon she left. But I discovered I had in the meantime lost my mood for Arthur Krock for the moment, so I sat there thinking about the little girl finding "lots of dogs," which seemed incredible but still, I said aloud, "Maybe she really does. How do I know?"

Coming up the road, I could see the letter carrier. Obviously he was not carrying letters on the Sabbath, but he lives over beyond in a swaybacked house snugged against a stand of pine and often walks for pleasure. I think he is a cousin of Charles's wife, but I do not dare ask him again because, in explaining how it is, he goes into genealogical contortions and always loses me somewhere in the twice removeds.

I like the term "letter carrier." It seems more appropriate than "postman" because the former not only predates junk mail and refers to an era when everything you received was worth opening, but it also conveys something of the importance of the job. Long before each of us lost his name and became simply "Occupant" (a classic example of modern insolence and indolence), kingdoms were cannibalized, ladies consigned to the shark-filled moat, and plague germs inadvertently transmitted, all by post.

As a child, the only mail I received was at Christmas and on Valentine's Day, so I probably grew up thinking vaguely of the letter carrier as an amiable fellow with wings, a long white beard and a quiver full of arrows. But the point is that I liked him because it was exciting to watch a handful of envelopes drop through the letter slot and to see my name on one.

I still like letter carriers and when this one finally ambled abreast, I called out halloo and asked him if he would stop for refreshment. He said he would and that he would like, of all things, a cup of hot chocolate. I remarked that, when young, someone had told me that a steady diet of the stuff would clog the circulatory system.

He said "My nose is red because I am out in the wind a lot. What is more, if hot chocolate is going to clog my circulatory system it had better hurry, because I have been drinking it for about forty-two years and I do not know how much longer I can hang around waiting. And lastly, you drink what you want to, and I shall drink what I want to."

And so, in friendly fashion, we went on to other things. He is a good man to listen to; he has been away to school and he came back home to be a letter carrier, not because he had to, but because he wanted to. He said, staring at his spoon, "My family went away the other weekend, and I suddenly realized it was the first time in probably twenty-five years or more that I had been alone in my own house for an extended period. I suppose women are alone in their homes a lot, but it happens so seldom to men."

"I hadn't thought about it," I said. "I suspect you're right."

"Nor had I, but in the unaccustomed silence, I walked from room to room, letting everything I saw remind me of something, and thinking how many pieces of things you collect, item by item over the years, until finally it's together, and it's a room."

He went on, "The first thing was the ticking of the clocks, because you don't even notice that when people are talking, or the television is turned on. The clock in the dining room has hung in the same place for more than half a century; its brass pendulum has swung back and forth at the same rate in that room while the people who put it there grew old and finally died, and while my daughter was graduated from the wooden play pen on the floor beneath it to driving an automobile."

"However," I said, "the passage of time, of itself, ought not to be a saddening thing."

"Not at all. Neither was my tour of the house. On the contrary, I was glad to be reminded of things that I hadn't thought of for years. I found my copy of James Otis's *Runaway Brig*, a real thriller for boys once upon a time, and its spine was all splintered from reading and there were even old grass stains turned brown on some of the pages, because I used to read it in the backyard.

He took a long gulp of chocolate. "You remember those framed chromolithographs everybody used to hang? Ours said, 'God Bless Our Home' in letters fancy enough for an illuminated manuscript, and it hung in our kitchen when I was growing up, and now we've got it in the living room, which probably indicates something, but I don't know what. Anyway, it made me think of old man MacKenzie, because when I was a boy and he came to our house, he used to sit just under it, in the same straight-backed chair every time.

"He had been to sea, but in the later years, he sold vanilla extract, which he carried in a limp Boston bag. If he arrived at noontime he ate with us, and I always expected him to bend all the silver because he had enormous hands, but he didn't. He wouldn't eat with the people next door; he said they never served anything but olives and tripe.

"There were lots of things as I walked through the rooms, all from places to which you cannot return and should not want to, but it is good to think about them once in a while.

"The piano was sold to us at half price, because we couldn't afford to pay any more, by a man who loved pianos, and who loved people who wanted pianos, more than the money the pianos made for him, which wasn't much either. The other day I walked past the place where his house and piano shop were. It's a parking lot now."

"So few things are not," I ventured.

"Mmm," he agreed. "And another thing that stopped me — the front of our fireplace is blistered, and even though it has been sanded and repainted you can see where the flames once came up. I suppose, no matter how careful people are, that has happened at least one time to everybody who ever burned a log regularly. You just forget to open the damper before you light it —

"I did it when my son had just gone to the hospital. It was a Sunday, too. He was in the third grade then. The doctor was honest. He said they wouldn't know for a week whether the boy would live. I paced the floor, and thought a fire would be cheerful on a gray day. Almost burned the house down." He chuckled. "The boy lived. Last week he told me he weighs two hundred and five pounds. All muscle."

166

"And do you remember where people sat in your home — particular people?"

"Of course. And whole conversations, some good, some bad, most of which I can still reconstruct without great effort."

He finished the chocolate. "Must go," he said, rising. "Much obliged." He turned for the last word. "You know, I go to a lot of houses every day. What bothers me is how many you wouldn't want to be alone in, because they don't say anything about anybody or to anybody."

Which is true, of course, yet it may be that we are giving more thought these days to where and how we live. I say this because of an experience only a week or so before I began my vacation.

A bald young man with a nicely suntanned scalp was preceded through my office door by a long green cigar that was obviously too expensive to be given away to one's friends. He arrived without appointment, sat down without being invited, and began rummaging through his attaché case, monotonously humming something from, I think, Gilbert and Sullivan.

Meanwhile, he said confidently, "I am from Shaster Associates. We take public opinion polls. I would value your opinion."

That softened me. The last time anyone asked me what I thought was six years ago when a colleague asked me if I thought I could lend him five dollars.

Nevertheless, I said rather tartly, "I notice you are wearing a lapel button that says, 'Anyone Over Thirty Is a Creep.' Doesn't that interfere with your poll-taking efforts?"

"Not at all," he said. "In the first place, I never seek the opinions of anyone over thirty. And in the second place, this is my son's button. He has gone back to prep school and I am not responsible for his opinions."

Now since I observed my thirtieth birthday so long ago that

I cannot remember who was President at the time or if, in fact, we had one, I thought, "This is a sharp young man indeed, and before he leaves this office, I shall frisk him to make sure that he has not palmed my best ball-point pen and the new box of paper clips." I said in my most peremptory fashion, "I am over thirty."

He whistled in overdone amazement. "You could have fooled me," he said. "Now let's get down to business." And with that, he dragged forth a volume of forms in quadruplicate, and festooned one corner of my desk with them.

"You are, of course, aware," he rambled, "that Constantinos Doxiadis is one of the world's leading architects — "

"Yes," I began, "I once knew a fellow who — "

"And Mr. Doxiadis," the young man interrupted, "has criticized the American front lawn as a sterile extravagance. How do you feel about that?"

"Well, I have thought of the American front lawn in many contexts," I said. "Pockmarked with wormholes after rain. A repository for various types of cast statuary, including pink flamingos. Littered with croquet wickets to fell the unwary. But never as a sterile extravagance."

"Try to think of it in that context," he persisted. "Mr. Doxiadis is in favor of building houses flush to the street, with the front wall right at the roadside, in the European way. That would allow large backyards in which you could do what you want to do."

He waxed to his subject. "The twenty- to forty-foot front yard setback required of most American homes is a real waste of space and money. It's like a goldfish bowl. Noisy traffic streaming by. Pedestrians leering at you."

"Leering?" I asked.

"Leering," he said. "American women don't sit out there on the front lawn sunning and chatting and enjoying themselves.

168

The children can't be left out there to play alone. Even pets aren't safe on the front lawn. It is nothing but an unused, un-usable large hunk of land that has to be mowed, trimmed, clipped, rolled and watered, because if it isn't immaculate, everybody assumes the inside of your house looks the same way."

"Well, I — " I began.

The young man was filling in blanks furiously. He was using brown ink, which he remarked in passing resists fading in bright sun, and he did not even look up as he resumed, "Now, granted that you build a house right out at the street, even if your lot is relatively small you can fence in the backyard with wooden or wire structures or high foliage, and that way if you want company, you can invite your friends over, and if you don't, they can't wander over."

"You know what that makes me think of?" I said. "In the Normandy campaign of 1944, the American troops were hav-ing trouble getting through the hedgerows, which were tough, high and thick and generations old. There was this fellow, I think he was a sergeant, and he improvised blades for the front end of his tank that would lop off whole trees. Smashing suc-cess," I said.

"How is that relevant?" asked the young man. "Are you implying that your neighbors have tanks? Or that they would fight their way into your yard if you tried to keep them from coming in?"

"Well, since you put it that way," I said, weakly, "I guess —"

"Let's stick to the subject," he said, relighting his long green cigar and filling in a half dozen more blanks with brown ink.

"Now I think you will agree," he said, "that at a time when neither Americans nor anyone else can look forward much longer to the privacy of secluded buildings on large plots of land, the answer to privacy, including space and seclusion that we require increasingly in today's demanding world, lies in eliminating the front yard, and making a walled-in, extra 'room' of the backyard, where the family can do what it wants to without —-''

"Being leered at?" I risked.

"Precisely," he said.

"You have used the phrase 'the family can do what it wants to do,' " I said. "You make it sound positively orgiastic. I suppose one of the most daring things my family might do in the backyard is to read the *New York Post*. And how on earth are you going to hand a cup of sugar over a ten-foot wall if anybody wants to borrow one?"

He was repacking his briefcase. "You've been most helpful. Thanks for participating," and he left in a trail of long green smoke.

Sitting there on the step, I got to thinking of what the letter carrier had said about looking at objects and being reminded of things. One supposes that, consciously or otherwise, we may look upon as many as ten thousand objects each day, and it is tempting to wonder what each has meant to someone. I suspect to know would be unbearable.

A clump of blue flag, one of the commonest forms of iris, prompts this observation, for it is a monument of sorts to a woman I never knew, yet with whom I have an inevitable empathetic communication. These fragile blue flowers are at the base of a high brick foundation, on which rests a house old enough to be both historic and neglected. Increasing numbers of automobiles have worn tracks almost to the iris, yet it still blooms, testifying to the surprising stubbornness of delicate things.

170

What I remember about the woman, whom I never saw, is a newspaper clipping, so yellowed that I knew I would be the last person to unfold it, or to read it; it fell to pieces in my hands. With the story there was a picture of her, wearing overalls and holding a saw. This is extraordinary, considering that in her time the use of lipstick was daring, and women were not expected to have opinions on anything other than recipes. At the time, she was renovating the interior of her house, and this usurpation of the male prerogative would have been singular in itself, but that she should have permitted a newspaper interview on the subject reveals uncommon individuality.

When photographed she was constructing a corner china closet, with glass-paned doors at the top, and a drawer for flatware and a cupboard below. As far as I know the closet is still in the house, in the northeast corner of the ancient living room. I have seen it, and it is a very creditable job of fitting and joining. Even in the rains of spring and the fogs of summer the doors do not stick; the woods are nicely accustomed to each other, well-found, and the mitred corners are as tight as they were when she drove the last nail and countersank it.

I should like to have heard her speak, not because I think she would have said profound things but because there are not many neurotic carpenters, and I suspect her voice, like her face, reflected an inner composure. Overalls and saw notwithstanding, she appeared womanly and poised, and gave the impression that, far from seeking public attention, it was good manners, graciousness, and a positive attitude toward her fellow man which prompted her to admit the intruding reporter.

What she did for the house inside, with care and love, was complemented by her attention to its grounds. I do not know whether anything grew there before her arrival, but soon thereafter she brought forth life and color everywhere. Along the back wall, white and purple lilacs clustered, heavy with blooms in time for Memorial Day. Beside the back-porch stairs, there was a Japanese quince, with a profusion of scarlet blooms. North of the house, there were rows of bright Chinese poppies as big as teacups, peonies with enormous blooms, and rambling blackberry bushes for the catbirds and their kin.

The place was not an estate. It was not, as a matter of fact, even a very large house lot, and heavy traffic rumbled by much too closely. Yet the woman succeeded in creating an atmosphere peaceful and apart, although she built no fence and planted no hedge. She accomplished this by introducing beauty where it was natural for beauty to be, and by transmitting, even to the house, the calm that derives from care and sensible disciplines.

So much time has gone by now since she lived there that it is difficult to know what happened. With each year, the task of discovering the whole truth — even if I wanted to, which I do not — becomes increasingly less possible. Those who might have known it have drifted away somewhere, wherever it is that people drift to as time passes.

A neighbor, now dead, suggested that "something happened" to the woman's marriage, a euphemism in keeping with the gentleness of the house and land as she influenced them. A banker who knew something about the matter once said to me, "We would have carried her along, you know. She could have paid just the taxes and interest indefinitely. But we didn't even know she was in trouble. She never came to us, or to anybody, as far as I know. The first thing we knew, she was ready to sell the house and had a buyer. I don't know where she went. I don't know that she ever told anybody where she was going."

Possession of three or four automobiles may indicate American affluence to a European, but the truth is that in this country, the appearance of a fleet of cars in the front yard, whether they are old or new, is the first evidence that the property is sliding downhill. Principally, that is the sort of thing that has happened to this place since the woman left. Its architectural uniqueness is gradually being obscured by a layer of neglect and here and there, by desperate jimmy-hammer efforts to postpone the worst of what is happening to the house.

It is not precisely fair to suggest that people have done everything destructive that has happened. If you incline toward such thinking, you may choose to believe that nature, too, conspired toward the ultimate destruction of what the woman had created, since she could no longer have it. In fact, the first ravaging was by hurricanes, without precedent for decades, which uprooted the magnificent elms and forced the beginnings of new starkness on the land.

Then came a succession of tenants, transient and ruthless, and Philistines among them, armed with chain saws, leaky crankcases, and barbaric children who poisoned, cut down, pulled up or trampled out of existence virtually every living thing, including most of the grass.

However, if there is a tragedy in all of this, it is, of course, that of the human relationship, not of the flowers. Realistically, I suspect the last time the woman looked at the iris it had already lost whatever meaning it possessed for her. Thus, even though it is the sole survivor of what was, I suppose it really does not matter whether the blue flag comes up again next year.

Yet I am not sure of this, not sure at all, and perhaps it matters far more than I know.

In part, what happened to the woman refutes the popular notion that people in small towns are always closely knit; obviously, she lived unto herself, perhaps unfortunately so. Moreover, I

173

have found a heartwarming reaching-out between strangers in the city, and I will tell you how one of these affairs came about, so that you may see what I mean.

It was an ugly fire in a small place.

Now this is the late-winter shape of the crooked street, jammed into Boston's anonymous press of movement; it is not far from Harrison Avenue, and the faded letters of the battered red-and-white sign slung over the sidewalk read, "Wai Wai." The time was ten thirty in the morning; the dirty three-inch ice was black in the gutters, and two blocks away, bright billboard bulbs announced that it was nineteen above.

This is Chinatown, tight province of tumbled contrast, wall jumbled against wall, and suddenly one dreary display window blackened like a lamp chimney when the wick is too high. There was a quick, breathless puff as the glass shattered and black smoke, like a wild, thick rope, poured upward through the jagged hole.

A woman, old enough to be my mother and agile enough to be my daughter, shiny black hair in a tight pug, came running out of the burning building carrying a bent snow shovel, and with the fear and agony of all time in her face.

It will be a moment before anything else happens.

Look about you, for the kinds of contrasts there are. Here, with modern concrete balcony under dull green pagoda, is the twentieth-century headquarters of the Chinese Merchants Association and over it, snapping in the March westerly, is the flag of the Republic of China. It is also red, white and blue, but with certain differences. The flag has a white sun in blue sky, over crimson ground; the twelve points of the sun, starlike, represent the twelve two-hour periods of the day and, collectively, symbolize the spirit of progress. The three colors represent the three principles of the people: blue is *min chuan*, democracy; white is *min sheng,* people's livelihood, and crimson is *min chu,* nationalism.

In the street below the flag, there are other things. Why a cat howls behind a splintered green door, down four stone steps littered with trash that leads into a puddled basement, I do not know, and I am glad that I do not. On the corner, under the Coca-Cola sign, with pale yellow shirt, tight pants and transistor radio, a handsome young man smokes and listens to his music; strokes his long hair affectionately, and watches the girls pass. They are, virtually without exception, pretty girls, clear-eyed and neat, and here is one with white, calf-length boots and a blue airplane bag from Pan American.

The thick smoke, and the woman wailing, trying futilely to get a shovelful of ice to throw on the fire, are attracting passersby. Here is a group of young Chinese men, one of whom is attending the Massachusetts Institute of Technology, and he is interested in the structure of matter. Students all, with green book bags, sketch pads, T-squares and briefcases, they pause to watch — not dispassionately — and one of them speaks in Chinese to the woman. She halts her ineffective shoveling and stares at the smoke with empty eyes, seemingly unaware that, in this cold, she is wearing only an unbuttoned sweater over her dress.

The students are good-looking, not only because they are young, but additionally because there is ordinarily a civilized composure in the Oriental face. I think how interesting it is that here, where they live, are the characters and configurations of an ancient, foreign civilization, yet only minutes away are the universities of new America, to which they are going.

Do not be impatient. It is only seconds since the front of the shop blew out. It always seems a long time until the fire apparatus arrives — although it is not — because you can see the orange flame curling, and hear its hungry crackle.

In the grocery next door that is Kai Wing's, two split smoked ducks, thin and wide as boards, hang by the bills between strings of red-and-white layered meat like necklaces, skewered on a black iron hook. Across the way, there are windows full of brass and lumpy bright beads, chopsticks and bamboo, and a sign on one says: "Wok sold here." If you do not know, a wok is essential to Chinese cookery; it is an iron kettle shaped like a salad bowl so that the heat is distributed evenly throughout the vessel.

Now the snarling sirens are in the near distance. A Chinese woman of about thirty, wearing black slacks and buckskin gloves, pulls her GMC truck with New Hampshire plates hard over to the crumbled slates of the slippery sidewalk. She opens the back doors to unload, and there are the pink and marbled legs of dressed lamb, wrapped in white cheesecloth. She lights a cigarette, waiting for the firemen to have done with their affair.

Within the burning shop, something pops; too loud for a bottle; perhaps something like a sealed gallon can. Now, into the narrow street roars Engine 26, sweeping a quick path through things and people, its red, gold-lettered snout high, powerful and exciting. The booted crew swings down from its gleaming efficiency; they are like quiet generals of an army, swift and knowledgeable, and suddenly, there is water bursting, hard and foaming, from the throbbing nozzle. The engine's big pump beats like a heart; water freezes in glasslike twists down the building front and quickly the smoke turns white, and this means the fire is beaten.

As if returning from far away, I remembered abruptly that I had an appointment. But the gutters now ran deep with dirty water from the hose and, with neither overshoes nor rubbers, I found myself marooned on a chunk of hard snow and rubbish.

In all that, for what reason I do not know, the woman in the unbuttoned sweater whose shop was gone, saw and understood

176

my problem. Wordless, she held out her snow shovel for me to step on to cross the swirling street. Turning to thank her, I sensed that she did not speak English, but we smiled for one triumphant second before she turned back to look upon the ashes of her livelihood.

THE TENTH DAY

T HE wind was southeast again today and the rain came
slanting in from gray clouds low enough to knock a man
off a horse. In town for groceries, I went looking for a second
cup of coffee and an escape from the puddled sidewalks; I turned
into the nearest sanctuary, an unpainted place with its frayed
awning still lowered against last summer's sun, and I found
there, hunched over a doughnut and a newspaper, a solid citizen
who spends much of his life haddock-hunting in knee boots.

I know this fellow, who claims the first sounds he heard on
earth were the thundering guns of bloody Jutland — and that is
an awful way for a baby to begin. But he has turned out well
for all that. As a matter of fact, he has pink cheeks and blue
eyes and looks younger than I did when I was a sophomore in
high school.

He rose to the attack immediately, by which sign I understood that he was in good spirits, enjoying his doughnut, and his

last trip offshore was more profitable than he had expected. Crushing the defenseless tabloid in one enormous hand he said, "I don't care what they say about inflation. Banks don't really want you to pay your bills."

"That is close to heresy," I suggested.

"Heresy and be damned," he said, pointing his bent and dripping spoon at me. It was one of the few times I ever heard him swear. "Just let me tell you what happened," he said, biting off each word carefully.

"Now about fifteen years ago, we had a line storm and it rained for three days. And this church where I go had a leaky roof, so we found out.

"So they came to me and some other fellows in the church and said, 'Can we afford a new roof?' And we looked at the thing and told them, 'Never mind afford it. Get a new roof or one of these days the ceiling will drop around your neck.'

"They did so, and took out a mortgage to pay for it. And once a month everybody gave something for the mortgage and just the other Sunday, what do you know, the pastor said to us, 'We have paid off the mortgage.'

"Very good for a little church in only fifteen years, I thought to myself. Maybe it is that this country is not going to you-know-where in a handbasket after all."

He buried his sunburned beak in the china mug, emerging refreshed like a breaching manatee. "Now then, pastor said to me, 'You will be chairman of the mortgage-burning cere-mony.' This seemed like a lot of fuss and feathers to me, and I said, 'Do we have to go through all that? Why don't you just heave the mortgage in the wastebasket?'

"But he said, 'No. These people have worked hard to pay this bill. It makes them feel part of the church; the church belongs to them as much as they belong to it. They have a right to a special moment for having done this good work, and it will give them a lot of satisfaction.' "

This fellow stared at his boots and sighed. "I didn't know it was going to be such a project but anyway, the three of us men and a couple of ladies who were on the committee figured we ought to have a rehearsal — just to see how everything would work out.

"So I went to the bank and I got some pieces of their paper, just the same size and thickness as the mortgage. And we got a fancy brass kettle from somebody to build the fire in, put a sheet of asbestos under it and put it on a table. Then we went through the program — you know, a prayer and a short talk from the head deacon and that sort of thing, and then it was my job to set fire to the paper.

"Well, when it came time, I did, just the way I would do it in the real ceremony. And the fire was just right, not too big, not too small, but in a minute, we realized that the burning paper smelled awful. 'Smelled' is no word for it. I have smelled some smells in my time, including an outdated whale and bottom mud that's been festering since the days of Noah, but this was awful enough to interest the Defense Department.

"I hove a pitcher of water into the kettle and put out the flame, but we had to open all the doors and windows and two days later, the place was still discouraging to go into.

"So I took the mortgage to the bank and I said, 'Is this printed on the same stuff you gave me for the rehearsal?' And the man in the bank checked it and said, 'Let me see.' I told him who gave me the paper and what happened when we burned it, and he clucked some, and said how sorry he was.

"Then he called in a vice-president and they talked, and finally they said I had been given the wrong kind of paper, that the mortgage was printed on something entirely different and would not make any smell at all.

180

" 'Good,' I said. 'I appreciate this,' I told them at the bank. 'I am not very good as a church member, but still, there are those in the congregation who at least wish me no harm. And I do not want them to change their minds because I make their church so that they can no longer enter it in peace and comfort.' They assured me all would be well.

"On the Sunday in question, we had the ceremony and when it came time, I took a deep breath and put the match in to light the paper. The match went right out and I thought it was a draft, so I asked them to please close the doors at the rear, and the organist began the piece over again that she was going to do while it was burning. Then I lighted it three more times and it still didn't catch, and the organist stopped playing until I could get it going.

"Anyway, what happened was that I used up half a box of wooden kitchen matches and didn't get any fire at all. I burned three fingers, got a black smooch on my new white shirt, and scorched the church table. By and by, the pastor said quietly that we should conclude with a short prayer and leave, and we did.

"Now, I have the God-damned mortgage paper at home. Pastor says he thinks it is my problem. The bank people don't want to talk about it any more. Next time I have a mortgage, you see if I hurry to pay it!''

My friend returned to his coffee, indicating that he did not want to talk further, although he asked how my father was. My father also once hunted haddock, and they are a closely tied breed, these offshore people.

On the way home I meandered some, since the rain was drying up and the sky lighter, and I got to thinking about my father, because Christmas and his birthday are coming and all that and, his tastes being simple, he is difficult to buy for. By the time I got to the four corners at the end of Main Street, I had about decided the best present I could give him would be to declare war on Italy, and I suppose that requires a little explanation.

My father never would be mistaken for the late Al Capone, because he is taller, has blue eyes and is nonfelonious, but they share one thing and that is an affection for the broad-brimmed fedora. For the benefit of those readers born after the repeal of Prohibition, this type of hat, with brim snapped down over the eyebrows, was a trademark of the sinful, ginful twenties, when they called a Thompson submachine gun a typewriter.

Most of the defendants in Chicago-style rubouts wore them, and I have seen simple country people cross to the other side of the street when they saw a stranger wearing one of these hats coming toward them. As a matter of fact, one summer evening my father, who is kind to everything from grasshoppers to grandmothers, swung through the doors of a local hostelry in a snap-brim fedora and scared a public prosecutor out of the lobby, up a flight of stairs and, possibly onto the fire escape for all I know. It was a case of mistaken identity in the low glow of twilight. An accused, who wore the same kind of hat, had threatened to inhibit the prosecutor's odds for survival if they ever met.

That's how touchy things were in those days. We did not have the atom bomb to worry about, but danger was a personal thing, Dodge City style, and I think, frankly, that kind of threat gives you much more of a feeling of participation. Don't you?

One day, my father's hat blew overboard, or something of the sort. We went to buy another and discovered, alack, that Americans no longer sold or wore the Caponian version.

It was like this: we entered a posh metropolitan hattery and a

182

smiling young man came forth with an armful of narrow-brimmed, high-crowned creations. He handed one to my father and asked, "How do you like this, sir?" Without even raising his voice, my father replied, "I wouldn't be seen walking through hell in it." We departed, leaving the young man's arms full of unwanted hats.

As a result, my father's next two hats came from Italy. I add a hasty footnote to the Internal Revenue Service that this is not as high-flying as it sounds. He just happened to know a couple of people who were going anyway, and who bought him a hat. The first was broad-brimmed and eminently acceptable; he has had it relined twice, and I think it makes him look most satisfactorily like a well-fed counterintelligence agent. The second, perish forbid, was narrow-brimmed and so we got the cruel news that Italy doesn't produce the broad hat any more, either. The company just stopped making them.

So what I propose is this: I will declare war on Italy. I see no need of involving the U.S. Government, because that just means carbon copies of everything. Instead, I shall get off some kind of letter to Rome, probably on fancy paper, pointing out in dignified fashion that the situation has become intolerable; this is slightly anticipatory, but, on the other hand, nobody frustrates my father indefinitely with impunity.

Nor do I see any need of actually having the war. Apart from the fact that everybody is busy at this time of year, the war is not what I am after, but rather, the postbellum situation. It seems to me, therefore, that once having declared an official state of belligerency, we could then get right on with the peace treaty ceremony, and I have a couple of ideas on this.

I should like to see simultaneous gatherings held in the middle of New York's Verrazano bridge, appropriately named for a Florentine navigator, and in Rome, either beside the splashing waters of Trevi, or in the flower market at the foot of the Span-

185

ish Steps. Speeches ought to be cut to a minimum, because ours is an age of terrible speeches, in whatever language. They are either too long, or put together by people who handle words as if they were automobile parts, or both.

I was thinking of having Danny Thomas say a few words, but his ancestors were Lebanese, and that means declaring war on another country in order to get him involved, and I am not that fond of writing letters.

I do think we might have some nice background music, both contemporary and traditional — we could start with "Santa Lucia" — and serve all hands Chianti, dry and red, and prosciutto, which is wonderfully translucent ham, with melon. Maybe even favors for the children, I don't know, although probably it would be much more peaceful if everybody under ten stayed home since they don't wear hats much anyway. Do they?

At this point I intend to involve the United States Government, although not to large extent. I would like to get someone like Sophia Loren (on second thought there is, of course, no one like Sophia Loren) to appeal to the American Congress for funds to aid Italian industry in the wake of the war that we would have just concluded, this rehabilitation assistance being a well-known U.S. custom. I can visualize the legislators on both sides of the aisle, impressed by Miss Loren's elocution, virtually stampeding in the race to appropriate the requested funds.

Actually, of course, the only Italian company for which I desire financial incentive is the one that used to make the broad-brimmed hats. I hope we might give the firm a check, in the name of helping a former co-belligerent return to economic normalcy, that would inspire management to dust off the Capone molds and produce a couple of yesteryear's hats for my father.

I did a little figuring and it seems to me the whole thing could

184

be accomplished for under three hundred dollars, and there might even be enough left for an all-day picnic for the employes.

Really, that is so inexpensive that we can't afford not to do it and besides, do you want my father to be happy on his birthday or don't you?

I do not know why on earth everybody has to look just like everybody else, simply because the people who make hats and other things say so, and I intend to do what I can to stiffen the will of the dissidents. That is why, when I got about three quarters of the way home, I took a detour; I had to. I had topped a rise and there, with knotted tail streaming, rising against the pale, washed sky out of the brushy wilderness, was a massive kite. It was just incredible. What kind of man flies a kite in the fall?

The sandy, rutted road was labeled only "No Dumping Here," and I observed with pleasure that it took an immediate bend behind wind-twisted scrub so that I could not see where it led. It was the beginning of just the kind of small adventure that freshens the spirit, the more so because it was a surprise and possessed a mystery.

Occasionally, I looked up at the steady kite to check my bearings. I supposed the half-filled footprints in the ruts belonged to its flier. There were no other tracks but these and I decided, because they were deeply planted, evenly spaced and unwavering, that I was about to meet a man of quiet, yet firm purpose.

Around a blueberry bush I came upon him, standing in the yellow-grass clearing on the top of a low hill. He was about sixty, of generous proportions, red-cheeked and bald, and he wore a dark-blue Navy surplus jacket. I decided he must be a retired dentist or an Episcopalian bishop.

"Hello," I said. "I saw your kite flying and couldn't stay away. I hope I'm not intruding."

"I heard a jay yelling at you," said the kite flier. "I suppose I feel about the same way toward you that he does, but at least you didn't bring a clutch of noisy kids and besides, this is public land." He didn't even look at me, but concentrated on the kite and knowledgeably let out more cord with smooth and easy motions.

"You made the kite?"

"Every year I make one. Usually in August. Then I fly it in September, months before this place gets full of other people who want to fly kites. This country's not too small or overpopulated. It's just that everybody wants to do the same thing at the same time in the same place. Ever go to a public beach at seven o'clock on a Monday morning? It's empty. But on Sunday you don't even dare eat lunch there for fear of getting somebody else's sandwich in your mouth."

"I used to make kites," I volunteered. "What kind of newspapers do you use?"

He began to show a little interest in the conversation. "Funny you should ask. Most people think one newspaper is as good as another. Nothing like old Nantucket *Inquirer and Mirrors* for the part where the string goes through, because it's quality paper stock, and tough. And I use some Pittsburgh *Courier*, because it's orange, and some Page Ones of the Washington *Post*, because they use color photos. You can make some pretty good color patterns if you think about it a little."

We stood in appreciative silence, listening to the wet and reedy call of a black duck, complaining in some marshy pothole about the state of his wild-rice lunch.

"You see that?" asked the kite flier, pointing with his big crepe-soled foot at some extra papers he had brought along for patching, if need be. On top was a two-page spread in the New

186

York *Times* that advertised an American Airlines jet plane of the near future.

The ad said, "If you can imagine an airliner with a penthouse — a penthouse with staterooms and offices — you will have an idea of what we are planning. There will be a spiral staircase to the upper deck, room for a special theater section, and even a drawing room that can accommodate sofas and club chairs."

Accompanying illustrations showed a businessman in one of the staterooms dictating to his secretary; a twin-bed room with a mother reading a story to her daughter before retiring, and a fellow in evening clothes, obviously overfed, descending the spiral staircase. In the background there was a lounge, including potted palm.

"Fantastic," I said.

"Eyewash," replied the kite flier. "All I know about aeronautics is right on the end of this string, but that stuff is preposterous."

"Why?"

"I'll tell you why. These days, you spend less and less time in an airplane because it goes faster and faster. So what's in it, except comfortable seats, becomes decreasingly important. Potted palms and spiral staircases belong in hotels. Penthouses belong on top of buildings. But if an airline is going to spend all the money that fairy tale implies, you know what I'd like it to do?"

"What?"

"I'd like to see it publish a two-page ad that reads: 'Within the next few years, if something interferes with the main propulsion system in our airplane, it will not come down like a twelve-pound ball in a shot tower, smash all to hell, blow up, burn, and kill everybody aboard. It will come down gently, and if it lands in water, it will not sink like a damned stone. It will float, maybe for a week, and you can still get a drink at the bar while waiting for the Coast Guard, or write your will, or take out more insurance. Spiral staircase, bah!"

And he let out more string in impatient jerks, looking, I decided, much more like a bishop than a dentist, although that may not be fair to dentists, because I have known some dentists with a lot of moxie.

I thought some about that when I got back to the house because I discovered that Charles had left me a couple of tautog, and while I was skinning them and otherwise building a chowder I fell to reflecting on whether the clergy is up to the times.

A while back, I was discussing with a member of David Susskind's staff some people who might possibly appear on one of his shows, and I mentioned a clergyman. The staff member said quickly, "Ministers are a bore," which probably means that in terms of show biz they are too low-keyed to stir up much adrenaline, but still, you don't want everybody to yell.

There is, for example, this man of the cloth, now wise and graying, who distinguished himself when young and first assigned to a parish by the effectiveness with which he dealt with three teen-age rebels who were disrupting a ladies' church bazaar. He persuaded the three to come to his study, which they did in surly and irreverent fashion, and there he acquainted them with the necessity for self-discipline and for assuming one's responsibilities to orderly society.

Then, perhaps in part because he had been No. 2 man on an Eastern university wrestling team, he banged their heads together and suggested quietly that they depart while they were able, which they did. The bazaar raised the unprecedented sum of $356.27.

Aware of this segment of unwritten (until now) ecclesiastical history and its clue to the cleric's spiritedness, I was not surprised one day during the Johnson administration when this fellow said he wanted to talk to me about the Rev. Cotesworth Pinckney Lewis of Bruton Parish Church in Williamsburg, Virginia.

You will remember that when Mr. Lewis learned the President of the United States was to attend worship services at his church, he amended his sermon to include remarks about Vietnam. What Mr. Lewis said was that this country had not been given a satisfactory justification for the war. This upset the White House staff very much because, they said, the President does not have to listen to any opinions he does not want to hear. Why, they asked, should he be subjected to such remarks in church?

What astonished me (and, I gather, my clerical friend) was that most of the published reaction from press, public and church appeared to agree with the White House implication that Mr. Lewis had abused his position by taking advantage of the fact that the President was momentarily part of a captive audience.

When my friend appeared, it was obvious that he felt seriously about this matter. His excellent manners notwithstanding, he did not inquire about the state of my health, but thrust a newspaper clipping at me, demanding, "What on earth is the matter with us these days?"

It stated, "The Bruton church incident has reminded everybody in the White House that total security against unenthusiastic opinion is jeopardized by the President's habit of attending church.

"Henceforth, to protect the President, agents will call Saturday night upon the minister of the church he plans to attend next morning.

"Personal interviews will be held to ascertain whether the clergyman sees eye to eye with the President on key issues of the day — Vietnam, poverty, civil rights, dissent, education, etc. If the minister betrays signs of disagreement with administration policy, he will be required to submit a text of his sermon to the White House for review before midnight Saturday.

"The White House speech-writing staff will be available through the night to supply an alternate sermon if the original cannot pass review."

When I finished reading, I was aware that my friend was tapping his well-shined shoe in deep anger. He said, "I am drafting a letter to the President. I do not know why a thousand others, both in the church and out, have not already done so, but I will do it, even if I am alone in doing it.

"I am saying to the President that everyone else in this nation, man, woman and child, has to hear things he does not want to hear every single day.

"The little boy wants a nickel to buy candy, or he wants to go out of his own yard to play with somebody. And his mother says, 'No,' which upsets him because she disagrees with him.

"The mother goes to the teacher to find out why her child is getting poor marks. The teacher says, 'Your daughter is lazy, and that is because you allow her to be so.'

"The father says to his employer, 'I think I should have had that raise rather than the fellow who works next to me.' And his employer replies, 'No. He is doing a better job than you are.'

"All of these things are unpleasant. One would rather not hear them. But the fact is that they insure the perspective of realism and they are, therefore, of greatest importance. At least half of all truth is unpleasant and if you ignore this, what you have is not truth."

His big knuckles were white on the rolled newspaper he gripped. "I am disturbed that the men in the White House have adopted this policy of 'see no evil, hear no evil' for the President who must lead us, thereby guaranteeing that he shall have a blind side. For the 'evil' in this case happens to be honest opinion, no matter what you think of it or how valid you think it is.

"But I am even more distressed that nobody seems upset about it. They don't even seem to think it illogical that the President has one of the biggest captive audiences on earth — and we are all in it — yet he doesn't want to be in ours."

He rose to leave. "In my letter I am suggesting the creation of a new Cabinet post: Secretary of Opinion. Its holder and staff would have one function — periodically, to make the President listen to all the things he does not want to hear, especially dissident views as expressed by the American public. I don't suggest that would change his mind at all, but it would be good for him and bring him closer to us.

"In the meantime, should the President honor my church by coming to it, and if his agents should come to me in advance, I will say, 'If you want to know what I am going to say on Sunday, you come and sit in a pew on that day. You get no text of mine; I accept no text of yours. Separation of church and state is a two-way street, and I want the government to keep its well-manicured hands out of my pulpit.'"

I am not aware that he ever got an answer from the White House, but then, the President did not visit his church, either.

Now you may think this minister friend a bristly fellow, yet actually, he, of all people, is dedicated to the proposition that most gaps between people are bridgeable; he has believed that for a long time and with increasing conviction since the night of what this community still calls, "The Church Fire."

There is no sound, not even the trump of doom, I suspect, more chilling than the bray of a small-town fire alarm at one in the morning in a midwinter blizzard. In this case it was December, below freezing, and the acres of white flakes, driving and swirling from the northeast, already had festooned roofs and drifted high across the outer roads.

Interminably, the ugly horn roared its alarm, the sound now choked in the wind, now clear and frightening. Behind the yellow curtains of the snowbound houses, lights winked on, for every able-bodied man in the community was, of necessity, a volunteer fireman. Six miles of tidewater separated them from the nearest help and whatever was burning, they had to put out by themselves, win, lose or draw.

As always, it seemed forever, but really was no more than a few minutes, while men roused themselves from sleep, shivered in their largely unheated bedrooms, pulled on their clothes and said to their anxious wives, "Ring Central. Probably Beth Fairbanks is on tonight. Ask her what it is. And if it's much, bring coffee in an hour or so."

Then the booted feet in the empty street, hoarse voices muffled in the storm, and finally, the bull-throated engine of the first pumper, siren screaming, as it rolled out of Saxon's garage with nobody aboard but the driver, and he driving with one hand and still pulling on his coat with the other.

You did not have to ask where the fire was if you were outdoors. From the hill on Madison Street a wound of orange rose against the low black sky, and even to windward, the terrible sound of hard-driven flames could be heard two blocks away. It was the church of my friend, the Methodist church, green-shuttered and white-spired, with the gold-handed clock in the tower, the gentle striking of which could be heard as far away as the Four Corners and, on a still day, even on Hammett's Ledge, where the lobsterman hauled his pots.

And now it was neither pretty nor peaceful, but a creature in torment, and even while they struggled with soaked mittens and half-frozen hands to couple the hoselines, the tall windows buckled and blew out, and a column of raw fire erupted through the roof.

The white paint browned, peeled, and turned black; charred rafters crashed into the flaming wreckage and showers of sparks whipped to leeward. Water turned to ice as it struck, and the men, half-scorched on one side, half-frozen on the other, slipped, scrambled, struggled for footing, worked in as close as they dared, fell, cursed, and rose again to man the throbbing hoses.

It was obvious from the beginning that the building was lost, and all they could hope was to keep the fire from spreading. By daybreak there was no flame left and no church, either, only the blackened bones, half-encased in glistening ice, and here and there still wisps of stinking smoke rising. Already, the church ("Built 1823 A.D. by the parishioners of . . ." the plaque by the door had read) and its flaming end were half legend. "Were you there when the steeple was ready to fall and the bell tolled and tolled its last, as if someone were ringing it?" they asked each other. "And did you hear that the Bible on the pulpit was the only thing not to burn, and it was opened to the Psalms, the part where it says, 'We went through fire and through water'?" one said, although this they were not sure of.

But what they were sure of was that the church, church of their fathers and grandfathers before them; church of worn and shiny pews; church born of and perpetuated by generations of bean suppers and cake sales; church of children in little chairs repeating, "Our Father, who art . . ." and many of the children now grown and even long dead — this church was no more.

It may be different in cities, I do not know, but in small towns everyone tends to grieve with the aggrieved, because there are no strangers. And it was that the town felt for the Methodists, even those, frankly, who could have taken John Wesley or left him, if they had, in fact, even known who he was.

My friend the minister looked tired and old when he went to

the post office next day, and because of fatigue and preoccupation, he almost collided with Father Ferreira of Saint Peter's. They said hello, and the minister said to the priest, "John, we're going to rebuild from the ashes." Then he smiled wryly and added, "It's going to take a lot of work and money. I don't suppose that the Roman Catholic Church would like to contribute to the rebuilding of the Methodist Church."

Father Ferreira smiled a little; then he stopped smiling, and said, "What on earth do you suppose the bishop would have to say about that?" They parted.

In the next day's mail the minister received a letter that began: "To our friends of the Methodist Church: Whereas Christmas, and all that it should mean to men, soon will be upon us, and, Whereas, it is assumed that you will have to demolish your present church before you can start building a new one, and Whereas, it might be that the bishop of this diocese would object to our supporting the construction of a new Methodist church, but would have no fault to find with the destruction of the present one, we, therefore, contribute the sum of $100 toward the cost of tearing down the present Methodist church."

Then the letter said, "Merry Christmas," and it was signed, "Rev. John Ferreira and the parish of St. Peter's."

It is significant that, some time later, when Father Ferreira was ill for months with terminal cancer, he received as many cards and letters from Methodists as from Roman Catholics. The nurses remarked upon how singular this was.

I cannot think about ministers without thinking about Pop Chase and the time I heard him recite from the pulpit John Hay's "Jim Bludso," which I suspect was rather daring for those days. You will remember, "Jim Bludso's ghost went up alone in the smoke of the Prairie Belle," and that line concluded one of the most understanding sermons on man's frailties I have ever heard. Both Chaucer and Bret Harte would have approved of it and that, I submit, is quite a span of time and intellect.

Pop Chase's son John is a professor and a paleontologist and all that, and I have recently been pleased to renew acquaintance with the family because, of all things, of the matter of man going to the moon. Frankly, I have looked with misgivings upon the project from the beginning, but I did not expect to find myself so personally undone by it so quickly.

Some eight or nine years ago, Dr. John Chase was browsing among the cliffs at Gay Head and found a fragment of an oddly sculptured glasslike disc. It was bottle green in color and of an original saucer shape suggesting that it cooled rapidly while spinning in space. Subsequently, it was identified as tektite, the third specimen to have been discovered in this hemisphere, and its age was placed at 33,600,000 years. People of scientific eminence, including Dr. John A. O'Keefe, formerly of the National Aeronautics and Space Administration, and now an astronomer for the Goddard Space Flight Center, long have supported the view that tektites come from the moon.

Now I am not a scientist. As a matter of fact, I well remember the morning in Biology II when I was meandering confusedly through the insides of a frog and the professor leaned over my shoulder, clucked in dismay, and remarked, "I hope you're not taking this course seriously." Yet my relationship to Dr. Chase and his to tektite have proved to be of inestimable value to me in recent years.

Any number of times, having been invited to some sort of social bash, I have found myself, after about twelve minutes, nudged into an out-of-the-way corner with the only homely woman in the room, or the only man so unprepossessing that the host forgot to introduce him. Once upon a time, I should have

195

given up under such circumstances and fallen to muttering and studying the wallpaper design but not, believe me, in what I have come to call my Chase-Tektite Period.

Clearing my throat loudly to interrupt the conversation of those within hearing, I would begin by saying, "I have a friend who found a thirty-six-million-year-old piece of the moon on Martha's Vineyard . . ."

The effect was usually electric, especially since everybody else was talking only about Tiny Tim's marriage or Jacqueline Onassis' marriage or Joe Namath's barroom anyway, and all their bifocalar eyes would be riveted — that's a strong word for the eyes of anybody over forty; perhaps glued would be better — on me.

I would go on, saying, "You realize, of course, that what is now the moon was once ripped out of the hole that is now the bed of the Pacific Ocean . . ." And they would say, "No?" in breathless chorus and begin to draw near, like summer flies around the bung of a molasses barrel.

I am not so sure the moon actually was ripped out of the Pacific Ocean bed because this was told to me by a drunken bridge builder who was ousted from the professional fraternity for creating an expensive two-piece drawbridge that proved to be one foot short of meeting in the middle. Yet he was, after all, a convincing fellow and he did have something of a scientific background, didn't he? I mean, you have to in order to build bridges, don't you?

Anyway, by this time I was surrounded by all the introduceable men and nonhomely women in the room and the evening usually went on to become a smashing lunar success.

Now this whole gambit, and along with it my social life, are in jeopardy. Analyses of the many glass beads found by U.S. astronauts on the lunar surface have struck a heavy blow to the

196

theory that tektites ever came from the moon. Dr. Elbert W. King, a University of Houston geologist, has said, "the tektite subject should be entirely dead as far as the moon origin is concerned."

Really! How casually, almost cavalierly, Dr. Chase and I and tektite are thus dismissed — and as a matter of fact it isn't even a very nice thing to do to Martha's Vineyard. Yet true to my Anglo-Algerian background, I do not propose to give up this easily just because I am outnumbered, outgunned and up against the wall. Too much is at stake; I don't mean scientifically, for that frets me not, but socially.

Besides, I think one must stand up for one's friends in times like these. That's what friends are for. So regardless of the capricious shiftings of the scientific community, I will continue to believe and declare that my friend John Chase found a piece of the moon on Martha's Vineyard. I owe Dr. Chase and the island, for that matter, that much.

Well, so it goes, yet this is not all I have lost. In finding their moon, the astronauts, albeit with neither malice nor intent, have cost me mine. And I am not certain where I go from here, for new moons are hard to come by.

The moon that was mine was thoughtfully shaped and colored by several centuries of imaginative people who looked upon it as something that boys and girls in love could walk under, and cows could jump over.

"*The moone is made of a greene cheese,*" wrote John Heywood and, wistfully, I thought it would have been nice if Bob Hope could have been one of the first to make a lunar landing, since he was prepared to exclaim upon alighting, "Gad, it really is made of green cheese!"

I do not know what an examination of the moon rock speci-

197

mens will reveal, but nothing, I suppose, as non-scientifically exciting as well-aged Camembert.

Even if given an opportunity, I am not sure what I could say now to Shelley, who wrote to Jane: *"Sing again, with your dear voice revealing/A tone/Of some world far from ours,/Where music and moonlight and feeling/Are one."* For moonlight now has been automatically transferred from the category of the spirit to that of the laboratory; it is no longer mind, but matter, and I brace myself for that day when we shall know exactly what it is and, more awful, what it is not and never was.

It is fortunate that Edward Lear wrote when he did: *"They dined on mince and slices of quince,/Which they ate with a runcible spoon;/And hand in hand, on the edge of the sand,/They danced by the light of the moon."* For wonderful nonsense no longer has a place in the moon world, which suddenly has become an amphitheater of gargantuan heroism and almost terrible seriousness. Besides, we now know that one does not dance by the true light of the moon, but rather lopes or hops, and this is due not to lightheartedness but to unique gravitational features. And what on earth rhymes with "gravitational features?"

I envy Nathalia Crane, who once could write, *"When the moon comes over Brooklyn/On time with the borough clock,/'Tis the same that saw Palmyra/And the walls of Antioch."* That was true then, but it is not now. Ours is no longer the same moon as that of yesterday, or of our ancestors.

No, Virginia, there is no man in the moon, nor is the moon a goddess. We know, for we have stepped into the moon's boudoir and observed it naked, and do you know what it is? It is a pitted, dead gray expanse that rejects life and love, an old and empty place whose monotonous items we shall now subject to a cataloguing so exhaustive that there will remain no lunar corner where doubt, or mythology, or green cheese, or romance, or Santa Claus, can lurk.

As one of the millions of *Vineyard Gazette* readers all over the world, I was reminded by its editor, Henry Beetle Hough, that my father, Joseph Chase Allen, once wrote: "*When the moon walks upon the water,*" in recalling those years when he went down to the sea in ships. I am not even sure that he would dare write that line now, for fear that he would get a terse postcard from NASA ground control in Houston informing him: "The moon really does not walk upon the water. This is an illusion."

Edouard Vuillard once painted a portrait of Theodore Duret. It is a picture of a man of gentle countenance and sensitive hand, who is seated, holding a cat. His surroundings are colorful and interesting but generally disorderly, being dominated by heaps of papers, books and pictures; the impression is one of warm clutter, of delightful intellectual meandering, one suspects punctuated by imaginative thought and bright conversation without bounds. Because it is a painting of soft lines and equally soft colors, one comes away with the idea that both man and room typify the profound but imprecise among us, that they symbolize that important area of life to which the slide rule may not be applied, since its very creative existence demands the right of inefficiency and error.

By contrast, the new moon we have discovered and the new world it opens to us cannot, in the name of protecting human life, afford error. A few minutes before the astronauts landed on the moon, they radioed this message back to earth:

"Roger, AGS residuals: Minus zero decimal one, minus zero decimal one two, minus zero decimal seven, and we used the PGNS noun 86 for delat-VZ which was niner decimal five, which is yours which is nine decimal one, and I believe that may explain the difference. Apogee five seven decimal two, perilune nine decimal one, sun check, the three mark noun two zero minus noun two two, plus zero minus one niner plus zero decimal one six plus zero decimal one one. Over.''

That, of course, just about banishes forever the moon that was frivolous enough to walk upon water. But perhaps even more important, although this message is in my native language, I do not have the faintest idea what it means.

Moreover, I suspect that even if someone who does know spent quite a lot of time in patient explanation, I would still not be very clear about the matter. Obviously it is not sufficient to memorize definitions; a whole body of knowledge of which I am unaware is necessary in order to make this message have meaning, and to understand its causes and results.

I do not, of course, stand in the way of progress, if for no other reason than fear of being trampled to death. It is simply that I do not know where to find a new moon with which I can feel at home — a moon that is, in fact, poetic, rather than scientific. What I wonder in the larger sense is what kind of role, if any, there will be for the nonmathematical man in the new world we have begun to build.

And now the onions are nicely yellowed in the stick of melted butter; the potatoes are well-done; the fish is sufficiently poached as to fall in flakes at the fork's touch. I shall sprinkle crisp bacon on the top and find certain consolation in the fact that, even though there no longer is a moon, there is still chowder.

THE ELEVENTH DAY

I THINK we do not demonstrate much inner composure in accommodating so poorly to what we like to consider the idiosyncrasies of weather, but which actually are much more normal reactions to natural causes than are our own. This thought comes as a result of more rain. On this morning, the water almost matches the sky in its monotone of light whiteness and the rain pours straight down, its sound as monotonous as the color of the day.

Now there are some people who have a right to be upset when what passes for daybreak brings a gray deluge. The farmer has a sufficiently hard time as it is, without having to watch helplessly while his plantings are flattened and flooded. The innkeeper in a resort town has only a few weeks in which to make much of his year's income, and every day when his lodgers cannot go to the beach, soak up sun, and sail means money out of the bank.

But most of us are neither farmers nor innkeepers, and much of what we do can be done as effectively whether or not it rains.

Yet we have small patience with low pressure areas, and it takes only a few hours of drizzle to make us petulant, if not pessimistic. This reveals something about us as a society.

Once upon a time, I knew some thoughtful people who used to play a game called "Psycho" in the sidewalk cafés of Europe. I was introduced to it by a Viennese grandmother who wore white, calf-length boots and had carried a machine-pistol through the Spanish civil war. I think she never said which side she was on, and I neglected to ask her. The game can be played in many places, but sidewalk cafés are preferable because you are able to see so many people at one time. Also, you can sit for a long time without spending much money.

The game is very simple. As soon as a tableful of new customers arrives, you make a small bet with your associates as to which of the recent customers will display the first mannerism and what it will be. After you have done it for a while, categorization becomes fairly simple, because most people are no more original in their mannerisms than they are in their other habits. Principally, they twine one leg around another, or around the chair legs; play with the napkin or the silver; indulge in multiple hand games, including drumming, tapping, gesticulating, clasping one hand with another, or repeatedly touching their face, clothing, or the person whom they are addressing.

Coin jinglers and water-glass tippers are fairly commonplace but, as with bird watching, occasionally you will make a rare find. I still remember with considerable satisfaction the fellow in the blue beret who stabbed two forks into a wine cork and balanced the whole business on the rim of his glass without even losing the thread of his obviously vigorous argument. However, you must not expect to see things like this immediately, or every day; they come only with patience and experience.

Eventually you will be able to evaluate people rapidly.

202

When you get to be an old hand, you will look at the newcomer and say to yourself, "Hm. Balding. Fiftyish. Executive type. Perpetual frown lines. Probably ulcers. High tension. Low boiling point. Probably begin by jiggling foot under table, then opening and shutting cover of match folder, and follow up by playing leapfrog with a pair of spoons across the tablecloth." However, because ulcer types vary a lot you will not bet more than a dime on this one. Put the big money on safe ones, such as the woman who obviously doesn't want to wear her glasses, but can't see without them. You know very well she will be opening and closing the bows all through lunch.

I like rain, and this morning I paddled into the village and had breakfast in a place operated by a former boatswain's mate who has a purple lighthouse tattooed on his left forearm, underneath which it says: "Alice." I was the only customer, and we watched water drizzling down the pane. He said, "I think America is on the verge of a national nervous breakdown. We have a few hours of rain and everybody is ready to bite everybody else's head off."

"Why do you say that?" I asked, applying myself to the English mustard.

He reached under the counter for a piece of brown wrapping paper. "We had a spell of rain a while back. During the week, I asked my customers, 'How do you like the weather?' and I made some notes here on what they said. Look." He handed me the piece of paper, on which was written:

1. Rich old lady. Connecticut plates. Said, "Young man, your apron is dirty, and why don't you mind your own business?"

2. Tuesday. Man with four kids. All pale and in foul mood. He said, "Lookit, buster. I spend six hundred bucks to get here, and get established in a beach cottage. We sit in a couple rooms and stare at each other. The sand is wet. The bunks are wet. The

wood is wet and won't burn in the fireplace. Three of us have colds and the house is clammy all day.

"My wife hates me because she wanted to go visit her folks in Wisconsin anyway, and I had more tan from the YMCA sunlamp when I got here than I have now. How the hell do you think I like it? I'll be glad to get back to work."

The boatswain's mate said, "They're all like that. Jumpy. Nasty. Uptight. Say 'Boo' and there they go, right through the ceiling. What'll they do if something really bad happens, I wonder?"

The point is, as we discovered with "Psycho," that most of humanity is a bundle of nerves.

In two years of playing the game, the only subject I ever saw who had no mannerisms at all was a Cherbourg docker who was so drunk that he fell asleep as soon as he sat down at the table. I lost twenty francs on him, having been certain that he was an earlobe puller.

After I got home, I ducked out between showers and leaned over the front fence, oiling the strap-iron hinges of the gate because they had taken to wailing like something out of Dante. Thinking about the wailing gate hinges as sounding like something out of Dante reminded me of a personal crisis; it was a reference to Dante that brought me to the juncture of roads taken and not taken.

It was a Saturday morning in spring and long enough ago so that I was sitting on the tailgate of a Model T truck that had a brass radiator cap, and we were bound for West Chop. I was wearing a disreputable white apron, and we were making the 7 A.M. milk and cream delivery. Up front, Henry was driving, and he was singing with considerable spirit, "I'm looking over a four-leaf clover that I overlooked before."

This was years before the supporters of Senator Robert A. Taft decided to make a campaign song out of it.

The air was so soft, the day so promising that I thought probably if the rear wheels spun a rock at me, it would prove to be a gold nugget. We went down a sandy lane toward the harbor, a place where roses would flood over white fences soon enough, and I jumped off the truck carrying a pint of this and that, and ran into a customer's kitchen.

She was down from Boston to begin opening her house for the summer. She looked as they always did, spring-hungry, delighted to be in a place where you could smell the water again. Filled with the joy of returning, she said to me, "Come see my new cesspool."

Now if this seems odd to you, it is because you have never had a new cesspool. I stepped out back with her and surveyed its fine workmanship and especially the sturdy iron cover. It was a good job, and that was no surprise because I knew who had built it. When he had built ours, he was down in the hole and I was on top watching, and he said, "Ain't everybody can do this, but I can," and he was right.

I said to the woman, "It's fine. It reminds me of Dante's *Inferno*." I said that because she was pretty and because, at that age especially, if you know something, you find a way of dragging it into the conversation so that people will know you know.

"Why?" she asked, smiling and a little puzzled.

"Because there are pictures in *Inferno* of tortured spirits attempting to crawl out of holes and out from under heavy covers."

She said, "How do you know about Dante's *Inferno?*"

I knew about it because we had a heavy volume of it at school that I had used for pressing leaves for a general science notebook. I found the text so difficult that I gave up trying to understand it, but the illustrations portrayed such awful things as to be fascinating; I had, as a result, already decided not to become a sinner.

But I just said, "Oh, we have it in school."

She appeared greatly interested and said, "I think you deserve advantages. How would you like to come to Boston and live with me, and I will see that you get an excellent education?"

The thought was overwhelming and I mumbled that I would let her know, tripped over my apron and an iron doorstop, and fled to the sanctuary of the truck.

That afternoon I told my father and he said sharply, "How old are you?" and I said, "Eleven."

"Well, how old is this woman?"

"Older than you are."

"Hmm," said my father. "Well then, let us assume this is a platonic proposition, even though that may be the worst mistake since General John Bankhead Magruder tried to take Crew House Hill. It is, in any event, a matter that requires a lot of thought. Obviously, she has money . . . more money than I have."

"Aren't you going to say I can't go?" I asked.

"No," said he, "I am disqualifying myself in this case on grounds of conflict of interest. You must decide."

I remember sitting on the back steps and looking at the budding blue flag, and the pear tree and the quince tree, and where the tiger lilies would be, when they got ready. By and by, my cat jumped on my shoulders and lay across the back of my neck and went to sleep, which she usually did while I was doing my homework. She smelled of pink salmon, which she ate by the canful, and I said to her, "It is a hot day for a fur collar," but she did not answer, or move either.

The salmon reminded me of smelt, because it would be time for them soon, and I could not remember whether my net had a hole in it, and might have to be mended.

I called to my father and said, "Do the smelt run in Boston?"

He said, "Not on your life. They know better."

So I tried to think what it would be like to go to school in Boston and it was difficult, because I had never been to Boston and besides, I didn't even know what part of Boston she lived in.

I thought it odd that my father had not said I couldn't go. It made me somewhat petulant. I thought he should have said it. I hollered in, "Do you want me to go?"

"No comment," said my father.

Tad, who lived next door, came bicycling down the lane and leaned up against the fence. He said, "I hear they're going to have cake and ice cream after Christian and Devils meeting tomorrow night." This was a very small joke; it was what we called the young people's Christian Endeavor group. "Fine," I said, continuing to think, and he went riding on, whistling, "Maryland, My Maryland," which we were learning to play in the school band.

I got to thinking about what I would say to this Boston woman at breakfast and nothing occurred to me as a reasonable subject of conversation. It seemed to me that breakfast was a key test of a human relationship; if it worked, you ought to be able to say everything, anything or nothing without jeopardizing it. The thought of facing her at breakfast scared me.

Thinking about breakfast made me realize I was getting hungry. I said to my father, "I'm not going."

"Good," said he. "We're having liver and onions and hot rolls tonight. Go wash your hands."

My cat of those days is long gone, and so is that world, but still, there are other cats and other worlds. As of shortly after lunchtime today one cat in particular has left its mark indelibly upon me, although that is not at all what I intended.

It began in a good atmosphere; most of nature, human and

otherwise, was taking advantage of the midday interlude to lick its wounds, bask in its triumphs, fold its petals, or feed its young, depending.

In the leafy backyard, nothing moved. Nothing, that is, except an iconoclastic golden cocker, who came careening around the corner of the house as if it were daybreak. Obviously she was after something and she bore down on the target like a jet fighter strafing a truck convoy, except for a certain bounciness that goes with short legs and big feet.

By the time I arrived where the action was, it had assumed the form of dynamic tableau. The pursued, a Siamese kitten with blue eyes, hung in the crotch of a tree, fifteen feet off the ground. At the base of the tree, like ill-tempered andirons, were its father and mother. Facing their spitting wrath was the cocker who, sensibly realizing that it is impossible to chase something that does not run, sat down.

It was from any point of view a standoff, I decided. I thought of that old nursery tale: "Stick won't beat dog, dog won't jump over stile, and I shan't get home tonight." Obviously, in this case, the kitten, which was crying piteously, could not get down unaided. His parents, not knowing that the cocker could not climb the tree, were unwilling to abandon their guardposts and thus would not go up to help their offspring. The dog, moreover, given the slightest indication that the cats were inclined to retreat, would have been happy to resume the chase.

"I'll go up and get the kitten down," I said.

"Oh, he'll get down by himself," said the lady next up the road, who owned the cat. "Don't bother. That's how they learn." And she went off toward home.

"I'll go up and get the kitten down," I said to myself, because its eyes were so blue, it was so small, and it yelled so piteously for help.

208

I got up on the fence, from there to the garage roof, and reached up among the catalpa leaves for the kitten. It clung to the branch with amazing strength for something that probably did not weigh two pounds; but finally I hauled it loose and it swung toward me in the air, its flailing back legs searching desperately for something solid to cling to.

In that second, before I had a chance to do anything, the kitten had arched its back, swung its legs toward me, and sunk both sets of hind claws into my forehead, just over the right eye. I pulled them loose with considerable effort, experiencing a sudden rush of pain, dropped the cat on the roof, and said, principally to no one, "He got me."

Compulsively, I placed the palm of my hand over the wound, which was throbbing hard, and drew it away covered with blood. It seemed to me there was, in fact, a great deal of blood. It was running down into my eye, trickling across my shirt front, dripping onto my white shorts, and plopping onto the tarred shingles of the roof.

The kitten, pacing the roof, was crying loudly with each step because it still could not get down. Its parents, anxious and angry at the foot of the tree, were talking back to it reassuringly. Or, I thought, sensing something else in their voices, "Probably they are swearing at me." Blood was dripping onto my white sneakers. Obviously somebody would have to do something soon.

I bent over, making my head ache, picked up the kitten carefully, and dropped it to the fence below. All three cats thereupon disappeared into the foliage, reunited and blissful. The cocker flattened on the ground, nose between paws, for a nap. The animal aspect of the episode was over.

"Only the blood and I remain," I said to myself. Somewhat gingerly I got to the ground, went into the house, looked in the mirror, and said, "Damn." The right side of my face was soaked with blood. It was still running rapidly, an ice cube did not help much, and I decided I must make my way to the doctor's. En route, I held several layers of tissue to my head to avoid getting blood all over the car upholstery, and I decided I must look like something out of a John Wayne movie.

Lying on the table in the doctor's office, I looked up at the physician and nurse as they busied themselves with my head, meanwhile offering gratuitous comments such as, "Wow, did he really get you!"

Finally I sat up, something like a tetanus shot and a half later, and the doctor was winding a four-inch white bandage around and around my head, meanwhile including the tops of both ears. "Do you have to have such a big bandage?" I protested. "I can't go out among people with all that on my head."

"Makes you look distinguished," said the doctor cheerfully. "Like somebody out of a John Wayne movie. That cat hit a vein. The bandage will keep pressure on it. Think I want you to bleed to death while you're asleep?"

The doctor was waxing to his winding. He said, "You know that Revolutionary War painting. The three guys? Drum, fife and flag thing? Boy, that's you. You're the one with the fife. Work up a little limp to go with it, and you're made. Probably you'll never take this head bandage off; it's really the making of you."

I paid ten dollars to the doctor's receptionist.

"And by the way," said the doctor cheerfully, "next time you see a cat up a tree just remember: when it gets hungry it'll come down by itself. They always do."

The lady next up the road was most apologetic and offered to pay the doctor's bill but I said no, that was all right, although I did feel somewhat shattered and would settle for a drink of Scotch if she didn't think it was too early in the day. Thus we parted friends, even though I have known a time when a cat severely frayed what began as a satisfactory human relationship.

A most unnerving experience in this category occurred only a few months ago. It was something like seven thirty in the evening, and the day was beginning to sag decently into submission after having been unspeakable for about thirteen hours. The phone rang, and it occurred to me without great cerebration that it was a thoroughly offensive sound; being mildly misanthropic at the moment, I assumed somebody wanted me to do something, and I was right.

On the other end of the line was a fellow who has freckles, a big nose and a penchant for whittling. He cannot really whittle anything; he doesn't know how, but he shapes never-ending pieces of pine into never-ending points that get shorter and shorter until finally he has nothing left but a pile of shavings and a satisfied smile. He says he does it because he came from a small town and he wishes he were back there instead of having made a success of himself.

In any event, he said I had to go to his house and help him, but he wouldn't say help him what. "If I tell you, you won't come," he said, and I suspected he was correct. So I went, but not without uncouth mutterings and a great deal of surly scuffing along the empty sidewalk. I said to the lonely darkness, "It's nice to be neighborly, but who wants to make a career of it?" There was no answer.

He met me in the hall, obviously agitated, and said, "Follow me," in a funereal voice. We went up the stairs to the second-floor living room and there the whole family was assembled: his mother, who lives with them; his wife, a son, Stephen, and a daughter, Lucille. All were standing and staring.

211

What they were staring at was their tiger cat, who is about four feet long stretched out, weighs something like twenty pounds, will bite your leg right down to the tibia at the slightest sign of insurbordination, has cool green eyes, and is named Sam. Sam was stretched out, with his eyes closed, diagonally across a large square table.

My friend said in a hoarse whisper, "He's lying on the puzzle."

"Puzzle?"

"Jigsaw puzzle, stupid. It has more than eleven thousand pieces in it and my mother has been working on it for five and a half months. It's the Battle of Missionary Ridge. I mean, that's the picture on it. You know, General — "

"I know," I interrupted, "and I don't want to know any more about it."

"For months," he said, "we've kept the door shut here because Sam always likes to sleep on that table, but today somebody left it open and there he is — all over the puzzle. It wouldn't take anything to make him break it all to pieces and there goes all that work."

He looked at me as if I were somehow responsible. "My mother is beside herself," he hissed. "I'm afraid she'll have a heart attack. We've got to do something."

"We?"

"We," he said firmly.

"What have you tried so far?"

"Nothing, because everything we think of is so risky. In the first place, he's stretched out and on his side. Whatever you do — call him, shoo him, put a dish of milk down, the first thing he's going to do is roll on his belly and brace his feet to get up. I think that would scatter the puzzle in all directions."

Lucille said irritably, "I can't get my homework done with all this going on."

212

His wife said, "I haven't even started supper."

"How did you happen to call me?" I asked.

"I tried everybody else first and nobody would come," he replied.

His mother said, "I can just see Sam now, kicking that whole thing into thousands of pieces with his big clumsy feet. And after all that work. I don't know how many hours, night and day . . ." Her voice trailed off, drooping with despair.

"Well," said Stephen, "are you desperate enough to try anything?" and they all said they were. So then he looked at me and said, "I select you to help me because these people are all shook and perhaps you are objective enough to have calm nerves." That was quite a speech right there for a boy of his age.

"In physics," he said, "we placed a tablecloth on a table, put a goblet of water on the tablecloth, and the teacher whipped the cloth out from under the goblet without spilling the water."

"So?" I said, raising an eyebrow.

"I think it would work in reverse," said Stephen. "I think we could whip something off the top of something instead of whipping something out from underneath something. I think if you took one end of Sam and I took the other, you know, very quickly, we could sort of shoot him off the table onto the floor without really touching the puzzle at all."

"What was the law of physics you said applied to this?" asked his father doubtfully, and Stephen told him. His father mumbled something disagreeable, low enough so that his mother wouldn't hear it. Then everybody said, in unison, "Go ahead and try it, but we aren't going to watch," and they all left the room.

Stephen gritted his teeth and got at one end of the sleeping cat, and I got at the other. Sam started to open one eye and

Stephen said, "Grab him and swing him before he starts to get up."

My friend's mother was so right. Sam kicked the puzzle into thousands of pieces with his big clumsy feet.

"All to hell," said Stephen, surveying the Battle of Missionary Ridge, which was now more or less wall to wall.

I went home.

This afternoon I went to the beach, and I will write something about it, but more because it ought to be written than for any pleasure in the recording. If what occurred had happened on television or in a poor book, which is about the same thing, the elements preceding the climax would have been tidily arranged, so that there would have been only one obvious thing to do. But it was not so; in real life it seldom is.

The matter at hand involved breaking and entering and theft. Now as almost everyone knows, there is a proper atmosphere for this sort of thing. It ought to be done at night — preferably, very late — and if the wind and rain are such as to keep honest citizens at home, so much the better. Furthermore, the culprit ought to be an ugly sort, clearly a danger at large — a snarling, antisocial fellow who shaves irregularly and for whom it is difficult to feel sympathy. You know, broken nose, mouthing obscenities, all that.

Finally, he ought to be stealing something from someone who had befriended him or who might even have been willing to give it to him had he asked. You can see him, can't you, working away in the archbishop's library, a pencil of light guiding his whirring drill? He knows well where the wall safe is, just there, behind Lucretius's *On the Nature of Things* and Bacon's *Essays and Advancement of Learning*, because the kindly gullible cleric has shown him, during the many afternoons of sharing tea and cakes. What this ingrate is stealing, of course, is Lady

214

Faverwell's brooch, graciously donated to make possible the building of the much-needed parish house, with a day nursery in the basement for the care of poor children whose parents must work.

Under such circumstances the course of action is quite clear, isn't it? You can't wait to do your duty, can you, either directly ("Up with your dirty hands, Gaspar; this is a 45-caliber Colt automatic, and I'm not afraid to use it!") or indirectly ("Constable, you might pop round to the rectory; all's not right there. You're welcome, sir, really no more than a citizen's responsibility,") your approach depending on temperament.

But the fact is that what happened today was breaking and entering and theft nevertheless, and it was nothing like the tidy classic case at all.

In the first place it was midafternoon and a time of several bounties, all calculated to buoy the spirit. Salt lay sweet and sharp upon the air, still bearing the sea's coolness; the sky was so gently patched with gray and blue as to appear fragile and distant; and from the rustling stalks of the marsh poured round bird notes in plump circles of tone.

Also, there were several people walking the beach; not interfering with each other, yet passing and repassing. But people do not see, for the most part. Or rather, they see only what they expect to see, and they are not very quick to realize when they are looking at something that ought not to be happening.

Near where a little clear brook crosses the beach to the sea, there is a beach house; I have walked past it more times than I could count. This time as I came abreast of it, I realized, without looking at the building directly, that I had seen a face inside, near the window. Now obviously, what was wrong with this was that there was a padlock, securely fastened and plainly visible, on the cottage's only door.

I knew, because I had been there before, that there was a back window in the house. Presumably whoever was in there had gained entry that way.

If you make an effort, you can recall much of what the eye recorded in such an instant. I thought, "Whoever it was, was taking things out of the kitchen cupboards, probably canned goods." There had been that kind of arm motion, and something in the hand.

It had been a young person. Male or female? Instinctively, I had not dared look too long for fear of alarming the intruder, who could have been either, I decided; long hair, granny glasses, faded yellow shirt. A thin, pale, unlined face; a gentle, harmless, hungry face, with a little pointed chin.

"Harmless?" I chided myself. "Grow up, my friend. This is burglary. Somebody worked to pay for that stuff that's being stolen."

Maybe the kid is on drugs, I thought, stealing things to pay for the habit. Maybe a hippie type, roaming the nation, broke and hungry. What had they said on the radio the other day? Something like four or five thousand young girls reported missing from home and wandering.

The face had looked intelligent and — I tried to remember precisely what its quick glance seemed to convey to me — it looked in need, as if it were in need of . . . Of what? Love?

"Oh, stop it," I said to myself. "So we have social problems. And we have a lot of kids in trouble because they need love, or understanding, or something. And I'm sorry. But you can't just walk past a man's house and watch a burglar looting it and not do something about it. Suppose it were your house? Wouldn't you want an eye witness to do something responsible if he saw it being burglarized? And suppose the kid decides to set fire to the building after he has taken what he wants?"

216

The face, I said to myself, did not look like the face of an arsonist, or of a thief, either.

"You are a fool," I told myself. "This is, in fact, a thief. And what arsonist looks like an arsonist, pray tell? And if you are really concerned about this young person, do you think you are helping him by letting him get away with this? Whose feelings are you sparing, his or your own, if you choose to make believe that you have seen nothing?

I went to the roadside phone with no enthusiasm, dropped in a dime and said, "Operator, get me the police. Quickly."

The day was suddenly cool and my hands were damp with perspiration and I wished I had not come that way at that time.

THE TWELFTH DAY

ABOUT a half mile from my house, there is a green hill. I was sitting on it this morning with a country fellow who is my age, but appears much younger both because, bumpkin that he is, he insists on breathing air that contains no carbon monoxide, and because the only thing he has to worry about is how to make a barnful of dreamy-eyed cows earn him a living.

I would think the latter might be difficult but, paraphrasing the philosophy of Rudyard Kipling's Disko Troop (who caught lots of codfish because he went looking for them in places where he would go if he were a codfish), my friend says that all you have to do to be a successful dairy farmer is to think like a cow, an exercise that he professes to find calming.

We were talking about the fact that old houses have more creaks at night than in the daytime and if you know why this is, pray do not tell me, because I think we lose a lot of potential poems by pursuing the poetic thought to its scientific conclusion, which is inevitably prosaic. If I wish to think that old houses have more creaks at night because bony-heeled ghosts are stamping about, burning their Revolutionary War draft cards, permit me to do so.

Abruptly, my friend said, "They're making a big mistake if they think that making trains go faster will pull the railroads out of their financial difficulties. They ought to make them go slower, not faster."

I said, "That is a thought that verges on anarchy. Obviously, daisies won't tell and neither will I, but I think you should not voice such a sentiment beyond the sanctuary of this meadow. What leads you to such an apparently witless conclusion?"

He sighed with satisfaction. "I thought you'd never ask. I have to begin my reasoning with the story of the New York, New Haven and Partridge Railroad."

"You've been nipping at the kitchen sherry?"

"No. There actually was such a thing. When I was much younger, three or four of us ran a child-size railroad on the outskirts of town to help pay college expenses. You know, it was an amusement park sort of thing — a little shiny steam locomotive, a couple of open cars, and about half a mile of track."

He stuck a straw in his mouth, which farmers are supposed to do when they talk to city people.

"Yes?"

"Well, the thing didn't make a nickel and we were greatly discouraged, until one day a pair of quail made a nest in the grass beside the track, subsequently laid eggs, and hatched a family.

"At first, we were going to move them, so they wouldn't be frightened or hurt, but since they seemed to have chosen the site to keep away natural enemies, we finally decided to leave them there. The birds became very friendly; we had to shoo them off the track, and I almost got the male to ride in the locomotive with me a couple of times."

"And what happened?"

"You wouldn't believe how business boomed. Everybody, young and old, took the ride to watch the mother and father take care of their offspring, and to follow the progress of the little birds as they grew. Even though they were quail and not partridge, we felt we owed them so much that one of our directors suggested naming the railroad the New York, New Haven and Partridge."

He paused, "You know, sort of a joke, because 'partridge' . . . I mean, it sounds more like 'Hartford' than 'quail' does."

I said, "The deeper we get into the autopsy, the less enthusiastic I become. Let us simply acknowledge that where you come from, they laugh at things like that. What does this have to do with making the nation's railroads take longer to reach their destinations?"

"Just this. I think railroad trains ought to meander more. All the cars have windows, dirty or otherwise, but the route never gives you anything to look at. I mean, who is inspired by the back piazzas of tenements, a lineful of laundry, or a rusty mountain of junked cars?"

"What would you show them instead?"

"Well, now you take the run from Boston to New York. If I were routing it, I'd send the train through Connecticut so that you'd hit Granby."

"What on earth for?"

220

"There's a copper mine there that supplied ore for some of the first coins minted in America. During the Revolution, they used the mine for a prison, and put some of the captured enemy in there."

He poked his finger at the top button of my shirt for emphasis. "But that's nothing. I'd give them a look at the Yale quadrangle, the state capitol at Hartford, made of splendid Connecticut marble; the tobacco fields stretching to the horizons — I'll bet you've never even seen a tobacco field, and they're virtually in your backyard — and I'd show them the Wesleyan campus at Middletown, the national park at East Rock, outside of New Haven . . . Not just a ride, but a life experience."

He paused for breath. "And what's more, I'd have a guide, you know, sort of a lecturer, with a microphone in each car. He not only — and maybe I should have pretty girls dressed in colorful uniforms representing the four seasons," he interjected reflectively. "Anyway, these lecturers would describe and give the background, not only of the buildings, historical sites and so on, but they would identify birds and foliage.

"Any number of people, whisking along at sixty miles an hour in a train, have caught a glimpse of a flock of bluebills or something bobbing in a marsh and mused, 'I wonder what they are,' and then, of course, a seventy-four-car freight train cuts off the view and by the time it's gone, you're in another state."

I looked at him. "There's only one thing wrong with your whole idea. The passengers would spend days meandering and just never get to New York."

It didn't faze him.

He fixed his pale lime eyes on me and said, "Over the years, I have concluded that at least eighty per cent of the people en route to New York did not want to get there at all."

My own view is that, in lieu of changing the scenery, riding in public transportation would be much enhanced if management could find a way to provide compatible seatmates. If you're lucky enough to get one, the resultant communication may well be the high spot of the day, especially if you dislike traveling and really do not want to go where you are going anyway.

On the way back home after visiting my dairy farmer friend, I stopped at Mr. John Claverly's for a dozen eggs. Although I have known him for many years, I still refer to him as Mr. John Claverly, because that is the way he introduces himself to strangers. As a nation we no longer think much of "Mr." but in the tradition of freedman, property owner and quarterdeck, Mr. Claverly knows what the word has meant over the centuries, how many thousands never were entitled to it, and he uses it with a fierce pride of possession. Similarly, he will reprimand anyone, whether he knows him or not, who refers to a doctor as "doc," saying, "The man has earned an honorable title. Don't make it sound like a nickname."

Mr. Claverly, plump and neat in somewhat formfitting overalls, was on his hands and knees, climbing out a second-floor window into the broad daylight. With much wheezing and little agility, he crawled onto the porch roof, peering down like Thornton Burgess's Jolly Round Red Mr. Sun, and clutching in his arms an American flag, flagstaff, and halyards.

I stood there watching him, thinking that most people do not have to crawl out of a window to put up their flags. He went at it very theftily, as Liverpool Jarge would have said, and had the staff in the socket and the flag in the breeze in no time, although not without a dribble of perspiration on his pink chin, for it obviously was going to be a warm day.

Then he peered down at me, cleared his throat and went on, almost in a monotone, as if he had been asked the same question a thousand times. "I climb out of the window to put up the flag because it is easier than getting a ladder. I do not put the flag any lower because if I do, somebody will steal it while I am at the other end of the house. One day they stole my front doorknob, which was brass, and I couldn't even get back into my house until I bought a new doorknob. I put up the flag every day except when it rains, because I think it is about time somebody did."

I said, "I suppose you are tired of hearing people criticize the United States. That's why you hoist the flag every day?"

He sat down on the roof and pulled a black pipe with a chewed-off stem out of his pocket while he thought about that. The tableau that we presented, talking up and down to each other, reminded me of Lewis Carroll's Alice, grown tiny, who conversed with a hookah-smoking caterpillar seated on a toadstool, although Mr. Claverly looked more like Tweedledum than a caterpillar. I could see it would be a while before I got my eggs.

"No," he replied, in answer to my question, "I just think flying the flag is a healthy thing. I like to see it blowing around. As a matter of fact, I criticize the United States myself."

"For example?"

"I'll tell you. Just the other day, the United States House of Representatives passed a bill authorizing the Secretary of Commerce to study the advantages and disadvantages of introducing the metric system in the United States. This," he said, pointing at me with his pipestem, "I assume I do not need to remind you, is a system developed at least as early as the eighteenth century, which now is in use in every civilized country except ours.

"Almost two hundred years ago, Mr. Thomas Jefferson urged this nation to adopt the metric system. Nobody listened."

Mr. Claverly paused to untangle the flag, which had wrapped itself in neat folds around the pole.

"So here we are. I understand measurements of length are now so precise that man can measure one one-hundred millionths of an inch; pressures as low as one one-hundred billionths of a pound per square inch, and weights down to one one-hundred thousands of an ounce. So I am told," said Mr. Claverly, adding, "on good authority."

"Yes?" I said, not knowing what else to say.

"Well, sir. Here we are, able to calibrate the complex factors and forces that must be measured in order to shoot something into space and hit the moon lightly enough so that the impact will not crack an egg. Soft-shelled egg, even," he said with certain belligerence.

"Yet we measure distance like the primitives who built Stonehenge on Salisbury Plain. You know what a foot is? It is the length of a man's foot, or the king's foot, if you will, something between eleven point seven and twelve point four inches, depending on whose foot and what language."

Mr. Claverly tamped his pipe vigorously. "You know what an inch is? The breadth of a man's thumb. You ever look at the difference in breadth between a butcher's thumb and a bookkeeper's thumb? And a yard. What's a yard? Why it's the distance from the king's nose to the thumb of his outstretched hand. What king, I ask? What nose? De Gaulle's?"

"De Gaulle was not a king," I protested.

"You wouldn't have dared to say that to him," snapped Mr. Claverly. "And the mile, that started out being a thousand Roman paces, which incidentally, were two steps, not one, varies, according to country, from eleven hundred to twelve thousand yards. It's a wonder to me that we don't go back to determining distances with measuring worms instead of yardsticks."

"May I have my eggs now?" I asked.

"No you don't," said Mr. Claverly. "You brought up this subject and you'll hear me out. I have one other thing I want to criticize."

"You'll make my lunch late."

"I want to talk about stamps."

"What on earth is wrong with our stamps?"

"Think of it this way. In a nation that spends billions on pills, medicines, doctors and hospitals to keep healthy, that has found cures for diseases and has greatly increased longevity, here's what we let happen every day:

"The government prints a stamp. Are you going to stand there and tell me that everybody involved, printer, engraver, apprentice, clerk and all, washed his hands before he touched the back of that stamp? Bosh! And then it's packed, sorted, handled and manhandled, and finally shoved into a crumby Post Office drawer that has held germ-laden stamps through the damp and dank of the ages.

"And there, all sorts of people poke that stamp about, and it mingles with crumby paper clips, elastics, misplaced hair ribbons, broken fountain pens and old grocery lists, for all I know. Then the postal clerk touches it again when he tears it off the sheet. And after all that, you put it in your mouth and lick it.

"Thus," said Mr. Claverly, "we live on the threshold of epidemic. You mean to tell me a country that can split an atom can't devise a sanitary postage stamp?"

He paused and untangled his flag again. "Now I'll get your eggs. And while you're eating them, you might see fit to reflect upon what I have said."

The eggs, as always, were excellent. I made an omelet, with sharp cheddar, lightly fried onions, and sautéed mushrooms; it browned and rose so beautifully (they don't always) that I

225

wished I could have shown it to somebody, but there was no one within hollering distance. I have a special appreciation for food and am grateful for being able to eat virtually anything, for it was not always so. Subconsciously or otherwise, there is a day that I remember whenever I begin a meal.

On the particular day, I felt pale and old, if one can feel pale, and I sat hunched on the front steps, chin in hands like a small boy, feeling rather than seeing that there was nothing in the empty street but the knife of wind that still had winter about it. I was cold, but too listless to get up and go into the house; in any event, I was impatient with the frailties of the body and reluctant to cater to its discomfort.

At quarter of eleven the night before, the doctor had informed me that I was to have an ulcer operation, that I was not to work meanwhile, and that I was to endeavor to think nondisturbing thoughts. Principally, I had thought since then, "I am scared. Why did it have to happen to me?" and I had not been able to get beyond this to anything less disturbing.

It was unhinging not to be at the office in midmorning. They had called, intending to be reassuring, and said that everything was going fine, but this served only to remind me that I was dispensable. The low-level growl in the midriff was a constant reminder of my condition and it made me ill-tempered.

A bright yellow truck drove up and out jumped a burly, red-cheeked fellow in khaki who whistled a few bars of nothing, clanked some steel tools furiously, knelt in the street, pried up the manhole cover, squinted down into the black opening, and said loudly, "Ah ha!" Then he proceeded to unreel a long wire snake that went on and on, down into the hole, and apparently was supposed to unclog it, if indeed it was clogged.

I did not feel like speaking to him, or to anybody for that matter, but I watched, first idly, because there was nothing else to do, and gradually with a sense of envy. The storm drain

226

cleaner, head cocked on one side watchfully, sometimes grunting pleasantly with effort, clearly knowledgeable in the use of his equipment, obviously enjoyed what he was doing.

There was nothing frantic about his movements; not a thing to suggest that he was bowed down by the balance-of-payments problem, Vietnam, crime in the streets, or the cost of living. He looked reasonable, civilized, as if he enjoyed getting up in the morning, and there was an altogether wholesome and peaceful quality about his scrubbed ruddy face.

I thought, "Why did I have to go to college, become a professional, whatever that is; get into the socioeconomic rat race that is American business, and tie my insides in knots? Here is a fellow who is at peace with life and himself; I don't care what he makes, but I will bet that he gets more out of one day than I do out of a year of rushing from crisis to crisis, most of them phony."

By and by, the noon whistle blew, a wavering bray upon the crisp westerly. The drain cleaner straightened, pulled off his heavy gloves, slapped them together and said loudly, "Well, lunchtime." He took a brown paper bag and a Thermos off the truck seat, walked over to my steps and said, "O.K. with you if I sit here and eat?"

"Go ahead," I said, but not very cordially. I was hungry all the time and knew very well that if I ate it would make me ill. I braced myself for what I anticipated would come out of the paper bag; probably a wonderful thick slice of meat such as I had not been able to eat for weeks; a couple of hard-boiled eggs, with salt and pepper . . . The saliva ran in my mouth, and I cursed silently.

I watched the drain cleaner bite into a sandwich of pale white bread and asked in astonishment, "What are you eating?"

"Cream cheese," said the red-cheeked fellow.

"What in hell are you eating that for?"

"I've got ulcers."

"You're kidding."

"I wish I was. I almost can't eat nothing. For years."

"Do you mind if I ask you a personal question?" I said.

"Ask already," said the drain cleaner. "My life ain't so interesting l got anything to hide."

"Why do you think you have ulcers? I mean, here you are, outdoors every day, no pressure, whistle while you work and all that . . ."

"I don't have to think why I got ulcers. I know why I got ulcers. I got ulcers because I can't stand my wife."

"What's the matter with her?"

"I know everything she's going to say before she says it, but she goes ahead and says it anyway. Ten-twenty years of that is a pain in the head. If she would just say one thing that would surprise me, like, 'Well, dear, I have just set the house on fire, and how do you like them apples?' I would feel better."

He uncorked his Thermos.

"What do you drink?" I asked him.

"Warm milk and cream. I hate it. You say I whistle while I work, hey? When I'm away from home and working is the only time I feel decent. It's so bad when I get through work, and I always work overtime without even charging the town for it, I almost can't bear to go home and open the door. There she'll be, saying, 'Oh, you're home, hey? Well, today's been some day, let me tell you!' Every day she says that."

"It's not any of my business, but why don't you get a divorce?"

"I go round and round on that one. Maybe it's because of the kids or because I can't afford it, I don't know; that's why I have ulcers. You're smart. I can tell by the way you talk, you been to school. If you got problems, you got brains enough to figure out the answers. I ain't. So I got ulcers."

228

The drain cleaner folded his sandwich paper neatly and tucked it back into the bag. "How come you ain't working today? Day off?"

"I'm sick," I said.

"You don't look very sick to me," said the drain cleaner. He went back to the drain.

After I had finished my omelet, washed the dishes, and refilled the backyard birdbath at the demand of a noisy jay, I had an unexpected visitor whom I have known since she was about a foot high. She is a moppet matron and it is hard to know whether woman or child predominates, because she weeps for joy and laughs at adversity and both the very young and the very wise do this.

She came to return a recipe for beef stroganoff, and began by saying, "Do you believe in miracles . . . I mean, really believe that they can happen?"

"I believe that some things are fortuitous and that occasional coincidences are exciting enough to make conversation pieces, pardon the expression."

"That's the trouble with your answers," she said. "They don't answer anything. But I want to tell you something that happened to me, and it's related to the beef stroganoff which, incidentally, came out very well even if I never had made it before.

"And I did the whole thing, you know, with my grandmother's lace tablecloth and candlelight and Beaujolais in crystal goblets. It was wonderful; the table looked just like a magazine cover. I really should have invited you, but honestly, I didn't have that much . . ."

"You're forgiven. I'm pleased that it went well. And were your husband's father and mother impressed with your talents?"

"Wowed. Absolutely wowed. But that's not what I wanted to tell you. You know, there's all this talk in the newspapers and everywhere about an affluent society but really, there are loads of us — especially young people just starting — who have to count every nickel. People don't realize this."

She stared like a serious child. "The thing was that I couldn't invite my husband's parents to dinner without having three pieces of the living room furniture reupholstered. They looked awful, just awful, and we had been putting it off because we didn't have the money, and I didn't think it was fair even to mention it to Fred, because it would have fretted him.

"Soooo, I wound this dilemma around and around inside my head for about a week and what do you know, one afternoon while I was bathing Andrea, buttoning John's snowsuit, letting the dog out and the cat in, and turning off the teakettle, which was boiling — the phone rang. That's always when the phone rings, didn't you know?"

She went on, "By the strangest coincidence, it was a new upholstering company. The man said they had just moved into the area and were trying to attract customers by giving the first few some amazing bargains. The prices he suggested were fantastically low and I couldn't resist. I asked him to come to the house, to look at our things, and make an estimate."

With a womanly glance she added, "I told the man to come when Fred was at work. I didn't know exactly what I was getting into and I thought there was no use in worrying both of us. Does that make sense?"

"Well, obviously, you're still married and your husband hasn't broken your arm. I suppose things that work make sense and whatever you did seems to have worked."

"Yes, but it wouldn't have except for the miracle." She took a deep breath and rattled on. "The man came and before I knew

it — he wanted to take the furniture away. I didn't know what
to do, but then the phone rang again and it was Fred. He had to
go out of town for a couple of days and he wouldn't be back
until the evening when we planned to have his parents for
dinner. That decided me. That and the fact that the man told me
I would have six months to complete payments. I got him to
promise he would have the pieces back in time, and let him take
them."

She waved her arms dramatically. "They swept in with the
furniture on the morning of the day that we were to have the
dinner party. They had done a beautiful job." She grimaced.
"They also handed me a piece of paper that I seemed to have
signed, pointing out that I did have six months to 'complete
payments,' but that eighty percent of the total bill — or a
hundred and fifty dollars — was due on delivery of the furniture."

She held her head in both hands. "I had been had. I was sick
about it. I didn't have a hundred and fifty dollars or anything
like it. And my husband wasn't even available. The only way I
got them to leave the furniture in the house was to promise them
that I would pay them the money by five o'clock that afternoon. It was ten in the morning already."

She shook her head in painful recollection, shiny hair flying
like a little girl's. "All day, I died over and over. I thought of
borrowing the money and I didn't dare. I even thought of
stealing it, but I didn't know anybody who had that much.
Here I was, trying to take care of two kids and put together an
especially important dinner, meanwhile trying to figure out
how to keep my living room furnished without going to jail, or
something equally awful.

"Finally, I decided that nothing must upset the dinner, that I
would go just before five, tell them I couldn't pay them then,

and it would be too late in the working day for them to take back the furniture.

"I did all my housework, all my cooking. I felt as sick as if I were pregnant again, but at 4 :45 P.M., I went to the upholstery shop. I was so scared I was green.

"It didn't look like much. Shabby neighborhood. And there was a policeman there, locking the door or something. He said, 'Do you have business here?' and I was just so upset, I told him the whole thing, as if he were my father."

"The policeman said, 'You're one of the lucky ones. Ninety percent of the people they did business with paid in advance and never got the work done. They used the first few satisfied customers for word-of-mouth advertising. They're wanted in about a half a dozen states and we picked them up fifteen minutes ago. As far as I'm concerned, you don't owe them a nickel.'

"I flew home," she said, "on my very own wings. And the stroganoff was unsurpassable."

My friend Perley's wife dropped by late in the day to see if I would like a half dozen newly baked blueberry muffins (I took three, because they are good for the soul and bad for the waist-line) , and we fell to discussing food generally.

She said, "I will tell you what happened to me last evening, and it would not have happened at all except for my appetite."

The place was a typical town through which a concrete highway passes, unzoned, undistinguished, its night sky spattered with neon and its architecture ranging tastelessly from late-Industrial Revolution to atomic-age split-levels, with a dash of marked-down Disneyland.

Yet she was hungry, having had no lunch; there was a long evening ahead because she was taking an education course with the idea of going back to teaching when the children were grown, and it was the nearest community to her destination. It is appalling to think of the number of places visited for similar reasons that would not be otherwise.

"Fine Foods" said the bright blinking sign over the aluminum diner, although it did not say that exactly, because the second "o" was not illuminated and produced an effect like an open mouth with a missing tooth. She drove in, tires crunching the white gravel, suspecting vaguely that the pale purple lights over the parking lot made her look as if she were suffering from an advanced case of jaundice.

It was 7 P.M. She checked her car doors to make certain they were locked, pushed down the button on the driver's door to lock it, and slammed it shut. Walking across the lot, she was trying to decide what to eat (eat too heavily and the best lecturer will make you drowse, especially in an overheated schoolroom) and had about chosen bacon, lettuce and tomato when she heard a couple of clinks on the gravel and realized the chain she held in her hand was broken and she was dribbling keys as she walked.

"Holy Toledo!" she said under her breath, stopping to recover them, and realizing with increasing concern that there must be two or three other missing keys, including the one to the car. "If I backtrack carefully," she said hopefully, "I'll probably find them all right. It's very light here." She walked back slowly. No luck. And standing at the car window, she could see the missing keys — three of them, including the car key, shining on the front seat.

"At least I haven't lost them," she said, trying to encourage herself. "At least I know where they are." Then she said, "Phooey! So I know where they are. What good is it going to to do me?" She looked at her watch. Seven fifteen. Her class was at eight. Her eating time, if any, was going down the drain rapidly. "Damn and double damn!" she said, and stomped toward the diner.

At the counter, she managed a smile when the proprietor, armed with toothpick and wet cloth, swabbing as he went, came to ask her what she would like. "Help," she said in a small voice, "and after that, a bacon, lettuce and tomato sandwich."

He listened to her, scratching his ear with a hairy arm, and when she had finished, said, "You ain't got all that problem. How much time you got?" She told him and he said, "Lemme make a phone call and then I'll get your sandwich. You got nothin' to worry about."

He dialed the wall phone and said, "Hello, Tony. Howza boy, Tony? Now lookit, Tony, here's where it's at . . ." Then he told him the problem and concluded by saying, "Lady's in a rush, hey Tony?" and she did not know the counterman's name, or who Tony was, but she was deeply grateful to both of them. She thought, "So many things men know how to do . . ." and felt, with a twinge of conscience, that there really is more of man's humanity to man than one realizes sometimes.

Her conscience was involved because, no more than a half hour before, a reckless driver had cut in sharply ahead of her and, as she watched, there poured from his windows a shower of beer cans and litter. She had condemned him, and man generally.

"But most people aren't like that, of course," she thought, and suddenly was aware of the counterman, smiling behind his toothpick. "Police dispatcher is a friend of mine. Sending a cruiser right over. Take care of you in no time. Now we'll rustle up that sandwich. How do you want your coffee?"

Seven thirty. The cruiser rolled into the drive and two men, one in uniform, got out. She left the counter, sandwich in hand, and went out to meet them. "I'm the one," she said lamely. "I locked myself out," and she led them to her car.

The men walked around it, peered through the window at the

keys, and the patrolman hummed a little, and then he said, "What do you want, Jack?" Jack said, "For this one, a coat hanger." So he went into the diner and got a wire hanger from the coatrack; then he came out and said to the policeman, "George. Pair of pliers from the tool kit." George opened the trunk of the cruiser and produced them.

She watched in fascination as Jack straightened the coat hanger, leaving a slim curved hook on one end. Then he wiggled it past the rubber insulation of the triangular vent window. He said, "George, get on the other side and tell me where it's going."

George squinted through the glass on the other side and said, "Little to the left. Now right. Lower it about two inches. Easy now; lift it a little. Good boy, right on." Jack hauled up slowly, lifting the inside door handle and suddenly, there it was, unlatched.

"All yours," Jack said to her, extricating the coat hanger. As he started to walk away she said, "I'd be glad to pay somebody something. It was a great help to me." But the policeman said, "No charge," and he thanked his departing friend. "Oh, anytime," Jack said, and wandered off into the night.

"Is he a policeman?" she asked, while finishing her sandwich.

"No ma'am," said the officer. "Matter of fact, he steals cars."

"Really?"

"Cross my heart. He's out on parole and he has to keep in touch with us anyway so that we'll know whether he's being a good boy. We usually know where he is, and he likes to help. The most interesting thing is that he could've picked your lock, but he didn't want me to see him do that.

"I suppose I can't expect him to show me everything it's taken him years to learn," sighed the patrolman, and he too departed, whistling a little.

It was 7:45. She thanked the counterman, who would not take anything extra either, and drove off, newly thoughtful.

I thought about it, too, that evening while eating one of her muffins, reflecting upon the many and curious ways in which our lives interrelate.

THE THIRTEENTH DAY

SEDUCED by the high temperatures and benign sky (both somewhat unseasonable) I went swimming today and, because we are creatures of rigid pattern and formidable habit, found it exciting thus to defy the calendar, for summer is long since a faded memory. It is passing strange in these latitudes to lie about in warm salt water marveling at the brilliance of turned leaves along the shoreline and watching a meandering V of southbound brant wobble across the sky.

It was a day of such beauty as to cry for a poet (you will remember, Millay wrote, *"Thy woods, this autumn day, that ache and sag/ And all but cry with color! . . . World, world, I cannot get thee close enough!"*), of such crystal silence as to suspend time, of such vastness as to place man in becoming perspective. Small wonder that such an interlude inspired a thought, and it did so specifically because the seven-mile, white-sand beach that is filled with beach balls and banality in July was preciously empty, from land's end to land's end.

I thought that it must have been much like this for the first man, at the start of the world. What has happened to us since, I suspect — especially war — stems in part from the virtual disappearance of peace and privacy such as this autumn beach provided.

A gull swept overhead, a reminder that gulls, or for that matter apes and monkeys, are reluctant to kill their own kind, particularly when confronted with gestures of appeasement or submission.

I recently asked an ornithologist whether he thought the aerial battles between migrating storks and eagles that are reported each year in Asia Minor actually take place. Some think they do because of the quantities of dead birds that are found. He believes the birds are struck by lightning and thinks it unlikely that they battle, because only man, the inventor of war, is known to participate in such practice.

Increasing interest in aggressive human behavior has given rise to a new science; polemology. It is the study of conflicts, taking peace as the normal, "healthy" state of mankind and war as an "epidemic," the causes of which can be learned and perhaps cured.

Once, long ago, while ironing my Sunday shirt, Hattie Tilton remarked with breathtaking understatement that it "would be nice" if we could abolish sin. I feel the same way about "curing" man of war. Someday, someone will find a way of measuring the subconscious burden that a man who has killed for country bears because he has done so, contrary to the precepts that have governed most of his life. I suspect it exacts a heavy price, payable as long as he lives, and costlier to him and to his society than the dollar bills spent for guns and ammunition.

What man is trying to discover is why he fights and kills, especially in groups, or, more basically, why he wants to. Perhaps related to the answer are experiments conducted by Dr. John B. Calhoun, a comparative psychologist at the National Institute of Mental Health in Bethesda, Maryland.

Dr. Calhoun allowed rat colonies to outgrow the space available to them. The result was radical disruption of behavior. Mothers, defying one of the most powerful of instincts, neglected their young to the point where, in one experiment, 96 percent of the offspring died. Some male rats became tyrants, bullying others; some males became pariahs, skulking on the edges of the group. Rats subjected to constant defeat through crowding collapse and die for no obvious reason.

The suggestion then is that man's nature changes if he is denied adequate room, that group aggression tendencies develop and one group often seeks to eliminate or reduce the other by fighting.

As an extension of this thesis, I submit that thousands of people in today's rapidly growing America are ill-tempered, inefficient and frustrated because everybody wants to do the same thing at the same time, which produces largely unnecessary crowding. Trains, buses, subways, beaches, parks, golf courses, supermarkets and department stores — all linked to patterns involving working hours, days off, pay days and school systems — are largely empty many hours a day, and jammed beyond description during the relatively limited period when everybody uses them. Highways and parking lots are just two of many institutions that cause migraine headaches, ulcers, poor digestion, apoplexy and divorce because everybody has to go to the same place at the same hour.

What should be recreation becomes irritation if you have to drive miles bumper-to-bumper to get to the beach and once there, can find neither sand nor water because of the people. A weekend experience such as this produces adverse effects that last for days, ranging from lackluster work habits to depression and mayhem, because the subject feels that he had no weekend at all. Some foundation ought to find it worthwhile to award a grant to a cross-sectional community that would try to stagger its "patterns of usage" so that no more than a limited percentage of the total population would be using a facility or service at one time.

At the end of a year, psychological testing, divorce statistics, productivity, police records and similar sources ought to indicate whether the residents were better natured than the national average because they had not had to push and shove for twelve months. If this were measurably so, then it would be time to think about applying the principle to the world and the "curing" of war's causes.

So much for the joy of swimming out of season at an empty beach. There is, however, one small footnote to the experience : I felt a twinge of selfishness, wishing that everyone I knew, and many I do not know, might experience such a moment at least once. But the odds are against it, and much more heavily than they used to be.

I am aware that on July 29, 1893, the New York *World's* correspondent at Buzzards Bay, Mass. (then the location of the summer White House) wrote: "Cloudy and rainy weather prevented President Cleveland going fishing today. He remained indoors.

"There were no callers except the newspaper representatives. To these, President Cleveland said there was no news, and he had nothing to say for publication."

Now you may say with reason that this was Victorian isolationism which ignored domestic inequities, wars fought and unfought, worldwide needs, conservation, and the fact that the horse was soon to be replaced by the you-know-what. I agree.

But how dear, how wonderful, in a sentimental musical comedy manner, to have a day on which "there was no news." How uncluttered and unburdened, at least superficially, an age in which the President of the United States had nothing to say for publication, and not one reporter at the press conference snarled, "What do you mean you have nothing to say for publication?"

Last summer, wistful for an era without flak, fallout, the Iron Curtain or campaign oratory, I went in search of a similar world where there "is no news," knowing in advance precisely where to find it.

Not far from the house, there is this place on the shore of a lake, a boys' camp, not of the posh variety, but where youngsters with little money, or even no money, can come and get sand in their sheetless beds without being scolded, burn marshmallows black, and toss each other into the drink at will. I drove slowly down the road, the fine sand rising from the ruts, spinning halfway up the car wheel and pouring off in a golden stream. Low pine boughs thumped the top of the car and cooler air on the cheek betrayed the presence of the deep, icy lake that appeared around the bend.

I let the car roll to a stop in the middle of the grassy field, watching how the blades shimmered in the sun, and I said to this barefoot fellow in a brown skin with a Band-Aid on his knee, "Are you aware that the negotiations in Paris are stalemated?"

He continued to squat over an anthill that he was watching and replied, "Are you kidding?"

In this place, especially at midday, all the creatures, including the human kind, are quiet and casual of movement, having

241

been well fed and well sunned. The cicada is noisiest and he only briefly; somewhere among late honeysuckle bees buzz, but that is hardly a noise, being more of a sedative.

This is a microcosm and, as in any world, many things are going on simultaneously, seemingly without pattern or discipline, yet all orderly and obviously within a framework in which the rights of the individual are protected and the older and more experienced assume responsibility for the younger. I like it because there is no business of lining up on the hour every hour for the next activity when you would much rather do something else, or perhaps nothing.

Here is a boy with a towel over his head, on his way to the lake, and when I say "Halloo!" at him, he has to lift it up to see me. I think he was trying to see whether he could find his way to the water just by looking at his feet and the ground beneath them, and I suspect he did not wish to be interrupted. He wants to know whose father I am and we talk and I ask him what happened on the most important day of his life.

Without hesitation, he said, "It was last Memorial Day. In the morning, I recited Lincoln's Gettysburg Address at the cemetery, and blew Taps, and in the afternoon I went in a track meet, ran the hundred, and got a medal for second place."

"Whew," I said.

"You bet," he said, and went on to go swimming.

On the hillside, some loping young males are beginning to pass and shoot a basketball and I marvel at their eager tirelessness and the piston patterns of their smooth muscles. At the shoreline, a boy sits on a wooden box, scraping dry, white barnacles off the coppered belly of a small catboat. Beside him in the grass, a smaller companion sits with his chin on his skinned knees saying earnestly, "What's five times five?"

I asked them, "What is new since I was here last?"

242

They thought, and the older one said, "A fellow ran away. He went to Hyannis, but he came back. He went to the movies. The movie he saw was cool. He told us all about it. He said there was this guy . . ."

"Why did he run away?"

"Well, Uncle Harry — you know, that runs the camp — had to leave early last Tuesday because his daughter was in a class play."

"She wasn't in the play," said the other boy. "What she had to do was pull open the curtain for the class play and close it."

"All right. Anyway, he left early and this fellow swore out loud when Uncle Harry's wife — she was taking his place — asked us to come up from the waterfront and get ready to eat."

"Then what happened?"

"She said he had to wash out his mouth with soap. Well, he ate the whole cake and that made her mad. Then he asked for a second cake of soap because he said he liked it. When she wouldn't give it to him, he ran away."

"Do you think he really liked it?" I asked.

"Oh sure," said the older boy.

"He was showing off," said the younger.

I left them arguing about it. Apparently even in perfect worlds there must be occasional differences of opinion.

My own feeling is that the soap-eater was showing off, but on the other hand, I do not know what kind of soap it was.

I am mindful of a conversation I had the other day with an insurance fellow with whom I was having morning coffee at a lunch counter. He is in the deadly middle ages, that is, old enough to hold a mirror over his head each morning looking for sparse spots in the thatch and sufficiently young to be depressed when he discovers one. He began with certain impatience, slamming his spoon into the saucer. "If you can bear it, I want to show you a sad commentary on American education and/or my family heritage, as revealed by letters of my ten-year-old daughter written from camp this summer. Here. You read. I'll attempt to translate as required."

(*Dear mom, and Dad of couse,*

I am having a realy time. The grils in my tent are Daffy Duck, that's the one you saw with the pony tail. Then Debbie Freckles and Mo. There all real neat Kid. We always eat a 6:00. We go to be a 9:00 and get up a 7:00 but are tent got up a 4:00. I took my test and red cap is the losest, then green then blue and white. I got the green wich is the 2.)

"That," he said, "means she took a swimming test and emerged in the next to lowest of four categories, designated by colored bathing caps so the lifeguards know who's most likely to sink. Now try this letter, but have a little more coffee first. Or frist, as my daughter would say."

(*We are going on a hic in the wo-ods. The conseselers name is called Nel. She's duche.*)

"As in Netherlands, that is," snapped the father, reaching for the sugar.

(*On the fourth of joolie, we had a water canabull . . .*)

"Give up?" he asked. "Water carnival."

(*. . . and the blue and green caps whent in the water and tryed to get a big grecss water mellen . . .*)

"Greased watermelon. Who'd think of spelling it any other way?"

(*. . . I ran in but wen I got in, I came out agen. I had a nos blee. Somebody hit me but did not meant to. We didn't get the water mellin but lookout hill got it. Anne is in look out hill. In the night two people came from look out hill and aske me do you want watter million. I said yes of couse why do I get water* *mealon. they said i will get it becuase I had a noas bled and they had to cut it 3 times before I got wat I whanted. Please send stamps becuase my money is all brock.*)

"She means she's broke," he breathed over my shoulder. "One more, if you're able."

(*It shur windy her and a lot of bugs. We whent in row boars and I rowed and missed a consuler by this much. Any way thear is a bat on top of our tint and still is. I took too pichers of it but it wasn't coler because I use the color film al up. I got a leter from Grama and ther was a hole dolar in it. I am writing slopping because I am so escited.*)

"I think she writes on a slant because she's excited because she got a dollar." He stirred his coffee, thoughtfully, and finally he said, "Her English mark for the year wasn't very good, for reasons now obvious to you, and I had been inclined to make her go to summer school or a tutor. But at the last minute I remembered how I used to have to get a job every summer when I was a youngster, and I wanted her to be a child while she was one — get out in the sun, and all that.

"Of course, when these tortured letters began arriving, I realized I was producing a healthy, tanned illiterate and should have shoved her into a classroom for the summer. I don't know how many times I rehearsed my welcoming-home speech, and what I was going to tell the school principal, after I had polished off my backward daughter."

"Well, she came home," he continued, a bit more gently. "And she sat there, all brown and bright-eyed, and started to talk before I had a chance to say a word.

"She said, 'I had a lot of fun at camp. I was glad to be there and meet kids from other places. But near the end, it was enough. I began to get homesick and it wasn't just no hot water and things like that, either. I missed being home and in my own bed. And I always thought . . . that everybody felt like that.'

"That made me curious. I said, 'You mean everybody didn't?'

"She hesitated a minute. Then she replied, 'No. There was a camp rule that once a week you had to show a letter ready to mail home so you could get into the dining room.' She added quickly, 'That wasn't why I wrote home.'

" 'I'm sure it wasn't,' I said.

" 'Anyway, there was this girl in my tent and she showed them the same empty envelope with a stamp on it, all the time. We liked her and we tried to get her to write to her father and mother. We said they would worry about her and call the camp to see if she was all right. But she didn't ever write. And they didn't ever call, either — but you would have, wouldn't you, if I hadn't written at all?'

" 'You bet your boots I would have. And your mother would have, too.'

" 'And when it was time to leave camp, she cried . . . because she didn't want to go home. It was — awful, and we felt so sorry for her we almost cried, too.' "

He drank the last of his coffee. "Then she remembered I had asked to talk to her. She asked me what I had wanted to talk to her about. I looked at whatever it was that seemed older in her young eyes, reflecting on the obvious fact that there are many kinds of learning, and I said to her, 'I'm glad you went to camp instead of summer school.' "

I went this forenoon to visit a friend who has had an operation of some consequence and found him, in sandals and black turtleneck, lounging in his backyard among twittering sparrows and falling grapes, looking very pale and pure.

246

Having presented the jar of beach plum jelly I had brought as a gesture of good wishes, I remarked that the nearly five months of absence from his work appeared to have been beneficial, that there was a new composure in his face most of us do not possess. He began by saying, "Contrary to popular practice, I am not going to tell you about my operation, which I look upon as a fantastic job of plumbing, but hardly likely to succeed love as a subject for poetry, or sex as a subject for best sellers."

"Thanks," I said, "and may your tribe increase."

"But I want to talk to you about the approximately one hundred and thirty days that preceded and followed the hospitalization. To begin with, I am thirty-eight years old and that, I think, is especially pertinent to the experience."

"Congratulations," I said, "I cannot remember when I was thirty-eight, or if, in fact, I ever was."

"Don't interrupt. Many weeks ago, when it was discovered that surgery was necessary, the doctor gave me something calming and nonhabit-forming and told me to quit working until the whole business was over. I found astonishing the ease with which I withdrew from a ten-hour working day and many busy evenings. It was so much of a relief that I just sat on the grass out here for three or four days, reveling in the fullness of nothingness, as one might lie in a warm bath."

"Of course it wasn't nothingness," I ventured. "It was far more like everything."

"It was," he agreed. "First of all, for reasons related to the medication, I did not find it comfortable to use my eyes, and thus, reading was out. All I could do was think, talk, and look at things, and I found it an exhilarating simplification."

"Were you alone all day?"

"For a few days only. It was spring in the beginning, and I sat and walked in the backyard many hours. The sight of a male adult at home during the working day apparently was a novelty to the small children in the neighborhood — preschool age — and soon they came to see me regularly. It was only a step from that to telling them stories, mostly made up from things about us — dogs and cats they knew, names of streets, the shapes and colors of houses, thing like that."

"Did they listen well?"

"They not only listened, they became eager to add characters to the story, and to shape its course; principally, they did everything they could to keep it from ending, and one story — I think it was about morning glories that grew up an elm tree and into a robin's nest — went on for eight and a half days. We came to see things through each other's eyes; I found it delightful."

"Except for stubborn cases, such as libraries and some classrooms, we have lost storytelling," I remarked, "and I do not know whom I am sorrier for, the children or the storytellers, for, as you now know, the telling is a joy in itself."

"I do know. And that was only one facet of what I have come to look upon as my rebirth. With time standing still, I saw things I had never seen before — how the brown grass of winter becomes green, a little more each day; how the light flows through the edge of a bird's wing; the incredible engineering of a spider stretching a web between trees eight feet apart.

"And with it all, of course, a new questioning of the values of each thing and especially of what I had become, and what I was doing with my time and energies."

"Most of us have no such opportunity to reevaluate at that age," I said.

"I soon realized that. In the beginning, I had blubbered a bit in professional self-pity. Less chance for promotion now. Likely to be found expendable by the company. Getting out of touch in a quickly changing world. Things like that. But I

248

learned that I had been given the opportunity of a lifetime to think, at a time when I was old enough to have something to think about, and still young enough to effect meaningful changes if I desired.''

"What did you think about?"

"Did you ever read Samuel Pepys' diary?"

"Yes. Some time back."

"Well, I discovered that on March 10, 1666, Mr. Pepys wrote, 'The truth is, I do indulge myself a little the more in pleasure, knowing that this is the proper age of my life to do it, and out of my observation that most men that do thrive in the world do forget to take pleasure during the time that they are getting their estate, but reserve that till they have got one, and then it is too late for them to enjoy it.' "

"It still pertains," I said.

"More than ever. Now my idea of pleasure is neither frantic nor expensive. I like to read — I can now — and I am not reading anything new, but everything I half-read when I was in school. Including Mr. Pepys.

"I have just finished rereading Defoe's *Robinson Crusoe*. I don't suppose it's very intellectual — I don't care — but it gave me new thoughts about individual self-sufficiency, and not being afraid to be with oneself. Most of us are afraid to be alone. Most of us have to be entertained. Most of us are totally without ingenuity in the face of even the most minor problem."

"I await hourly the invention of a mechanical, electrically powered banana peeler," I said. "Peeling a banana is the last outpost of manual dexterity in an increasingly helpless world."

He ignored the effort at humor. "I also find pleasure in walking, swimming and finding places lonely enough to permit talking to myself aloud. I iron out a lot of things that way." He rose, to see me to the gate. "And I will take these pleasures. I will find time for them."

The sun being slightly more than straight up, I stopped by the house of a woman whose father and mother came from the Cape Verdes, and who makes sandwiches that she sells out of a slightly modified front window, now equipped with a counter. I bought a slab of corned beef with a slice of salt and peppered onion, the whole tucked into a crusted roll except for those generous chunks that overhung. I went to the dock and sat on a caplog intending to eat, but the panorama was too much; temporarily, I left the sandwich in the bag, and watched.

There is a painting by Jacques David, and it is less important whose regally attired young wife is thus portrayed than that her eyes dominate all else, expressing as they do the nucleus of life, which is to say, naked despair and stubborn hope.

The boy on the sunbaked wharf had such eyes and, as with most boys' eyes, they absorbed every detail of what was going on.

It was essentially a boy's situation. A flockful of late-season tourists, animated and colorful, buzzing and warm, laden and anticipatory, was waiting to board the steamer or had just come off it. A boarding trailer-truck, bouncing over the brow of the gangplank, had come apart in the middle, the "horse" unhooked from its burden, and what was necessary was to jack up the trailer and reconnect it before much could move either way again.

Meanwhile, the tourists stood about good-naturedly and many of them were as interested in the minor engineering problem as was the boy. "Wt. 10,000, Cap. 60,000" said the black markings on the silver trailer, so it was quite obvious how much had to be jacked up.

"I never saw anything like this before," said a tall man wearing a black baseball cap. He carried a tiny blond girl in a wicker basket on his back suspended by leather shoulder straps, and when the loudspeaker said hollowly, "Get your tickets, here,

250

folks, for a sixty-mile tour of the island," the little girl stared at the sky to see where the voice was coming from.

Now came one of the mates in khakis, sleeves rolled up to the forearm, and he stood at the caplog, hands on hips, feet apart, surveying the situation. Behind him on the stern of the steamer the American flag flapped languidly, and the man in the black cap took a picture of all this, squinting professionally through the finder. The mate, like a modern Merlin, bellowed once and waved his arms and two yellow forklift trucks appeared, one on each side of the stranded trailer.

The boy was temporarily diverted by the arrival of a black and silver motorcycle, which edged its way, engineless and guided by four bare feet, to the edge of the crowd. Six feet of galvanized chain, for securing it to parking meter posts, hung upon its gleaming handlebars and upon its black leather seats were a boy and girl. He had pink pants and a red beard; she was blond with braids, and when she put on her white helmet, looked like a woman of the twenty-first century, not unfeminine, but perhaps thermostatically controlled.

The man in the baseball cap looked down at the boy and said, "Have you just been to the island?"

"Yes," said the boy politely. "We go every year. We've rented a house down there every summer since I was small."

The man nodded appreciatively, probably thinking that the boy even now was no more than ten, but still, especially with boys, there is a time for accepting the fact that one is small, and a time for ending it.

With considerable thundering of engines that made the fat gulls squawk in protest and swoop off the spile-tops in search of quieter places, the forklift trucks jabbed their steel arms under the down-in-the-mouth trailer. The mate squatted down to make sure they both were under as far as the lifting arms would go.

251

"Now," said the man in the baseball cap, "the moment of truth."

"That's what they say in a bullfight," said the boy.

"Some of the same elements here," said the man.

He was right, of course. The mother with graying hair and the grease-spotted paper bag of popcorn; a baldish fellow with black and white striped socks and leather moccasins; the matron in a blue shift, with brown, bare legs and an Italian shoulder bag, and even the stout, pale people sitting on the bench against the white cement-block wall were watching with an intensity born essentially of the knowledge that something major might go wrong — that several tons of trailer might come crunching down upon men or machines beneath it. We are not so far removed from the audiences of the Roman amphitheater as we like to think.

"What do you like to do most on the island?" asked the man.

The boy responded eagerly. "There is a field next to our house, and it goes down to the water. In the summer it has flowers in it; pink roses all over the wall, and white daisies. Mice have holes there; I know where they are . . ."

He was interrupted. The voice of the mate roared, even above the engines, and the forklifts strained, their yellow frames squeezed low to the big, black tires. Slowly, almost gently, the trailer rose; the truck driver trod on the accelerator of his diesel; there was much yelling and waving of arms, and the two were mated once more. They lumbered up the gangplank, more cautiously this time, and disappeared into the cool dusk of the steamer's hold.

Now that the crisis was over, the boy resumed, "What I like to do is run down through the field because the wind is nice on your face when you run. I run right down to the water and jump in. There's a lot of room to swim and when you first get in it's cold, but after a few minutes it's just right and sometimes I stay there and swim around for maybe three or four hours."

The people were starting to go aboard. The man in the black cap nodded appreciatively at the boy and said, "That's wonderful. I'm glad you enjoy doing that," and he walked toward the gangplank.

I do not know whether there is even such a house on the island, or such a field or body of water. I do know that the boy was in a wheelchair. His legs are half normal diameter; he has never run or swum in his life and never will.

But his eyes are like those in the David painting and what he had to say suggests that courage may be the most beautiful aspect of man.

I was eating my sandwich, the general excitement being over, and this fellow I know who runs a service station came driving by and said, "You ain't doing anything. I got to go over to Baker's Ledge to my wife's mother's and get a bed she's giving us. C'mon along so I got somebody on the other end of it." So I got in, and we drove off to her farm.

Each year the number of countrywomen of yesterday's pattern decreases and this is undoubtedly a good thing, for, principally, they demonstrate that unrelieved drudgery and a Spartan existence age the body relentlessly and wither the spirit beyond redemption.

I am mindful of the romantic notion that pumping water at the iron kitchen sink or splitting an armful of sticks for the heat-warped cookstove builds character. Having stared into the eyes of more than one farm woman who was forty and looked sixty, I think such activities are much more likely to produce lumbago and an irresistible urge to run off with the tea salesman. So I am pleased that the styles in the Sears Roebuck catalogue continue to look more like Pauline Trigère and less like Mother Hubbard, and I will bet that if you saw some farmers' wives on Fifth Avenue tomorrow, you would not even know that they were from out of town.

Having said all this, I have to return to the countrywoman in particular with whom my friend and I transacted this matter of the bed, and reverse myself somewhat. She looked like yesterday, in its best aspects.

At seventy-something, she sat with such excellent posture that she did not need the back of the chair. Her hair, salt and peppered, was pulled straight back, sensibly out of the way. In such women, the leanness of body is contrasted with the generosity of feature — her mouth, ears and nose were larger than some ladies' magazines would like — yet her features became her, and were far more indicative than her clothes of what she really was. This openness of countenance, reflecting something of what is inside, often can be found among people who have always known which way north is and what kind of weather the current wind is likely to produce.

Above all, although she had neither classical face nor figure, and never had possessed either, the magnetism of her womanliness was in every gesture and attitude. It was more evident, rather than less, because of the total absence of trappings, scent or jewelry, that might have come between the woman and the beholder. She was, therefore, rather than just some female person, a woman in particular.

She was peeling apples into a worn, battered pan; those of her kind, from long training, do not even sit without doing something of value. I watched the peelings, each one of endless length, almost forgetting the conversation while I waited to see if she could pare an apple with one unbroken peel, which she did several times.

She caught me watching, and smiled. "You eye those peelings just the way my grandson does. I guess all males do, at some time or another."

"Yeah," said my friend, "tell him what happened to Jerry and you last week."

"That's my grandson, Jerry," she said. She resumed her peeling, not looking at me, but at the apple. "Well, in the first place, I know I ought to have a telephone in the house now that I'm mostly alone. My family keeps at me to get one, and they're right, but I haven't got to it yet anyway. One of the reasons I haven't hurried is that the phone company put up one of those roadside booths about a half mile down the highway. You passed it coming in."

I nodded.

"The other day, I was taking care of my little grandson — he comes over for the day every so often, and we're good company for each other. I was putting up some huckleberries and pretty busy, and he was on the kitchen floor playing. Just then something started to boil over, and as I ran to turn the heat down, I noticed he had a penny in one hand and a piece of hard candy in the other. I don't know to this day where he got either. By the time I got the kettle off and got back to him, both the penny and the hard candy had disappeared, and he was choking.

"I thumped him on the back, dumped him upside down and shook him, and I wasn't getting anywhere. I could see he was breathing some, but it was hard going, and he was scared and crying and that made it even harder for him. I figured I could leave him for a few minutes, but I needed a doctor. Oh, he didn't even know what I was talking about, but I kissed him and told him I'd be back in a minute and I ran out the door without even my sweater on."

She put down the knife and shook her head slowly, remembering. "You couldn't call me soft. I've helped get in the sheep when a blizzard was coming on, and I've walked more miles over this land than you'll ever walk. But I'm — when it comes to running anyway, I'm an old woman. And I don't scare easy, but I was scared.

"I ran so long and so hard I didn't think my heart could stay in my chest. I prayed for a car to come along, but there wasn't any. I wished the phone was a half mile nearer. I knew I could get Doctor Merriman to come if I could just get through to Dorothy, his wife. He's always good that way; keeps right in touch with her. You can always find him and he knows all the back roads. Gets there in a hurry.

"When I got to the phone booth, I was breathing so hard I didn't think I could talk. My hands shook as if I had the palsy. I dropped the dime twice." Then she said quietly, "You know what happened?"

"No."

"Somebody had plugged all the phone coin slots with chewing gum. I couldn't get a coin in any of them."

She resumed peeling. "Oh, it came out all right, or I wouldn't be sitting here telling you about it. I couldn't wait for cars to come by. I figured it was all up to me. I don't know how I managed it, but I ran all the way back to the house, pretty much expecting, I guess, that I'd find him dead.

"But he wasn't. He was laughing and playing. Right then, I saw the penny in a crack in the floor; I guess he'd been sitting on it before when I looked. It was the hard candy he had swallowed; it melted and unplugged his windpipe. If it had been the penny, he wouldn't be alive today."

She said, "I know when you get old it's easy to forget anything in your own time that you don't want to remember. But I don't know what kind of people put gum in the coin slots of telephones and I don't think we ever had anybody would do that kind of thing in my time. No sir, I don't think so."

256

When we left her, the last thing she said was, "I'm glad I ain't any younger. I'm glad I'm just as old as I am, because there's things about these times I don't understand."

There are, of course, things about these times that most of us do not understand; whether these are different from any other times I do not know, yet in concluding this day's journal I must mention the two squirrels. What happened to them is symptomatic of the confrontation between people and things that is a hallmark of our age.

At 6:30 this morning, there was the precious quietness, so soon and so easily fractured as the populace bolts its coffee and charges to the daily fray. It was still enough, even on what sometimes can be a busy road, so that the cocker's jingling license tag startled a tiger cat out of a nap, and breakfast-bound birds, rattling the leaves overhead, sounded like an airborne herd of small and disorderly elephants. In the road, there was the fragile emptiness of early morning; nothing marred its sunny, leaf-patterned surface but a mislaid jumprope minus one blue handle.

Suddenly, as swift and magic as light, the two gray squirrels appeared. Whether they came over a fence, through a hedge, or headfirst down a tree trunk, I do not know; the eye was not that fast. It was simply that, first, they were nowhere in sight, and suddenly, as if some footlights visible only to them had brightened, some orchestra audible only to them had begun its accompaniment, they flowed into the road like water alive, and danced.

For certainly, it was more dancing than running or leaping; it was ritualistic, a fundamental response to compulsions such as literally shake the earth in the change of seasons, and such as demonstrate each year the encouraging thesis that a blade of grass can crack a cement sidewalk.

Ordinarily squirrels — especially country squirrels — have one cautious eye for men and dogs, whom they know they must not trust. But this was not ordinary; they were aware only of each other, and jumped, bounded, twitched, halted, sat up and scampered, as if all the world belonged to them and what they were doing. In a sense, I think it probably did.

It was a splendid way to start a day. Even the cocker did not seem inclined to chase them but sat, head on one side, and wondered, I suppose, what kind of feet you have to have to climb a tree.

In midafternoon, when I came back to the house, there the two squirrels were — flattened, bloody lumps of fur in the middle of the road, about four feet apart.

The first thing I thought was, "If somebody had to kill them, I'm glad he got both of them, and simultaneously," which obviously was what happened. They must still have been dancing when struck.

Then I thought, "What a marvelous technology we have created in Detroit, an automotive capability related to precise wheel distance so that even a relatively unskilled driver can run over two skittering squirrels at once."

Richard Eberhart once wrote, "When I almost hit the squirrel, I pulled over to the right, stopped in a ditch and experienced a period of nervosity or illumination during which I felt clairvoyant. This lasted probably several minutes. I felt I knew and possessed, that is, experienced, all possible relationships between the small squirrel, myself as a slightly larger animal and the immense idea of God . . . ."

In his case, the result was the poem, "On a Squirrel Crossing the Road in Autumn, in New England," in which he wrote, "*He obeys the orders of nature/Without knowing them./It is what he does not know/That makes him beautiful./Such a knot of little purposeful nature.*"

Now you may say a squirrel is nothing but a rat with a bushy tail, and I will reply that a poem is nothing but a bunch of words, but I would not wish to be without either poems or squirrels, if, indeed, a squirrel is not a poem.

The point, it seems to me, is that the automated age has encouraged us to lose what Dr. Albert Schweitzer referred to as the reverence for life. I do not think that the average driver of an automobile, if given a stick, would choose to begin his day by beating two squirrels to death. That would constitute a first-person confrontation and I have to believe that most people are nonviolent and wish the creatures about them to live rather than to die. But driving an automobile removes one an important step from the front line of bloodshed and death. There is a moment when the well-waxed automobile hood and gleaming chromium stretching out ahead obscure that area of road where the precisely balanced wheels are turning at a rate that is faster than paws can run.

No driver can see his unintended prey in that last fraction of a second when its panic strikes, its last unsuccessful alternative is attempted, its last anything and everything are made.

The laws, which recognize that human life is worth more than any other kind, help us to achieve, if not callousness for what we kill in the road, at least good conscience in so doing, for we say, "To have come to an abrupt stop, to have slowed down, to have turned aside for this creature, might well have caused an accident." And the law affirms that causing an accident merely to avoid hitting something nonhuman is not an acceptable reason.

Of course it isn't. Yet there are two observations that one might make about all this. The first is that, having seen the squirrels run, I would suggest that whoever hit them would not have done so had he been driving at a reasonable speed for the area. We shall never meet, he and I, and I cannot prove it, of course, but I would be willing to wager a reasonable sum that wherever he was going, or whatever he was going to do when he got there, did not reasonably require the speed at which he was driving — or their deaths.

Second, I am filled with certain apprehension at the thought that life, any kind of life, may be coming to mean less to us than it did, or than it ought to.

THE FOURTEENTH DAY

THE many people who never expected me to amount to any-thing will be agreeably surprised to learn that, as of this morning, I have been asked to lead a campaign for funds to restore Marie Antoinette's bedroom at the Palace of Versailles. I hasten to add that the invitation was so unofficial I do not even know who extended it. Considering Mlle. Antoinette's role in history, however, a suspicion of mystery, even intrigue, is fitting. Moreover, the important thing is that anybody asked me at all.

What happened was that the phone rang and, like one of Ivan Petrovich Pavlov's more satisfactory mice, I answered it, having been conditioned to do so over the years. There was a woman on the other end. She never did say who she was; I tried to recall afterward what her voice was like and all I can say is that if Chanel No. 5 had a sound, that would be it. I tried unsuccessfully to interrupt her a couple of times to ask her who she was and finally we had been talking so long that the question seemed silly.

She called to read to me an editorial from the Paris newspaper *Figaro*. It seems that an American has given two hundred and fifty thousand francs, which is about fifty thousand dollars, to help meet expenses of the proposed restoration, and this will cover approximately half the cost. For whatever reason, the American donor chose to remain anonymous and the lady who called me began the conversation by saying, "I don't suppose it was you."

I replied with agreeable vagueness, "I don't suppose it was."

In any event, *Figaro* thanked the American patron, in behalf of all those who love Versailles and concluded, "Thanks to this friend from across the Atlantic, half the money has been found. Could not the Minister of Culture [André Malraux] quickly find the rest?"

My nameless correspondent commented that, because the French franc has been having its ups and downs, perhaps M. Malraux could not, and she suggested that I would be "just the one," to employ her expression — because of my fondness for France and the French — to launch an appeal for more American funds for the project. Not being much of an appeal launcher, I have not yet decided whether I will respond positively to her blandishments or simply tuck the memory of them away with the pink hair ribbon that I took from the girl who sat in front of me in the fifth grade, and the bus check that once belonged to my blue-eyed English teacher in high school who, to my great consternation, married someone nearer her own age.

262

I have always felt certain compassion for Marie Antoinette, upon whose alabaster neck the bright blade of the guillotine fell before she was forty. But for the political and biological negativism of Louis XVI, I think she would not have had to resort to king-making and the distractions of discreditable companions, both of which led to what might be called her untimely end. Moreover, she is not alone in having cried "for madder music and for stronger wine" than daily life provided.

Mlle Antoinette, upon her arrival in France in 1770, being informed that the country people had no bread, is supposed to have said, "Let them eat cake." ("*Qu'ils mangent de la brioche.*") I don't happen to believe she said it, principally because Jean Jacques Rousseau attributed such a remark to a "great princess," in his sixth book of *Confessions,* which was written two or three years before 1770. But assuming that she did say it, and most people would rather assume so than otherwise because it makes them feel better about the fact that she was executed while the mob chanted approval, I have a suggestion for raising funds for her bedroom.

I think a committee of volunteers might profitably sell brioche, a versatile French cake, and I am willing to provide an authentic recipe with which I think Marie might even have been familiar, for it is very old.

The recipe came to me via John L. E. Pell, gentleman and author of consequence, from Captain William Budd USN (Ret.), who spent the summer of 1891 at Westport Point, Massachusetts. Captain Budd captured a British blockade runner loaded with cotton and rum during the Civil War. His share of the prize money was more than eighty thousand dollars, which then would buy a frightful amount of horse collars and stereopticon slides. Being a gourmet and an outstanding cook, he employed some of the money in gathering a collection of recipes from many nations.

Here is his recipe for "Gateau St-Honoré, Paris," a fancy brioche: "Boil 2 gills water, 3 ounces butter and a teaspooonful of sugar for 2 minutes, add one-half pound flour, mix until the paste is smooth and does not stick to the pan.

"Take off and add, one by one, 6 unbeaten eggs. Butter a pie plate and cover with a thin layer of this, then make balls of the rest and set on as a border, fastening with white of egg. Bake until a light brown, serve cold with a filling in center of preserves, and whipped cream on top."

If you do not know how much a gill is, I will say to you what I say to my children when I do not know the answer either: "Look it up, and then you will remember it."

I assume no responsibility for the recipe whatever. I would think that if you can deduce what it means, it might be rather appetizing if you do not care what happens to your waistline, and it probably would be a fine thing to serve at the next committee meeting held in your front parlor or any other gathering at which it is too early in the day to drink.

I am mindful of the fact that, if Mlle Antoinette actually did say, "Let them eat brioche," she was making of this harmless dessert a vehicle for righting social wrongs. Should you desire to employ it in similar fashion, I suppose you might have to improvise — say, adding to the recipe arsenic to taste. Happily, this is your problem, not mine.

And pray do not send me bagfuls of dollar bills for Marie's bedroom until I decide whether I am going to take the job.

Last evening, my next-door neighbor interrupted the process of closing his cottage for the season to come over for a minute for small conversation. He sells something, evidently quite successfully because his automobile is paid for, and he is a husband and father of a certain age, as the French say artfully, which means that when he shaves he can still see a resemblance to Leslie

Howard and he tries not to wear his glasses except to look up phone numbers.

"I got to thinking that maybe I was spending too much time reading newspapers at home," he volunteered.

"Oh?"

"You know, at the end of the day, I'd go home, pour a glass of lemon squash, and put up my feet. I usually bought a couple of papers and I'd really get engrossed in the news until dinnertime. I think it's every American's duty to know who's calling us names and who successfully overthrew him because he can call us better names. Don't you?"

"Um."

"Anyway, one Saturday — isn't it Saturday when everybody publishes small papers? I'm sure it's Saturday. Well, I read both papers completely and picked up a ladies' magazine. It was one of those that always has a woman on the cover who looks like a Russian wolfhound, and who has a long neck and big feet. She stands as if her hips were out of joint, wearing something that seems to have been dropped on her, and obviously she hasn't eaten for a long time."

"You sound like Schopenhauer. He hated women, too."

"I only hate women who scare me. In any event, that is not the point. In the magazine there was an article about family 'togetherness.' It gave me a twinge of conscience because I was — well, withdrawn, as it were, just reading for my own pleasure and not, you know, sort of sharing myself with my family when the opportunity was available."

"What makes you think your family wants to share your frayed, irritable, 5:30 P.M. self?"

He ignored the remark. "So I knew my daughter had gone the day before on a school trip to Boston and I thought, 'It's selfish not to show an interest in this. Let her tell you about it; you know, dad and daughter are pals.'

"So I said, 'What happened on the trip yesterday?'

" 'Mildred and Katharine aren't speaking any more,' she began breathlessly. 'It was because they got assigned to the same bus instead of separate buses, because if they hadn't, it never would have happened.

" 'But in the same bus, they both wanted to sit with Henry — you remember, the tall one with red hair that you saw playing in the game the other night — and they got so mad they almost cried and now they aren't speaking . . .'

" 'But I wasn't asking . . .'

" 'And,' she went on, 'Mary and George went steady . . .'

" 'You mean Mary next door — your age? How long has this been going on?'

" 'They went steady all day. And,' she rushed on like the brook in the lower meadow, 'Jeannie couldn't decide whether to walk with John or Frankie, but neither one likes her anyway, so they tossed a coin, and John walked through the State House with her, and Frankie walked through the Old North Church with her, and I ate lunch with her, because she was alone by then . . .'

"When she stopped for another bite of jam, peanut butter and marshmallow sandwich," the father related, "I pounced on her, saying, 'Didn't you learn one single, worthwhile thing during this whole day of unique opportunity?' "

"She looked reproachful. 'You didn't ask me what I learned. You asked me what happened.'

" 'All right, all right. Didn't you learn anything about this government of ours that began in 1620, that men have fought for, that —'

" 'Of course, Daddy. The first government, other than that of the Plymouth settlement, was based upon the charter of 1629, which was intended to be merely the charter for a commercial company, but which was shaped by the colonists into a political constitution . . .'

266

"This went on," the father related, "for almost five minutes and she obviously knew a great deal about the subject. Abruptly, however, the open magazine caught her eye, and she stopped, seeing what I had been reading."

" 'We had a debate on that "togetherness" action in class,' she said.

" 'What did you conclude?'

" 'Well, I'm going over to Susie's at seven to listen to records. You don't want to go, do you?'

" 'Of course not.'

" 'I don't want you to, either. And the boys said they were embarrassed when their fathers insisted on playing ball with them, because —'

" 'I know,' he interjected. 'The game is slower because the fathers get out of breath, and all the boys are afraid somebody's father will forget how many years have passed, and break a leg, and the boys have to watch their language —'

" 'Yes,' she said simply. 'We decided there was no reason for adults to try to force themselves to be interested in teen-age things or vice versa. It's just boring for everybody and probably could make parents and children hate each other. I like to come to you when I need you, when I know that you know something I don't. Why should you learn Massachusetts history all over again just because I'm learning it?' "

"I now read my newspapers with greater peace," he said. "And I wrote a letter to the magazine editor and told her she didn't know what she was talking about. What's more, Mildred and Katharine are speaking again — and somehow, I knew they would be."

When my neighbor had gone, I got to thinking about human relationships and wondering in how many similar instances we overlook simple things that would improve them greatly, because we know that man is complex and erroneously assume that every solution to every one of his problems must necessarily be complex.

I will show you what I mean:

Enter a weeping man, age forty, as they say in stage directions, but be careful of leaping to conclusions, because men weep for many reasons, do they not?

This man is Eugene: height, five feet, nine inches; weight, one hundred and sixty pounds; principally bald; eyes, washed-out blue; acne scars on back of neck; tattoo on left forearm, "God Is Love." He has needed dental work for years and is self-conscious about opening his mouth, but this is not such a burden, because he has little to say and no reason to smile.

At the time of this episode, Eugene was an inmate of the Bristol County House of Correction; the charge: breaking and entering in the nighttime, and larceny of property worth more than one hundred dollars. He was older than many of the inmates, because forty percent of them are under twenty-one and fifty-five percent are under twenty-five. But he was very like most of them in possessing less than an eighth-grade education and insofar as he represented a symbol of social isolation and a lifetime record of no success.

You do not realize, until somebody like Eugene starts to relate to you the story of his totally unproductive and largely alienated life, by how many strong threads we attach ourselves to our society and, in so doing, build a frame upon which ego depends. If you haven't gone anywhere or done anything, it is difficult to tell anybody who or what you are. So it was with Eugene.

"Why did you become a burglar, Eugene?"

"I needed some money. Everybody got to have money, ain't he?"

"Why didn't you go to work?"

"I couldn't get no job."

"Why not?"

"First thing they ask you is put down on paper what you done, what you want. I couldn't put nothin' down even if I done somethin' because . . ." He put his hand over his mouth, an old habit linked to self-consciousness. ". . . because I never learned how to write and I didn't want nobody to know it."

"You went to school until you were sixteen; you had to, because that's state law. You mean to say you came out without having learned to write?"

He nodded. "It wasn't my mother's fault. She tried hard. She was the only one tried."

Thus, Eugene was alienated from society essentially because he was a functional illiterate. "Counterfeit Tiger," a poem written by another prisoner in his cell block, will give you an idea of what this feels like. The reference is to a man about to be released from prison: *"One day soon/he'll go his way/To find his rightful place/And walk among the tigers,/Within the human race."*

Starting with no staff and no money, Sheriff Ed Dabrowski established a school in the House of Correction where Eugene was confined. It is one of the least expensive investments in humanity in the nation (it costs about five dollars an hour), and it is nationally unique because, in an impressive exercise of the Golden Rule, the local community is paying for what really ought to be a county project, even though it could just as well have said no.

Dabrowski was moved to start the school because "these people already have all the handicaps, plus prison records. And what do we do? We isolate them.

"In the school, we have ceremonies for them. When we award them a certificate indicating eighth-grade equivalency, they cherish that piece of paper. If they're not in long enough to complete the classwork, we give them a certificate stating the number of classes they attended; something to hold, to keep, to show they have succeeded at something. For many, this piece of paper is the first good thing in their lives."

Originally, a prison guard who was a certified teacher administered the program. The fact that his title now is "educational director" is a major advance, for it constitutes official recognition of the project and its worth.

Naturally, it is not all downhill. Not everybody can be "sold" on learning, and sometimes upper-level red tape snarls up the process until a prisoner loses interest. But there are bright spots, and that brings us back to Eugene, who did, after all, choose to go to the prison school.

At age forty, he stood before the sheriff with tears trickling down his cheeks and he said, "I have just wrote a letter. The first one of my life. To my mother. Thank you."

More often than not, we do not pay such heed to those in need about us, even those who could be assisted by relatively little. This is what Alfred, the barber, and I were talking about this morning, because I have to think about getting back to civilization — if that's what it is — as of this evening, and whereas I do not mind my hair somewhat long, it was beginning to curl over my coat collar.

Alfred's is a small shop, dwarfed by a neighboring supermarket; its striped pole revolves cheerily to assure that it is open for custom, and in the window there is a potted red geranium, its stem serpentine from chasing the sun.

Alfred is bald and blue-bearded. When I walked in, he grunted affably, downed the last of his coffee, and swished the paper cup across the room with a deft underhand. It clonked precisely into the metal wastebasket, and he smiled appreciatively, and said, "Two points." Usually I read in the barber's chair, having been inspired to do so by a biologist acquaintance named Jack Rose (no relation, as far as I know, to the beverage of the same name), who once told me he had spent ten years reading the footnotes of Gibbons's *Decline and Fall of the Roman Empire*, principally while having his hair cut.

Being bookless in this instance, I risked conversation with Alfred. He promptly surprised me by ignoring the weather and other staples of social interchange, and commenting, "Well, pretty soon we will have had our election and on the same day the English will burn Guy Fawkes in effigy and time will tell which of us is ahead, but anyway, then we can all go back to work."

"You sound like Professor Herbert Marcuse," I said.

"Never heard of him."

"Well, he's a philosopher, and what I was thinking particularly was that Dr. Marcuse says he thinks democracy has a future, but he doesn't think it has a present."

"Hmm," said Alfred snipping away, and I thought for a moment I had dealt our conversation a mortal blow by injecting Dr. Marcuse's remark.

But then Alfred waved his scissors at my reflection in the mirror, which is a clever thing that barbers do when they are working on the back of your head and want to speak at you directly, and he said, "What's wrong with this country isn't going to be cured by voting."

"No?"

"No. O.K., so I never heard of this fellow Marcuse. You never heard of Benjamin Saunders."

"No."

"Well, I never saw him. I didn't ever meet him. I didn't ever know him. But I know what happened to him and that's why I never forgot his name. It was in the paper. Lived in Pennsylvania somewhere. Left his house in October to play golf in Wildwood. Never arrived at the country club."

271

Alfred stood back to survey my neck. "In the spring, almost seven months later, they found his body in his car, alongside the Garden State Parkway. He had been there all that time, right there in the middle strip of the parkway, and I'll bet you almost millions of people must have gone by him. Every day, they went by him."

Snip, snip went the scissors. "What I'm saying," said Alfred, "is that nobody stopped. Not one soul stopped to see whether anything was wrong. No. Swish, swish, go on by. I got my places to go to; never mind you, Jack. Right? That's the way we are." He paused. "Short enough?"

I waggled my head, and he went on. "You don't have to go to the Garden State Parkway to find that out, either. You just go right here in this town and it ain't very big, either. It's small enough so you'd think one human being would care something about another. But they don't, necessarily."

"No?"

"Damn well told no. I had a friend. Name of Frank Tanner. Used to drive an ice truck until everybody but barrooms stopped using ice. We used to go clamming together. He didn't have any family around here." He squirted a handful of warm lather, and waved at someone passing by.

"He lived fairly near me and one morning he woke up and didn't feel well. It was March — no, I take that back — it was the end of February, and there was snow on the ground. Been cold for days. So he started for my house. Wanted help, and didn't know where else to go. He kept to himself, mostly.

"Now get this. Here is a man, maybe sixty, sixty-two, clean-shaven, dressed in good clothes, shoes shined and all that, good appearance — and about halfway to my house, at say seven of a weekday morning, he felt faint. He was afraid if he fell down, he'd hurt himself or maybe even freeze there. So he backed up to a fence and hooked his arms around the pickets, to hold himself up.

"And he went dizzy, and maybe passed out, a half dozen times, still hanging on like that. Near as I could find out, he was there, on a busy street, almost three hours, until about ten in the morning. People went by. Cars went by. Everybody thought he was drunk. Nobody bothered to do anything. A little kid, seven years old, finally told a cop — I went round to the kid's house afterward and gave him ten dollars — and so they got him to the hospital. He was a real sick man, and half-frozen as well."

"Wet or dry?" Alfred said to me. Then he said, "Frank wasn't never the same after that. The doctor said he would have made a better comeback if they'd got him sooner. But it was more than that. Here was a man never took a drink in his life, not able to say a word, but knowing that all those people were passing him by. I suppose he had always figured people were better than that. You know, his ice customers used to like him."

Alfred jabbed the cash register keys, dumped in the bills I had given him and scooped out change. "Merry Christmas," he said, which is what he always says, no matter what time of year it is.

I know a couple of things about people — and about Christmas, for that matter — and this is an appropriate time to think about them because within an hour or two I shall be back in the world as it is, and I shall carry with me such thoughts as sustain.

Perley was telling me about a conversation he had with his daughter when she was home from school last year for the Christmas vacation. She sat by the window, a young woman of about nineteen, neither jaded nor ingenuous and, therefore, no longer simply a girl. The sunlight of December noon, pale and transient, illumined half her face and he thought, "So it is that today's youth must make its way through life, half in joy, half in sadness, and perhaps it was always so, but we thought less about it."

It was a quiet time, not a moment to discuss the gritty things; he sensed that, absorbing the security of the atmosphere, she was resting from the daily struggle. He remembered once peering over the gunwale of a skiff into the clear green water below and watching tautog, struggling against the current, slide out of its hard thrust to the quietness of a weedy ledge, where they could maintain their position with no more than a flip of the fin.

"So it is with all of us," he thought, "it becomes increasingly necessary to find the quiet places, the quiet times in which to rekindle the spirit and repair the battered armor."

Thus, he began the conversation innocuously. "All of your Christmas shopping done?"

She didn't answer the question, but looked at him with a thoughtful expression and said, "I want to tell you about the best Christmas present I gave this year."

She drew her knees up under her chin and hugged her legs, something he had not seen her do since she was little. But she was not, of course, little any more, he thought, except in a few delightful ways. On her sweater she wore a huge blue and white button decorated with hieroglyphics that she had said were Russian, meaning, "It's Friday, thank God!"

He had pointed out that Russians don't believe in God and she had replied with irrefutable logic, "I didn't make the button, I just wear it," and that ended that.

Her head was tipped forward slightly, so that her long dark hair fell over her face and he could not decide whether it was totally unbecoming, or the most becoming thing he had ever seen, because of its totally feminine artlessness. She said, "You remember that at school we can volunteer for a program to help people? Then you get assigned to somebody, usually a child from a poor family and you try to do things for him, like taking him to the park or the library to make his life, you know . . ."

"Richer?"

"Yes. Broader. Have more meaning, more variety of experience. And believe me, it's not hard to find something good they don't have. You talk about the seamy side of life. Some places we go, we go in twos and threes because we don't dare go otherwise. You know, basement apartment things, four-five blocks from a decent neighborhood, a telephone or a cop, and you find the old man home in midafternoon, sitting about in his whiskers and undershirt, drinking beer. And all you want to do is get in there, get the little kid and get out without a scene, and you say to yourself, 'I will not panic; nobody is going to grab me; I will be calm and dignified at all times.' Hoo, boy, I could tell you —"

"Color me coward," he said. "I am glad I do not know precisely the moments when you are in such situations, but I am pleased that you are moved to want to help people, and I want you to be aware that some people live that way and that it is wrong that they have to."

"Anyway," she went on, "for the Christmas season, we could take an extra, one-shot assignment if we wanted to. You get a name and go just once, to see if you can do something to make Christmas better for the person. You know what a morris chair is?"

He nodded. "Named for William Morris, the Pre-Raphaelite."

"Really? Well, so I got this woman. Maybe seventy-five. All crippled with rheumatism. Hardly move, and she sits all day long in a morris chair. She lives alone. Nice face. White hair. Not too much money, but nothing like what I usually see on these things. So what can you do for a lonely lady who can't move?"

He shook his head.

"I didn't know, either," she said. "We weren't just supposed to go out and spend money on them, and I didn't have any money anyway. They wanted us to do something special and thoughtful. So I asked her what she wanted most of all. You know what she said?"

"Couldn't guess."

"Well, we sat in her kitchen and it was small and neat and had blue linoleum. And she began by telling me that she had grown up in the country. She said she didn't suppose mothers brought up their daughters this way now, but her mother had spent a great deal of time teaching her to be a good housekeeper. You know, everything clean and nice. Monday, washing, Tuesday, ironing, and all that . . .'"

"I'm even old enough to remember."

"Of course. Then she said that was why it bothered her if everything wasn't just right and sometimes it wasn't, because she was so full of aches and pains she couldn't do some things, and she couldn't afford to hire somebody to do them. So I said, 'Tell me what you want done.'

"And she said, 'It doesn't seem right to ask you, but I can no longer do it. Would you wash my kitchen floor — as a Christmas present for me?'

"I said, 'I sure will!' and she started to cry a little, and I held her hand. Then I went to the room and got my jeans and sneakers, went back to her house and gave that floor what-for with a bucket of hot water and cleaner. If I do say so, I did a good job, way into the corners and everything.

"She kissed me when I left, and I walked back to school just thinking good thoughts. Sometimes it's like that — just good thoughts — isn't it?"

Perley marveled at how wise she had become so young.

And finally, I shall tell you what this place is like at Christmas, and specifically what it was like last Christmas.

If you go back to the land at the Christmas season, it is always still, because that is the time of year that it is, and that is the way the earth turns when it is between death and birth.

Here on this dry-grass hill, brightened with shiny, stunted pine, there is neither sound nor motion, and it is as if the total universe, from here to the sea, and from there to the pale line of the horizon, had stopped breathing for a little while.

It was like that with Mrs. Glennon, for whom I used to "run errands," as she said, when I was about eight. She was ninety-four and claimed to have read the Bible completely four times, although being troubled with forgetfulness, did not remember it very well if at all.

Periodically, she would say to me, "Now, who on earth was the father of Saul?" and usually I would not know, no matter what the question was. It is, I suppose, not to my credit that I would make up an answer to keep her from getting upset. I would say quickly, as if there were no doubt in my mind, "Elisha," or something similar, and she would be satisfied, principally because she had already forgotten the question and was thinking about something else.

But like the still earth in December, when I crept into her little house in late afternoon to see whether she wanted anything done, she would be sitting, straight-backed in a black dress, with her feet neatly placed side by side, and the Bible in her lap, and utterly without motion, even of hand or face. Almost every day, I thought she was probably dead, but she wasn't and I did not know then that only the earth and a very few people attain such composure.

Here on this hill, it is satisfying to think of Mrs. Glennon's composure, because if she could have walked up here she would have liked it.

Not one bird is flying; there is not one cloud in the smoky pearl of the winter sky, which is the color of a coachman's glove. Halfway to Boston, there is a tanker that also seems motionless on the bright gray bowl of the sea, and the black plume from its stack rises like a thin rod in the windlessness.

This fellow standing beside me is a wistful atheist, although he looks just like anybody else whose ancestors came from the banks of the Dnieper and clobbered the Romans at Salona a thousand years before the Pilgrims found Plymouth. Sometimes he is moody, but I do not mind, understanding that this happens because he is a Croat. We were talking about Christmas.

"Modern astronomers," he said, "are inclined to believe that the star of Bethlehem may have been a supernova, a faint star that exploded and shone brightly for weeks and perhaps months. Tycho Brahe saw such a supernova in 1572 in the constellation Cassiopeia. At its brightest, it was visible by day, and it outshone Venus. It was visible to the naked eye for sixteen months."

Across the gentle hillside that dropped a leisurely mile and a half to a purple marsh, there was no sound but that of his voice, hollow in the vastness of the time and place.

"As for the date of December twenty-fifth," he continued, "that was chosen by the church during the fourth century, A.D., a choice not dictated by any particular historical evidence, or even tradition, concerning the actual date of Jesus' birth, but rather by a desire to Christianize a Roman revel which marked the winter solstice.

"The biblical evidence plainly indicates that Jesus was born during the late summer or fall. That is the time of year when

Palestinian shepherds take their flocks into the field to graze at night."

Hard against the sea, the dunes lay like profiles of sleeping giants, an endless line of softly molded cheeks, noses and chins, from skyline to skyline.

"As for the 'three kings of Orient,'" he went on, "it is fairly evident that they were not kings, but probably priest-astrologers from Babylon. Their names, Kaspar, Melchior and Balthazar, are pure fiction, the good-natured invention of a ninth-century monk who thought they ought not to remain anonymous forever."

Halfway down the hill there is an old cellar hole, its crumbling, whitened brick falling by the year. Black raspberry bushes overrun it, providing food for the catbird and sanctuary for the cottontail, who sleeps, ears flat back on his shoulders, where the farmer once stored his preserves.

"Even the birth in the stable is unlikely," he said. "Perhaps a manger, which is a feed trough. But cattle in first-century Bethlehem were kept in caves hollowed out of the soft limestone cliffs."

"You don't believe in Christmas?" I asked. "Is that what you are saying?"

"A priest asked me that once," he replied. "You know what I told him? I quoted Robert Frost, you know that part about, 'Before I built a wall, I'd ask to know/What I was walling in or walling out.' I said to the priest, 'Don't try to keep me out of Christmas. Don't try to make it your personal property, because it's too big. You might as well try to fence in Niagara Falls. I belong here, too. It's mine if I want it, as well as anybody's.'"

"Of course it is," I said. "Nobody would argue against that. But I'm not sure that I understand what it can mean to you, if anything . . ."

On the hillside there was no sound, and nothing moved.

He said, "In a place like this, it is easier for me to think what it means to me than it is most times, and in most places.

"My fellow man is cowardly in his apathy, pathetic in his failures, and ignominious in his selfishness. Yet I cannot dismiss him and will not permit anyone else to do so without protest because, periodically, he is breathtaking in success, his generosity brings tears, and his bravery breaks the heart.

"At his best, he is magnificent. Very briefly, often very privately, he is at his best in the Christmas season. That is what it means to me, that is what this place means to me . . . man at his best."

Thus ends, without sound or motion, the fourteen days.

Books by Everett S. Allen
available from Commonwealth Editions

THIS QUIET PLACE
A Cape Cod Chronicle

CHILDREN OF THE LIGHT
The Rise and Fall of New Bedford Whaling and the Death of the
Arctic Fleet

A WIND TO SHAKE THE WORLD
The Story of the 1938 Hurricane

THE BLACK SHIPS
Rumrunners of Prohibition

MARTHA'S VINEYARD
An Elegy

EVERETT S. ALLEN was born in New Bedford, Massachusetts, in 1916. He moved to Martha's Vineyard when he was eight years old. After graduating from Tisbury High School, he attended Tabor Academy and Middlebury College. He was hired as a waterfront reporter by the *New Bedford Standard-Times* on the day before the hurricane of 1938, which became the subject for his book *A Wind to Shake the World*. After enlisting in the US Navy, where he served in Europe and participated in D-Day, he returned to the *Standard-Times,* where he worked until his retirement in 1979. The author of seven books, Allen died in 1990.